FEARLESS

FEARLESS

Harriet Quimby

A LIFE WITHOUT LIMIT

DON DAHLER

PRINCETON ARCHITECTURAL PRESS · NEW YORK

Published by
Princeton Architectural Press
70 West 36th Street
New York, NY 10018
www.papress.com

Printed and bound in the United States
25 24 23 22 4 3 2 1 First edition

ISBN 978-1-64896-035-2

Designer: Paul Wagner

Library of Congress Control Number: 2021953031

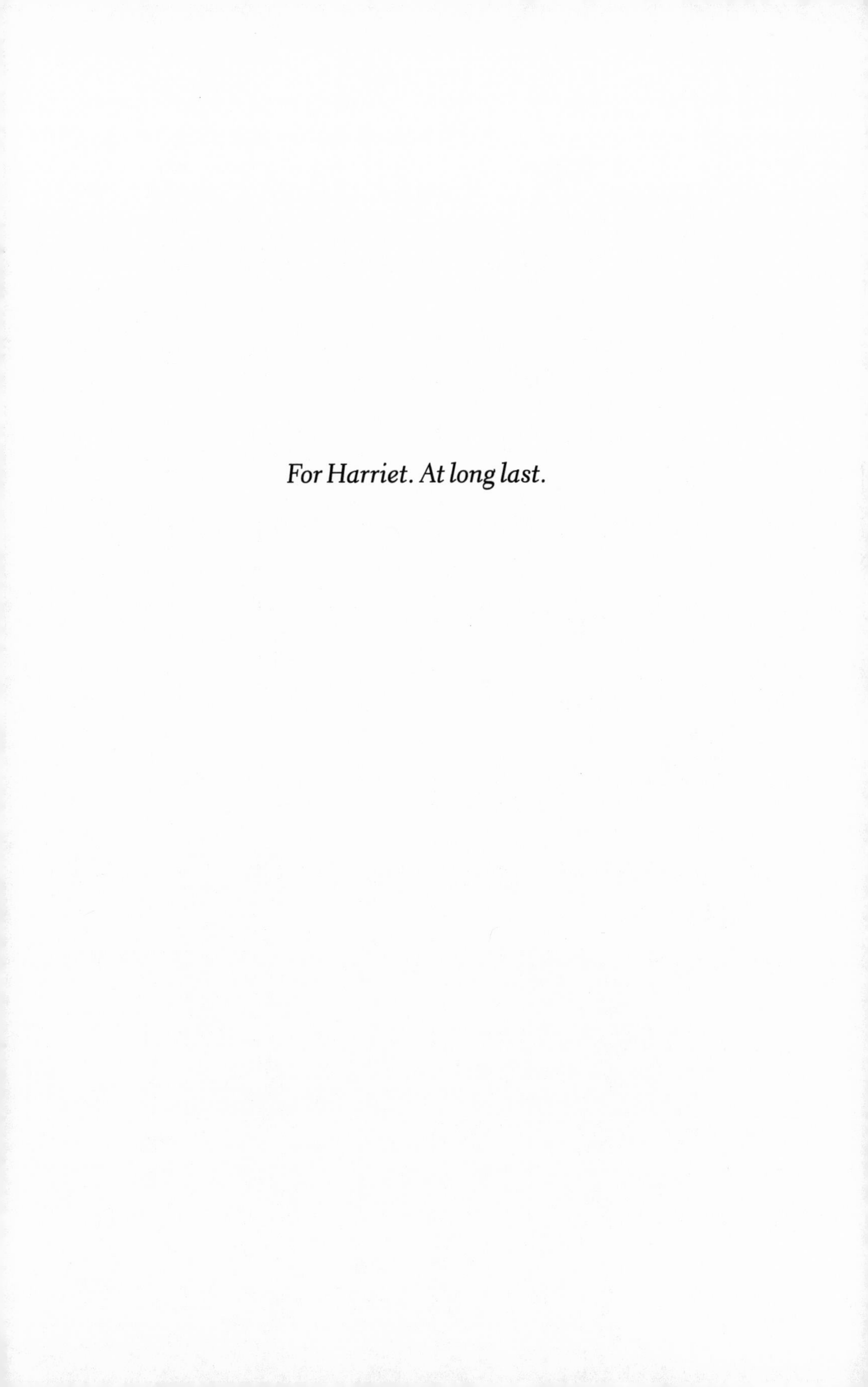

For Harriet. At long last.

I ride on the gale at my ease
The earth and the heaven between.

—Francis Medhurst, "The Aeroplane," 1910

CONTENTS

PART THREE

Harriet with a Moisant monoplane in 1911.

PROLOGUE:
If you are afraid, you shall never succeed

THE SEA BECAME SKY. Wraiths of heavy salt air floated across the White Cliffs of Dover, bestowing their wet caresses on everyone and everything that waited day after day for a break in the fog and lashing rain. But their petrichor marked a subtle change of fortune; there was something stirring in the damp perfume. Of those peering anxiously into the seamless gray wall was a tall, slim, remarkably beautiful woman with jet-black hair and blue-green eyes. Already an established drama columnist, travel writer, and reporter; already a woman who audaciously rode in a race car at over one hundred miles an hour; already a journalist whose investigations led to a public official's resignation, Harriet Quimby was about to take a literal, and literary, leap into the void. If she survived, and there was certainly no guarantee of that, her leap was to be a first for women, and another risk-laden challenge that some of those closest to her begged her to reconsider. Not even a heartbreaking betrayal would sap her determination.

Behind her, a monoplane's bicycle wheels rested delicately on the grass. Borrowed just days earlier from its inventor, Louis Blériot, because the more powerful version she ordered was yet to be completed, it sported a spindly frame made out of ash, fabric-covered wings that spanned twenty-three feet, and a 50-horsepower Gnôme rotary engine. An early observer of the racket that little motor made described it this

Louis Blériot, inventor of the monoplane and the first to fly across the English Channel.

way: "Take a motor bicycle, a rolling mill, and a buzz saw, and blend them, and you get something like it." The airplane was held together by a web of wires that made it look more like a marionette than something sturdy enough to cross twenty-two miles of the English Channel.

In 1912, aviation wasn't in its infancy; it was embryonic. Not yet a decade had passed since the brothers Wright trundled and hop-scotched their 12-horsepower biplane for all of fifty-seven seconds over the blowing sands of Kitty Hawk beach and into the public's imagination—*Caelum certe patet,* "the sky at least stands open." A spark that smoldered since the days of Daedalus and ancient Greece was ignited, and within just a few years, scores of young men were attending flight schools in the United States and Europe and plunking down thousands of dollars to buy rickety wood-and-linen airplanes, some of which were of questionable design and safety. The year before, a hundred pilots plunged to their deaths. Flight was a Faustian gamble between an early, often gruesome end and enormous fame, as successful aviators were the rock stars of their day, fêted by the press and followed by huge crowds of avid fans. Attendance at air shows numbered in the tens of thousands, some eventually swelling to upward of half a million. Fliers could earn thousands of dollars for less than a half-hour in the air. Imagine today's spectacles of the Super Bowl, professional wrestling, NASCAR racing, and gory octagon matches of mixed martial arts, and one gets some sense of the passion, fan loyalty, and, indeed, blood lust driving the early days of aviation. But with one addition: the Grim Reaper stalked almost every air show, often claiming at least one soul. "There's another good man gone," pilot Arch Hoxsey mused on New Year's Eve, 1910, after hearing of the violent death of a prominent flyer at a New Orleans event. He would perish himself moments later as he lost control while trying to best his own altitude record.

The first air show on American soil took place at Dominguez Field near Los Angeles not quite a year earlier. What was primarily a moneymaking endeavor for its promoters became the genesis of how Americans saw themselves and their future, reflected in the heroic images of brave aviators soaring and banking and pushing their machines to the edge of existence. It certainly made an indelible impression on one young woman in particular, whose interest in aviation would only continue to grow.

In ten days at Dominguez Field, men set records and became aviation legends. One of those was named Glenn Curtiss, who urged his biplane to the never-before achieved airspeed of fifty-five miles an hour. Glenn was emblematic of the anything-is-possible ethos of turn-of-the-century America. The dapper New York State youth—who sported suits, ties, and on occasion a neatly trimmed Van Dyke beard—left school after the eighth grade to provide for his fatherless family. Looking for adventure on the rutted dirt roads of the small Finger Lakes village of Hammondsport, he first made a name for himself as a bicycle racer and motorcycle designer. He fashioned a working carburetor out of a tomato soup can for his earliest attempt at building one.

By 1907, Glenn could claim the title of "fastest man in the world" with a run of 136 miles an hour on his own two-wheeled creation. That record established him as one of the leading motor builders in the nation. It was an achievement not ignored by the nascent aviation industry, such as it was. In June of that year, he flew over his hometown in a dirigible made by Thomas Baldwin and powered by his own engine. (The Wright brothers tersely, maybe enviously, rejected Glenn's engine design for their own use.) That marked his very first trip aloft. As soon as he landed, and true to his nature, the speed freak whom the press nicknamed Hell Rider set about figuring out how to make the dirigible even faster.

Glenn Curtiss, pioneer aviator and the man dubbed "Hell Rider." Photo taken shortly before he won the inaugural Gordon Bennett Trophy in 1909.

After Alexander Graham Bell himself came calling on Glenn to help create a heavier-than-air flying machine, the twenty-nine-year-old's name would forever be linked to humanity's quest to fly. Gone was his obsession with going fast over the ground; Glenn Curtiss wanted to conquer the sky.

Among many who were thrilled by Glenn setting the air speed record that January day in 1910 was a woman with "a brilliant smile" whose fashion taste "runs strongly to overhung bonnets and antique ornaments such as basilisks, amulet scarabs and the like, so that even in business attire her individuality is very distinctive." There is speculation that Harriet Quimby was at Dominguez Field to research an article about these novel contraptions and the daring men who flew them for one of the most popular magazines of the day, *Leslie's Illustrated Weekly*. As with many such assignments she convinced her employer to finance, it would have sprung from her own interests.

No one who knew Harriet Quimby, and who enjoyed Harriet's witty observations, stylish clothing, and unique jewelry, would have a clue as to her long-buried family history of poverty and heartbreak. Her appearance gave no hint of the nine years she managed to jettison from her actual age, or of the long, tedious passage to her success and financial stability. Harriet's fascination with flight took seed a year earlier, when she wrote an entertaining profile of a young inventor who was secretly studying the flight of buzzards at Biscayne Bay in hopes of building an aircraft based on their aerodynamics. The story she submitted shows an inordinate grasp of the various theories of flight: "the wings of a flying machine could be spread out or contracted so as to preserve its balance when meeting wind waves of varying velocities."

There's no way to judge how her usual readers greeted such technical vernacular. Harriet, through her writing and photographs, took them on various journeys around the world and introduced them to other cultures and customs, so perhaps they simply enjoyed another unusual literary ride. But John A. Sleicher, the editor of *Leslie's Illustrated Weekly*, seemed to have spotted a latent passion in his star reporter. Within a few months of the Los Angeles air show, Harriet had his blessing to ask the owner of an aviation school to teach her how to fly. Eventually she told her many readers about the adventure of becoming the first licensed female pilot in America. "If you are afraid," she once wrote, "you shall never succeed."

It was the beginning of a stratospheric personal and professional ascent that ultimately led her to the cliffs of England on that foggy April morning, as she set out in an oil-spewing contraption made of wood and fabric and hope for the far shores of France. In a time when human flight was still measured in minutes and dozens of lives were sacrificed annually for the advancement of the new science of aviation, Harriet's was a journey almost as audacious and perilous as a trip to the moon would be fifty-seven years later.

First, however, a little girl from a remote and failing Michigan farm had to find her way to a different reality.

PART ONE

This is believed to be the only childhood photograph of Harriet Quimby.

1

A TOMBOY FULL OF VERVE AND SPUNK

WILLIAM QUIMBY WAS THE kind of man for whom good luck was a foreign land he never stood a chance of seeing. A member of a large Irish farming family in Upstate New York, he was blue eyed, tall, and skinny to the point of lankiness. Hardworking but of chronic bad health William was unsuccessful at almost everything he undertook with one singular exception: he married well. The future Mrs. Quimby, Ursula Cook, was a diminutive force of nature, from an educated and enterprising family of physicians and entrepreneurs, who simply refused to accept the cruel randomness of life. It was she who eventually fashioned new and better prospects for the Quimby clan. The unlikely pair married in the presence of William's mother in Ovid Township, Michigan in 1859 as twenty-five-year-olds and remained a couple for the rest of their lives.

They had not yet celebrated their fifth wedding anniversary when William enlisted in the 188th New York Infantry Regiment, convinced to do so by a national recruitment push meant to bolster the Union's final efforts to defeat the Confederacy. On his enlistment letter dated September 29, the boilerplate commitment of three years is crossed out, and the word "one" is scribbled in the margin. The regiment included volunteers who stubbornly insisted they would serve only a single year.

Within a month of his enlistment, William's unit found itself in battle at Hatcher's Run in Virginia, where seven of its citizen soldiers were killed. After a few more bloody skirmishes at Fort Meigs, Boydton Plank, and Gravelly Run, William's Company B and the rest of the 188th took part in the final assault on Petersburg that April. But William never fired a shot. A permanent limp from a childhood injury kept him off the front lines, out of "bitter action," and in the company kitchen as a cook. There he, along with many other members of his regiment, contracted dysentery. He spent much of the rest of the Civil War bedridden, too ill even to attend the South's 1865 surrender at nearby Appomattox, during which the 188th received the honor of standing guard at the house of Wilmer McLean, where generals Robert E. Lee and Ulysses S. Grant shook hands. William managed to survive the intestinal infection, a full quarter of his unit did not. In fact, of the 370,000 mainly young men New York State supplied to the war effort, almost 28,000 succumbed to disease, not bullets.

The gaunt veteran eventually made his way home. As Ursula nursed him back to health, there were decisions to be made. In the weeks and months after the two war-weary generals doffed their hats in mutual respect and returned to their bedraggled troops, some 800,000 soldiers poured back into the North, most looking for work. But the Union, after having spent $3.4 billion ($106 billion today) dollars to defeat the South, began rapidly canceling government military contracts. With the exception of railroad expansion, the industrial engine that powered the wartime economic boom screeched to a halt. Factories began laying off workers. Above the Mason–Dixon Line, the economy shifted away from smaller subsistence agriculture and into large-scale operations with the help of machinery like the McCormick reaper and the Racine thresher—a future of might and steel and engines.

Given the uncertain economic times, and despite their solid East Coast connections, the Quimbys heard the siren call of the American frontier immortalized in the words of Walt Whitman:

Conquering, holding, daring, venturing as we go the unknown ways,
Pioneers! O pioneers!

William and Ursula packed their few belongings and moved west, eventually settling briefly in Coldwater, Michigan, then Manistee, then Bear Lake, before ultimately making their way to the wilderness along Lake Michigan, where distant relatives lived nearby, to try their hand at farming the rocky soil. There is every likelihood the couple had no idea what they were getting themselves into.

Through the Homestead Act, which was created by the US Congress in 1862 to encourage the settlement of the western territory by any adult "who had never borne arms against the U.S. government," William was granted 160 acres near the small town of Arcadia, Michigan. The site was along an old trail, which was little more than a horse path cut through the woods and grasslands by early Sauk people. The only condition was he and Ursula had to improve the land by building a house and cultivating crops. If they could hang on for five years, the property was theirs.

Along what were then the far reaches of mid-nineteenth-century America, there were no bulldozers or chainsaws, no tractors or backhoes or dump trucks to help clear the land. There were only the arms and legs and hands and muscles and backs of the landowners willing to labor for hours and days and years to wrest a living from the reluctant soil. Not even draft animals could help in the beginning, because they required pastures for food and fences and barns to protect and shelter them, all of which first had to be cleared or built. The virgin-growth forests of bur oaks and black gums, hemlocks and birches and red maples had to be felled, dragged along dirt paths by hand, and milled into usable lumber. Tall Michigan white pines eventually fed the lumber boom that helped build the emerging city of Chicago. Tools of the trade were the ax, the hoe, the ditching spade, and the scythe.

The Quimby homestead was twenty-five miles north of Manistee and three miles from Lake Michigan. A handful of other settlers lived nearby, clearing the land to scratch out a living in the thin, sandy soil. They likely grew little more than potatoes in the first year or two and depended heavily on hunting to supply their protein. One settler recalled, "We were hungry all the time." The cabins were typically single-room affairs, with blankets hung to create the illusion of separate bedrooms. Even the most basic of comforts were scarce: a few cherished pieces of furniture, beds with "springs made from crisscrossed rope and a mattress constructed from a tick filled with dry grass, hay, or straw. Tea, coffee, sugar and butter were rarely seen." There was nothing more important than the family fireplace, which served as the only source of heat and cooking and as the center of all social activity. Every family strived to, literally, keep the home fires burning or risk sacrificing one of the rare Diamond phosphorous matches that it cherished like precious jewels. Without workable roads, most people used the beach along the great lake as a sandy pathway to come and go to the nearest town by foot.

One can only imagine the tall, slight William and the petite but determined Ursula toiling away in the heat and the dirt, slashing through underbrush and poison ivy, facing bears and snakes day by day, aided by neighbors and family whenever possible. The most agonizingly vexing pest to the homesteaders, however, was the "omnipresent mosquito," which a long-time resident described as "large as those of York State and about as saucy. They are cannibals in every sense of the word."

There are no direct accounts of what the Quimbys' lives were like in those early years, but, fortuitously, a man named Daniel Stewart, who lived nearby in California, Michigan from 1868 to 1902, kept a detailed if sometimes indecipherable diary. He spent his days sawing wood, mowing hay, shearing sheep, butchering hogs, salting beef, and singing in church. He counted the deaths of friends and neighbors, the frequent births, and the occasional weddings. On a typical Saturday he borrowed thirty dollars from a man named Ezekiel French and paid $1.60 at the mercantile for a "Toledo" blade. Stewart dutifully marked the pleasant days and the frosty ones, during which he could conduct little work outside: "Mon 15. A wet loway morning. Cleared up about middle of a fore-n [?]. Drawed a load of wood for William Moore in morning. Fixed fence and cut corn the rest of the day."

This account undoubtedly mirrors the arduous existence into which Harriet, called Hattie by her family and friends, was born in 1875. She had a sister five years her senior, Helen, nicknamed Kittie, and between three and nine other previous siblings who, as a sad testament to the infant mortality rate of the day, all died of various diseases. A massive fire in 1871 in the town of Manistee destroyed most of the region's public records, so the exact number of Harriet's brothers and sisters is unknown. There is no account of how William and Ursula endured the horrific losses of their children, nor can one imagine the crippling burden of sorrow they would have to carry the rest of their lives. Did the couple lie awake at night, comforting each other's pain? Or did they stoically hold that such things are better left accepted and unmentioned? Harriet never spoke of her lost siblings.

Frontier life was harsh, punishing, and often brutally short. Joy was found in small indulgences—dinner with friends and gatherings at church where the hymns were lifted up past the rafters and into the "loway" skies. It is safe to say not one person who slid a spade into the soil of the Lower Peninsula of Michigan ever imagined they'd get rich doing so, or that their life would be one of fame and adventure. But after the penury many suffered during and after the Civil War, to be a landowner—with the opportunity to provide food for their family and leave some financial legacy to their heirs—was the original American dream.

In scribbled handwriting, the 1880 census of Arcadia Township mentions two children in the Quimby household: five-year-old Hattie and ten-year-old Kittie. They attended the nearby one-room, clapboard-sided elementary school that formed a solid basis for Harriet's intellectual curiosity that served her so well throughout her life. She was described as a "tomboy full of verve and spunk who was prepared to try anything." Hattie's and Kittie's days outside the classroom would have been filled with physical, exhausting work on the farm and an endless drumbeat of chores.

Judd Calkins, who grew up on an adjacent farm and went to the same school as Harriet, remembered his youth as filled sunup to sundown with all-consuming labor.

> Days were long, and nights were short. I did not learn to hunt, fish, or go swimming, to dance, play cards, or to smoke. After I was older and got away from home I had lost all inclination to learn these various accomplishments.

Yet, he said, the pioneer families prioritized education.

> Our country schools ranked very high compared to the average rural school of today. The curriculum included everyone, from the kindergarten to high school, with one teacher to handle all the subjects. Our teacher had no time for frills, but if a child was so inclined, he could get a good practical education if he could manage to remain in school until he was fourteen or fifteen. There was one diversion we really did enjoy, and that was the spelling school which was held once every two weeks. Each Friday afternoon the two best spellers would choose sides, stand on opposite sides of the room, and spell until no one was left standing, or until one person remaining was declared the

champion. This was rehearsal. The regular spelling school was held in the evening, and representatives from neighboring schools within driving distance would come and take part. Parents and small brothers and sisters were the spectators. After exhausting our old Saunders Speller with all the foreign, French, and catchwords we could find, we generally had to fall back on Webster to get down to the last contestants. As for toys which every child enjoys and longs for I had a little wooden cart and a small sled, both homemade. My books included a small copy of Mother Goose rhymes and a copy of *Robinson Crusoe*.

Harriet's skillful mastery of the English language and its rich vocabulary were brought into being within the walls of that schoolhouse.

In 1880 Ursula set about supplementing the family income by making and selling *Quimby's Liver Invigerator* [*sic*]. She based the herbal concoction on her father's recipe, which had been popular on the East Coast. It received an almost comically effusive write-up in the *Manistee Daily News*:

> Was used by many eminent physicians in their practice, very successfully in Chronic Diseases, which originate from the derangement of the Liver and Impurity of the Blood; as Biliousness, Fever and Ague, Jaundice, Erysipelas, Erputive [*sic*] diseases of the Skin, Scroufula, Scald Head, Salt Rheum, Pain in the Bones, Back, Side, Head Dyspepsy, Epilepsy, Thrus [*sic*], Canker, Sore mouth and throat, Bronchitis, Catarrh, Costiveness, Piles, Rheumatism, Diseases of the Kidneys, Heart, Stomach, Spinal affections, Female Weakness, in fact all diseases the human race is heir to.

And yet, despite this apparently magical cure for pretty much everything, Ursula's elixir didn't immediately solve the Quimbys' economic dilemma. Perhaps Costiveness just wasn't much of a problem along the shores of Lake Michigan. The family continued to scrape away on the 160 acres, hoping for a good crop, hoping for a change of luck. Maybe even hoping for a little assistance.

In the postwar years, the US government was anything but eager to set up expensive benefits for its military veterans. It wasn't until almost three decades after the Civil War ended when William finally began receiving a pension of twelve dollars a month. That might not seem like much money, but on a dirt farm in the late nineteenth century, any amount was manna from heaven. In response to this federal foot-dragging, independent organizations sprang up shortly after the war with the expressed purpose of supporting veterans and their families. One such was the Independent Order of Odd Fellows (IOOF). Documents show William signed up for Lodge 35 in Bear Lake, not far from the family farm, and Ursula later joined the sister organization called the Rebekahs. The IOOF's records of the Quimbys' diligent dues-paying over the ensuing years left a trail of bread crumbs along the family's next wanderings.

By 1884, the Quimbys had had enough. After a last-ditch effort by William to pad the family coffers by working part time at the local general store, the foursome let the farm go into receivership, packed what belongings they could carry, and joined the river of American humanity steadily flowing west. They stepped onto one train in Lansing, caught a Union Pacific from Chicago, and eventually climbed down onto the Oakland Long Wharf on the San Francisco Bay. A stagecoach took the weary family another 250 miles south to the coastal farm town of Arroyo Grande.

Why they chose Arroyo Grande is a mystery. Perhaps Ursula sought a milder climate than that of Michigan. Perhaps William thought the California soil was better suited for farming, or the opportunities there greater for their two children. Regardless, it is worth noting that Harriet never spoke or wrote about or even acknowledged her early childhood in Michigan. It was as if it never happened. When interviewed in 1911 she described herself as "a California woman, first, last and always." And, perhaps most tellingly, she eventually claimed the year she first set foot in the Golden State as the actual year of her birth.

The contrast in climates between their old and new homes must have been a revelation to the Quimbys after a decade of trying to make a go of things in the Upper Midwest. The days in Arroyo Grande average sixty-six degrees year-round, and rarely dip below forty-five. Sunshine painted the rolling hills and orange groves, the rains were regular and nourishing. Winters back in Arcadia were frigid and dark, often sliding into the teens with thirty inches of snow covering the obdurate ground, and the area's July heat waves of ninety to one hundred degrees were a savagely regular occurrence.

The family once again set about cultivating a life and future as farmers, but again it was not to be. Not even the rich Central California soil would respond to William's futile efforts, so once more he returned to running a grocery store, where the shelves were stocked with an abundance of fresh fruit and vegetables, Chicago Yeast Powder cost twenty-five cents, and four ounces of vanilla only a dime more. It is likely his daughters, now teenagers, helped around the place. That is, when they weren't wandering along Branch Street, window shopping and chatting, dodging the waves in the thundering Pacific, or daring each other to venture onto the terrifyingly high, 171-foot-long, swinging bridge one of the area's first settlers built over the Arroyo Grande Creek without bothering to add handrails.

Harriet spent hour upon hour on horseback, exploring the hills and fields at full gallop. The spirited girl loved speed, and she learned a horse is never faster than when all its feet are off the ground. There is nothing more in the historical record about what her life was like during those years, but by the time she reached nineteen years of age her mother had managed to form her into a well-educated, curious, and ambitious young woman.

As the end of the century neared, the US at last put its violent past behind it and strained in the harness of social and economic progress. The West finally bid farewell to its bloody wars with Native Americans after Geronimo surrendered (1886) and the Sioux were defeated at the Battle of Wounded Knee (1890). Barbed wire dissected the Great Plains, ending the age of the open-range cowboy. By 1900, 193,000 miles of railroad track spanned the continent from coast to coast, opening up new markets for Andrew Carnegie's steel. For forty dollars a person, families could travel cross-country in days, not months. These were bewildering, thrilling, intoxicating times in the nation, captured by the enthusiastic lyrics, "from sea to shining sea," in Katharine Lee Bates's 1895 anthem, "America the Beautiful."

It's not hard to imagine, for the first time in their hardscrabble lives, the Quimbys were experiencing happiness, some semblance of financial security, maybe even, dare to say it, dreams of a better future. But fate and events outside their control conspired once more to send them plummeting into crisis.

It began in the wheat fields of Argentina. In 1893, an unexpected and massive crop failure startled the international investors lured into South American speculation by the London-based Baring Brothers bank. At the same time, commodity values from South Africa to Australia began to collapse. As wheat prices crashed, European investors started a run on gold, bringing US Treasury holdings to dangerously low levels. America's Gilded Age economy was sustained by global commodity prices, and they began falling like trees off a crumbling cliff.

Two weeks before Grover Cleveland was inaugurated for his first term as president, the Philadelphia and Reading Railroad, which was vastly overextended from aggressive acquisitions, shocked the markets when it went into receivership and was forced to divest itself of the

Central New England Railroad and the Boston and Maine Railroad. It would not be the nation's last bankruptcy. Cleveland's presidency was doomed by the economic disaster he inherited.

As the extent of the global damage became apparent, regular Americans tried desperately to withdraw their money from the banks, forcing some five hundred savings and loans to close. Fifteen thousand businesses failed. Farms were abandoned. Railroads ceased their expansion efforts and stopped buying equipment. Stock prices plummeted. It was a financial crisis the US had never before experienced.

A quarter of Pennsylvanians found themselves out of work. The impact was worse in New York, where unemployment hit 35 percent, and worse still in the Quimbys' former state of Michigan. There, some 43 percent of citizens had no way to make a living or put food on their tables. Once thriving Americans turned to anything to scrape together a few pennies: chopping wood, mending clothes, and even, in some cases, resorting to prostitution. Soup kitchens sprang up in formerly middle-class neighborhoods.

When the economic temblor reached Arroyo Grande, the Quimbys were unmoored yet again. Over a period of six years they bounced from Arroyo Grande to Los Gatos, where Harriet likely finished high school, and then to Oakland, before finally settling in San Francisco. Along the way, Kittie eloped. William's pension application of 1898 gives his daughter's last name as Rassmussen and says she lived in Oakland. It has to be assumed her parting was not an agreeable one; no Quimby, including Harriet, ever mentioned her again. Little else is known about her.

But for the diminished, beleaguered trio of William, Ursula, and Harriet, fate finally smiled on them. Once settled in San Francisco, Ursula took the family's finances in hand and created a successful business, while Harriet found her voice, her talent, and ultimately the path to her historic destiny.

2

WEAVING SPIDERS COME NOT HERE

PHOTOS FROM THE END of the nineteenth century present San Francisco as a modern city of closely packed multistory buildings, with wide avenues dissected by trolley rails and church spires straining heavenward. Streetlights bore ornate globed tops. Pedestrians in long dresses and top hats strolled along broad sidewalks. That, however, is somewhat of a limited view. In fact, the city by the bay in which the Quimbys finally settled was a frenetic, noisy, smelly, and thoroughly fascinating mash of cultures, crime, chaos, and questionable characters. It all happened astoundingly fast. Such is the power of gold.

From about the time Captain John B. Montgomery fired the USS *Portsmouth's* big guns and rowed ashore in 1846 to plant the American flag and, a year later, proclaim the modest community of Yerba Buena would forever be known as San Francisco, *growth* became its defining quality. Thousands of eager-eyed prospectors—some of whom had little more than a shovel, a pan, and a dream—converged on the sandy little town in every possible conveyance. The population erupted from approximately three hundred in 1848 to twenty-five thousand just twelve months later. In the same amount of time, eleven visiting ships a year swelled to seven hundred, and San Francisco Bay became one of the busiest seaports in the world. Many of those ships were abandoned by crewmembers scurrying inland to find their fortunes, so the city eventually used the sunken relics as the foundation for an enormous landfill that became seven blocks of new shoreline.

The Bay Area's notoriously wet climate, coupled with steep hills, slick cobblestones, and a constant crush of carriages and overloaded carts, often led to gruesome disaster. One such particularly horrific incident in 1869 was witnessed by a suspension bridge–builder named Andrew Smith Hallidie. As he watched, a fully loaded horse-drawn streetcar began to slide backward down a hill, picking up speed as it went. The subsequent gory accident killed all five horses, injured countless passengers, and so affected Hallidie he went on to invent the first cable car system. By the time the Quimbys arrived in 1900, there were twenty-three cable cars threaded around the city, and, with the expansion of the city's electrical grid, some of these were already being replaced by electric versions.

Like 1899's mercurial Triple Crown–winning thoroughbred, Flying Fox, progress nationwide was bursting from the gate at a spectacular pace. Oil wells began sprouting in Kansas, Illinois, Oklahoma, Louisiana, and Texas. John D. Rockefeller controlled more than 90 percent of the nation's burgeoning refinery business, eventually feeding the growing demand created by the founding of the Ford Motor Company a few years later. Telephones were becoming commonplace, cities were stringing electric wires as fast as they could, and the Wright brothers were working out the details of their flying machine.

By century's turn, William, Ursula, and Harriet lived at 420 Montgomery Street, so named for the aforementioned captain, in an apartment described as not much better than a hovel. Theirs was an eclectic, somewhat sketchy, neighborhood near Chinatown and the infamous red-light district of Barbary Coast. The stretch of Pacific Avenue between Montgomery and Kearny was so plagued by theft and violence that it earned the nickname Terrific Street.

Chinatown held a special fascination for Harriet. From the moment the first three Chinese immigrants arrived in San Francisco in 1848, tens of thousands of Asians rapidly embraced the city while forming a distinctive enclave all their own, filled with hard-working families determined to carve a better future for their children. Perhaps it was that ethos and devotion that spoke to her most deeply. The aesthetics and customs of a foreign land beguiled her, and certainly one could be forgiven for mistaking photos taken in Chinatown during the late nineteenth century for the timeless alleyways of Beijing itself. But even the seedier sections of the neighborhood, which can be found in almost any sprawling city, did not dissuade Harriet from exploring. A map from 1885 details where visitors could buy cigars, get their laundry done, smoke opium, gamble, or spend a few furtive moments with a lady of ill repute.

Attracted to these new adventures and experiences, Harriet spent hours wandering the narrow warrens, soaking up the sounds and smells and images. To say her trips to Chinatown were formative would be an understatement; they were *transformative* to the now twenty-five-year-old. There she developed an intense, almost obsessive fascination with other cultures and travel, which she would in due time be able to indulge. Her horizons were expanded. The rigging of her imagination was set, the sheets were trimmed, and the lines cast free.

It was also around this time that Ursula altered the family narrative. She slapped a fresh coat of paint on their history of dirt farms, failure, and poverty, and what emerged was a *Jane Austen*-esque romantic tale of private tutors in France and New England and stately homes in California and New York filled with a priceless collection of English Staffordshire ware. William's curriculum vitae now included a stint as a member of the US Consulate Service. The ruse somehow stuck. Articles from as recently as 1982 cite the myth without dispute. And in countless interviews over the years, Harriet herself never denied being to the manner born.

There are plausible explanations for why Ursula was able to pull off this sleight of hand. Thanks to her good old *Quimby's Liver Invigerator* [*sic*], which William was selling up and down the Pacific Coast as far away as Oregon, and supplemented by prune sacks Ursula made for a fruit-packing factory, the family finally had some money for nice clothes and fashionable hats. Harriet pitched in by clerking at a neighborhood store. It's also likely that the young woman described as "stunningly beautiful" and "a willowy, beautiful brunette with green eyes" simply possessed the looks, intelligence, and grace to put any doubts concerning her background at bay. It was perhaps inevitable that the outgoing and spirited Harriet would be introduced to a loose affiliation of journalists, musicians, and artists whose raucous clubhouse was located near her new home.

"Weaving spiders come not here," reads the enigmatic motto on the brass plaque at the entrance to the Bohemian Club, which still exists on Post and Taylor streets. The saying is from Shakespeare's *A Midsummer Night's Dream* and is a veiled enjoinder to those who venture inside that no talk of business or politics is welcome. Although originally established as a place for male reporters and writers to gather, the club had fairly light membership requirements in its early years. Candidates would ideally be "young, as radical in their outlook on art and life; as unconventional, and, though this is debatable, as dwellers in a city large enough to have the somewhat cruel atmosphere of all great cities." Poet and early member George Sterling defined the movement further:

> Any good mixer of convivial habits considers he has a right to be called a Bohemian. But that is not a valid claim. There are two elements, at least, that are essential to Bohemianism. The first is devotion or addiction to one or more of the Seven Arts; the other is poverty.

That "other" prerequisite was abandoned over a century ago. What is now a men's club for the wealthy and powerful, including a handful of American presidents, was once a fraternity of intellectual and artistic progressives, some would say radicals, who enjoyed each other's company for long conversations about art, philosophy, or history, accompanied by a drink. Or two. Or five. Numbered among the early members were Jack London, Mark Twain, Ambrose Bierce (author of *The Devil's Dictionary*), artists Charles Rollo Peters and Maynard Dixon, and the editor of the *San Francisco Call*, Will Irwin. Rumors of "bawdy gatherings in Carmel and Monterey" during which the Bohemians "danced naked in the woods, feasted with wine and thrived on communal enthusiasm" undoubtedly laid the first bricks in San Francisco's eventual reputation as a home for liberal hearts, moral turpitude, and open minds.

Harriet immediately bonded with this extraordinary group of free thinkers and their equally curious female companions. Such was the former farm girl's trust and comfort among them, and perhaps her growing self-awareness, that she sat for a nude portrait by her new friend and likely photography mentor, Arnold Genthe. The photograph reportedly hung over the club's fireplace until its building was destroyed in the earthquake of 1906. In perhaps a Victorian-era attempt at revising her image as she became more famous, later accounts claimed the portrait of Harriet mounted in the club was a more modest one painted by her friend Ada Shawhan, in which the future aviator was fully clothed. Regardless, it didn't take much encouragement by this band of irreverent nonconformists for Harriet to become more of a risk taker and explore her creative side. She began modeling for artists and photographers around San Francisco and eventually dipped her toe into an avocation for which she had no previous training.

As the economic ship finally gathered steam across the US, so too did the public's interest in being entertained. Americans found themselves with a few extra coins in their pockets and a desire to experience new things, have a laugh, shed a tear. To meet that demand, a network of hundreds of theaters featuring traveling minstrel shows, acting troupes, and vaudevillians sprang up in cities large and small. The popularity of these performances cannot be overstated. New York City was the epicenter of theater life, but even in cities as far-flung as Toledo, Ohio, audiences at the Burt Theatre could watch the currently popular melodrama for thirty cents. An average of forty-five thousand people a month there attended four hundred and eighty-eight performances of sixty-four different plays. The golden age of theater was born.

On a late-May evening in 1900, the electric spotlight brightened at San Francisco's Sherman Clay Hall, revealing two people on stage. The audience quieted and shifted in their seats to get more comfortable. A voice was heard calling out from beneath a makeshift balcony:

> O, speak again, bright angel! For thou art as glorious to this night, being o'er my head, as is a winged messenger of heaven. Unto the white-upturned wondering eyes of mortals that fall back to gaze on him when he bestrides the lazy-pacing clouds and sails upon the bosom of the air.

The young actress playing Juliet, with long, flowing curls bathed in the beam of light as she perched on the makeshift balcony, was Linda Arvidson. Below her stood Romeo, gazing up at the object of unrelinquished love, reciting Shakespeare's timeless words, "But soft! What light through yonder window breaks? It is the east, and Juliet is the sun." Those words were said by Harriet Quimby, who was playing Shakespeare's tragic hero. As was customary at the time, both actresses were appearing under stage names: Lina Johnson and Hazel Quimby.

The two women treading the boards that night were most likely introduced through their mutual Bohemian acquaintances at the Clay Clement Company's Columbia Theater, where Harriet was working as an extra. They would remain life-long friends. Linda was one of the witnesses on the misty cliff who watched Harriet's Blériot monoplane disappear into a cloudbank over the English Channel twelve years later.

Linda, who went on to become a successful film star married to pioneering and controversial *Birth of a Nation* director D. W. Griffith, explained how they found themselves on the stage that night in her autobiography, *When the Movies Were Young*:

> My job-hunting pal, Harriet Quimby, a girl I had met prowling about the theaters, concluded we were getting nowhere and time was fleeting. So we hit on a plan to give a recital in San Francisco's [equivalent of] Carnegie Hall, and invite the dramatic critics hoping they would come and give us good notices.

But, as with most young actors' realities, the women's dreams were hobbled by a lack of financial resources.

> The Homer Henley Quartette which we engaged would charge twenty dollars. The rent of the hall was twenty. We should have had in hand forty dollars, and between us we didn't own forty cents.
>
> Harriet Quimby knew Arnold Genthe, and, appreciating her rare beauty, Mr. Genthe said he would make her photos for window display for nothing. Oscar Mauer did the same for me, gratis. Rugs and furniture we borrowed, and the costumes, by advertising in the program, we rented cheaply.

Still pathetically short on funds, Harriet and Linda ginned up the courage to approach James D. Phelan, the wealthy and "charitably disposed" mayor of San Francisco, and told him of their financial troubles. They must have made for an appealing team. Jimmy, a distinctively bearded man with an intense stare, inherited a fortune from his father but considered business a "sordid mess" and chose public service as his preferred occupation. He saw himself as a patron of the arts whose primary vision for San Francisco was beautification. He contributed thousands of his own dollars to the creation of decorative fountains and statues and pushed his upper-crust friends to do the like. Unfortunately, Phelan was also an unabashed racist who ran for reelection in the US Senate in 1920 under the banner: *Save Our State from Oriental Aggression—Keep California White*. He lost.

But on that day, Linda recalled,

> most attentively and respectfully [Phelan] heard us. And without a moment's hesitation gave us the twenty. So we gave the recital. We sold enough tickets to pay the Homer Henleys, but not enough to pay the debt to Mr. Phelan.

The mayor never got his twenty dollars back, but at least two critics did attend the performance. From the *San Francisco Chronicle*: "Peter Robertson...writes thus pleasantly of the dramatic recital of Hazel Quimby and Lena Johnston: Miss Quimby...gave an especially clever performance." And the *San Francisco Dramatic Review*: "Miss Hattie Quimby, a San Francisco girl of great dramatic promise... she is sure to be a success in time." It's probably no coincidence that review was penned by another close friend of Harriet's, schoolteacher Charlotte Thompson, who was an aspiring playwright and columnist for the *Dramatic Review.* There would come a time when Harriet was in a position to return the favor.

"But," Linda later admitted, "the recital didn't seem to put much of a dent in our careers." Harriet made a few other minor theatrical appearances, including as an extra in a scandalous production of *Sappho.* One of her fellow actors, Jean Patriquin, who went on to work for Mary Pickford Studios, remembered, "The first act of Sapho [*sic*] was a fancy dress ball, all of us in character. In our big dressing room was a lovely dusky girl with long lashes that shaded, I think, dark blue eyes, dressed as Roslyn. It was Harriet."

Had Harriet fallen in love with the smell of the footlights and the applause of the audience, her life could have taken a very different path. But it was not to be. The word "theater" comes from the Greek *theatron*, meaning, roughly, "a place to behold"—to behold the truths of the human existence; the ironies of life; the tragedies of love; the comedic twists of happenstance. Harriet ultimately beheld that she wasn't much of an actress. During some unexpressed moment of revelation—perhaps while gazing in the mirror applying makeup in order to affect someone else's face, recite someone else's words, convey someone else's thoughts and feelings—she realized that brief moments on stage portraying the pale imitation of an interesting character were no longer interesting to her.

Instead, she discovered in herself a passion and ability that would eventually lift her to breathtaking heights. Her two decades of watching, listening, thinking, forming opinions, asking questions, making new friends, stepping boldly into new situations, or simply having difficult or risky experiences—all those would become tools in the hands of a natural-born literary mason. She would build her own future on her ability to pave a path of words toward new adventures, for a considerable following of readers.

3

WHY, I JUST BEGAN TO WRITE

WILL IRWIN MUST HAVE felt like his office door was blown open by El Niño winds as the tall woman, a dervish of skirts and overhung bonnet, swept in and stood before him. She spoke quietly, with "a low voice and a brilliant smile." But Harriet Quimby had come to learn few could deny her an audience; fewer still could manage to say no to whatever her request might be. Like the tidewaters that still besotted the San Francisco before the Embarcadero was built, she was beginning to realize there was an inevitability in simply refusing to be constrained. On that day, her request was straightforward: she wanted to be a reporter.

The *San Francisco Call* was one of the most popular newspapers of its day, eventually merging with a competitor to become the long-running *Call-Bulletin.* William Henry Irwin, its young editor, happened to be a member of the Bohemian Club. He sported wire-rimmed glasses and a mop of unruly hair that rose and fell in waves on the back two-thirds of his head despite his best efforts to tame it, giving him the appearance of a man who had seen a few dozen more years than his birthdate would indicate. He was to become regarded as one of the best muckraking journalists and war correspondents of his day, eventually landing bylines in the *New York Sun, McClure's Magazine,* and *Collier's Weekly* before turning to novels and short stories. Will was as tough and ethical professionally as he was insubordinate in his personal life, having been kicked out of Stanford University for "beer drinking and inventive pranks" before finally returning to lock down a bachelor's degree against the better wishes of the faculty committee. He was a good fit for the Bohemians and likely either knew Harriet, or knew of her, before she walked in the door.

Whether or not he believed her to be up to the task, Will came to some sort of arrangement with Harriet, for the October 1, 1901 edition of the Sunday *Call* featured her very first article. It's easy to imagine Irwin gave her the advice all the best journalism teachers still do: *write what you know*. Because what she knew best was the world around her, which she explored with joyful abandon. Harriet's first published piece is entitled "Artists' Colony at Monterey":

> Slowly but surely the quaint old adobes, with their tiny barred windows, through which many a pair of bright eyes have flashed a message to the soulful orbs of Don Amourio, waiting below—the tumble-down ruins, half-hidden by the growth of jasmine: the old patio, with carpet of grass more luxuriant for the spaking of blood from the defeated toros, who ingloriously breathed their last within those four stone walls while cheers of the enthusiastic assembly echoed and reechoed, swelling with pride the breasts of the triumphant toreador—all these are with soft brushes and skilled fingers being transferred to canvas, for here in this little Venice of America can be found a genuine colony of artists.

What surprise did Will Irwin's eyes betray as he first read her submission? Did the facile choice of words, the visual descriptions, or the thumping pace that draws the reader forward to the next paragraph convince him here was a singular talent?

> Generations may come and generations may go, the quaint old adobes may be replaced with modern structures, but the Monterey of today will live on forever. Nowhere will you find the iridescent lights, now purple, now gray, that gleam through the mists in the soft tope [*sic*] so wonderfully beautiful as are found here.

That was the moment. Inside a cluttered office in the 315-foot-tall Call Building skyscraper came the inception of an unlikely career, which would define and enable and encourage a woman of exceedingly modest beginnings to constantly redraw the boundaries of society's expectations. When Will, who waded through a dozen articles a day, hundreds a year, and who wrote as many himself, set down the sheets of paper, looked up at her, took off his glasses, wiped them free of smudges, and then asked her to go write more stories as good as that, he had to be thinking he was witnessing something very special. And in fact, even years later, he praised her journalistic instincts.

That Harriet could so skillfully craft her first story, with at best a high school education, family mythology notwithstanding, is testament to three things: her intellect, her self-driven curiosity and voracious appetite for reading, and probably her mother's insistence that the Quimbys' only remaining child would never be limited by station or circumstance. One can see Ursula's revision of the Quimby family history as an unseemly deception, or one can see it as a staunch refusal to accept the sad lot fate imposed upon them. She proved to be the far better farmer than her hapless husband. Without a doubt, it was she who planted the seeds, nurtured the sprouts, and celebrated the emergence of a unique spirit. And in return, Harriet was determined to find a way to support her parents financially. Much of her ambition, work ethic, and, perhaps, courage grew from the years she spent watching them scratch a meager living from the ground and from failed businesses. That was their past; she would make sure it was not their future. The path to success would be built on adventure and words. As she explained to a reporter ten years later:

> Why, I just began to write. I always had rather a taste that way, and when I went to San Francisco, I began doing Sunday stuff for all the papers there. Occasionally I got things into the magazines, but the greater part of my writing was the sort that people lump under the general title of "newspaper work."

A few days after her initial meeting with Will Irwin, she roused herself in the middle of the night and made her way to the fishing docks for a story about the life of a fisherman. She was advised to get there early. "Two o'clock in the morning—ye gods, what an unearthly hour to begin one's daily work," she grumbled. A tugboat sat idling, belching out black smoke that "mingled with the veil of fog that hung over the water." The captain led her aboard his fishing vessel and directed her to sit out of the way as the fishermen stowed the nets and long coils of rope. In what would become her signature style of narrative, she cheerfully took the hands of her readers and brought them along with her to experience every aspect of the trip:

> Have you ever heard orders given from hurried men in Italian-French-American? If not you have missed a treat for those sons of the seas all have musical voices, strange to say. It may be the salty air or it may be the diet of garlic, for I have heard somewhere that the latter is excellent for the voice, should one have the privilege to use it. At any rate these folks have no nasal twang nor have they gruffy, throaty tones. Clear reverberant and musical through the fog came the mingled chatter, interspersed by an occasional laugh, for evidently the presence of strangers is a novelty and therefore somewhat conducive of

> good nature. Then perhaps we looked like green-horns, using nautical terms, that they anticipated seeing our complexions turn color when we neared the choppy water out beyond the bay.

After the gear was finally stowed and all hands on board, the boat pulled away from the dock and yawed out to open water, the lights of San Francisco twinkling behind them through the foggy dark. With the moist sea air in their faces, the crew chugged past Alcatraz Island, which, to Harriet, "looked like the huge giant with an eye in the middle of his forehead of our childhood's fairy tales, for the lamp in the lighthouse winked and blinked through the mist, which envelops everything in a sort of phantasm."

The fishermen busied themselves with prepping the nets with bait: beef liver or sardines. There were two sets of netting—large ones that hung off the sides of the boat, and smaller circular ones that held the bait. When they finally reached the fishing grounds the crew began lowering and raising the nets, which often contained "greenish creatures seemingly all legs."

> As it neared the noon hour everybody found a comfortable seat and waited for "breakfast"; did not wait very patiently either for the salty air gives one a royal appetite. Great round loaves of bread were brought out and sliced in no dainty proportions. Upon them, about an inch thick, were placed good-sized rounds of beefsteak. Another inch slice of bread was added to this. Then the novel sandwiches with an onion to each were passed around.

Credit Harriet with knowing instinctively that the general reader would be fascinated with every small detail. She went on to repeat a recipe for fish stew told to her by one of the crewmembers, and she performed her reportorial duties by describing what the typical catch was:

> fifty boxes, seventy pounds to the box, compiling all kinds—flounder, tomcod, seabass, codfish, and occasionally small sharks. Crabs, too, are taken up in the dragnets, sometimes an octopus, and not infrequently the nets are torn into shreds by some deep sea monster becoming entangled.

"A Day with the Fishermen" is a nicely crafted, descriptive, entertaining piece of first-person journalism. But this, the second of some two hundred and fifty articles Harriet wrote throughout her career, also contains an anecdote that defined her style of personal storytelling—a revealing glimpse of humanity buried near the end of the piece:

> One of the most popular characters of this little world all by itself is the Collector of wharfage rent, Luther G. Norris. For nine years he has held this post and the fishermen look upon him as a sort of godfather, angel, and good friend, which he certainly is. It has been his duty to see that each one of the 150 boats landing at the wharf pays to the State the proper rent, which ranges from 25 cents per week for the smallest skiffs to $1 a week for the largest boats.
>
> It is said that sometimes when continued rough weather prevents a catch with a profit, and some of the least lucky drop off on the luxury of macaroni and eat just bread with their wine, the wharf rent is paid promptly just the same, and sometimes a few dollars reach the toil-hardened palms when most needed.
>
> "And do they always pay back?" I asked Mr. Norris, when I repeated what I had heard. He was not anxious to discuss the subject, but

said that during all his nine years there he had "yet to find one of the fishermen that would go back on a friend."

It's the smallest peek into a proud, private man's kindness that only someone who knows what it's like to have nothing would notice.

1901 was a cacophonous riot of a year, where so much was happening it was difficult for anyone to keep track. Spindletop well blew in Beaumont, becoming the first Texas oil gusher. Baseball's Major League was formed. Queen Victoria died after sixty-three years on the throne, shortly before the public was made aware of the genocide of twenty-six thousand Boer prisoners of war in South Africa, women and children included, at the hands of British soldiers. William McKinley was assassinated by an anarchist and Theodore Roosevelt assumed the presidency. Alabama changed its constitution to require literacy tests in order to hinder black votes. The first trans-Atlantic radio signal was sent from England to Canada—the letter S in Morse code. And a German immigrant to America by the name of Gustave Whitehead claimed to be the first man to fly a powered machine, two years before the Wright brothers lifted off the sands of Kitty Hawk beach.

Gustave was twenty-seven at the time. His large ears clung to his head below the level of his eyes, like those of a charging elephant. As a boy in the fields of Leutershausen, Bavaria, Gustave (then Weisskop), the second child of Karl and Babetta, experimented with kites and trapped birds to try to understand how they flew, an activity the police did not take kindly to. He soon earned the nickname the Flyer, which would become ironic later in his life, especially to the family Wright, who used the same name for their first successful aircraft. At thirteen, he was orphaned and set about on a series of adventures that read like a Robert Louis Stevenson novel: bouncing between the homes of various relatives, landing a machinist apprenticeship, talking his way onto an

Australian ship and spending a few years as an itinerate sailor, and then briefly putting down stakes in Brazil before ultimately finding his way to Ellis Island in 1893.

With a newly anglicized name and a job as a kite builder for New York toymaker E. J. Horsman, Gustave began experimenting with putting motors on gliders at Harvard's meteorological station. He was eventually hired as a mechanic for the Boston Aeronautical Society.

On August 14, 1901, an article appeared in Connecticut's *Bridgeport Herald* that described, first-hand, Gustave piloting his Number 21 aircraft—constructed of bamboo and featuring a 20-horsepower engine—for half a mile, reaching an altitude of fifty feet. The article was accompanied by a drawing, not a photograph, of the craft he named the *Condor*, and for that reason the event has forever been clouded in doubt. Rumors of a photograph remain unproven. The Wright brothers disputed the account to their dying days, but they, of course, had plenty of reasons to do so.

Historical detectives believe that the unnamed author of the *Herald* story was likely the newspaper's editor, Richard Howell. Richard was an artist before he became a reporter, favoring illustrations over photographs. He described Gustave and another man driving the airplane like a car, with its wings folded up along its side. The reporter said he followed it on a bicycle and the contraption reached speeds of thirty miles an hour at times. It was obviously capable, in his estimation, of making the forty miles an hour necessary to take flight.

At the start of the experiment, Gustave realized some trees were blocking his way. "I knew that I could not clear them by rising higher, and also that I had no means of steering around them by using the machinery." His solution was to shift his weight side-to-side, yawing around the obstacles like a sailboat around a sequence of buoys. According to Richard, Gustave landed the craft "so lightly that [he] was not jarred in the least."

The story about the first flight of a human in a powered aircraft was international catnip, snatched up by more than two hundred newspapers. Even the respected *Scientific American* profiled Gustave and his accomplishments. A piece in the *New York Evening World* included a photograph of the inventor sitting on his airplane with a caption featuring the inventor's bold prediction, "Within a year people will be buying airships as freely as they are buying automobiles today and the sky will be dotted with figures skimming the air."

And yet, Gustave's claims were eventually rejected by the aviation community. The reason: no photographic evidence. A drawing would simply not satisfy the skeptics. The inventor pushed back. In a letter dated January 17, 1902, he promised the editor of *American Inventor* he would "send you some [photographs] of No. 21 [flying]" and that "this coming Spring I will have photographs made of Machine No. 22 in the air and let you have the pictures taken during its flight." He said he had already attempted to do this, but the weather was bad and the "snapshots that were taken did not come out right." Inexplicably, the magazine never received any photographs, nor ever heard from Gustave again.

Fame and fortune and historical approbation thus eluded him, but not from lack of effort. He found moderate success in building motors for other aircraft manufacturers, but he was more interested in creating his own flying machines and other contraptions than in getting wealthy. In 1911, Gustave invented both a sixty-bladed helicopter, which lifted itself off the ground without a pilot, and an automatic concrete-laying machine for road building. But there was an unfortunate, even tragic, chasm between his creative abilities and his business acumen. After eventually disappearing into factory work as a laborer to support his family, Gustave died in obscurity of a heart attack at the age of fifty-three, believing until the last that he was denied his rightful place in history because of a surge of anti-immigrant and anti-German sentiment in pre-WWI America.

Was the Bridgeport flight the Piltdown Man hoax of aviation? In the 1930s, several witnesses signed affidavits that they saw the flight, as well as subsequent successful attempts, happen. Harvard University economics professor John B. Crane published a 1936 article in *National Aeronautic* magazine that disputed Gustave's contentions, but he then reversed his conclusions after numerous eyewitnesses contacted him. And a group of aviation experts in 1986 reproduced the Number 21 airplane from Gustave's detailed description as a proof of concept. They successfully made twenty flights of up to 333 feet. (The Wright brothers' first attempt went to 120.) To this day, aviation historians are of two minds about Gustave's assertions. With little concrete evidence, the world may never know if the *Condor* did, in fact, fly on that summer day in 1901, and whether it was Gustave Whitehead, not Orville Wright, who was the first human to cast off the shackles of gravity aboard a manned, powered, and controlled aircraft.

It's unclear if Harriet ever knew of Gustave or his claims. She never mentioned him in any of the many articles detailing her own efforts to, quoting Shakespeare's Romeo, "bestride the lazy-pacing clouds and sail upon the bosom of the air." It might just be that in her years as a novice journalist, her eyes were not yet lifted toward the heavens. That time would come. But for now, Harriet found fertile ground for her new profession in the ripe fields of Chinatown. It was a subject she would revisit and write about time and again.

> Down on the fringe of San Francisco's Chinatown stands an old-fashioned domicile with barred windows. In front of it hangs a huge, almost transparent red lantern.... The doors are covered with long narrow slips of paper of that peculiar red.... Sacred from the

> inscription over the door, to the blue smoke that curls up and mingles with the fog. It is the sacred furnace of Chinatown, in the first of which are incinerated the papers, the discarded books, even the daily newspaper of the Chinese quarter. Their ashes are holy.

There was a moment, while wandering around the bubbling-potted, steam-billowing storefront Chinatown kitchens and the narrow streets that doubled as joyfully noisy playgrounds, when Harriet noticed that there was nary a piece of paper littering the ground. "There is everything else from fish heads to broken lanterns, rags, sacks, bottles, debris of every description, but a paper—no." So she did what she always did so well: she asked why. The story appeared in *Overland Monthly* under the title, "The Sacred Furnaces of Mon War."

> The letters of the Chinese are held sacred because Confucius and his contemporary sages used the same characters to reach the world with the words of wisdom which have immortalized their names. Letters that enter into any of the names of the Chinese Saints are reverenced, last and best reason of all, because the ancestors, almost from the beginning of time have used this silent method of communication. Out of respect to them their papers and letters are thrice sacred.
>
> "We cannot understand your attitude in regard to the literature of your country," said Mr. Ting, the pastor of the Chinese Baptist Church. "You are seemingly indifferent. The new arrivals from our land, never having seen anything like it done before, are surprised and alarmed when they behold you wrapping packages with newspapers, cleaning windows, kindling fires, or any one of the hundred uses that papers are put to every day."

The sacred furnace Harriet visited, the Mon War, which loosely translates to Furnace of the Beautiful Writing, was inside a cramped apartment. The oven itself was made of bricks and stood about five feet tall and four feet wide. Papers awaiting incineration were piled up on the floor like ink-stained drifts of snow. A "fierce-looking dragon" decorated the wall behind a lamp burning peanut oil. Clouds of aromatic incense spiraled toward the ceiling. The keeper of the furnace, tasked with transforming the sacred papers to ash, began reverently placing them into the raging furnace, then, when the cinders cooled down enough, shoveled them into burlap sacks. Harriet continued,

> Once a week these bags of ashes are taken by a Mon War wagon kept especially for the purpose to the water front, and there in a boat manned by Chin Ching and his assistants, are rowed far out near the Golden Gate, where the waters are pure and the tide runs swift. There they are emptied out, and on the crest of the waves are swept out to mingle with the salt of the Pacific.

Harriet recounted in the article that, as she was finishing up her interviews one evening, she noticed a stooped old man feeding a group of stray cats that gathered on his front steps. He told her they came every night at the same time, and he was morally obligated to feed each one, despite his lack of personal wealth. When she asked him why he made a regular visit to the butcher just for their welfare—after all, the cats weren't his own—he struggled to explain the contradictions of the beliefs contained in the well-worn Chinese-language Bible he held up and those of the more ancient tenets of Confucianism and reincarnation. He paused before responding. "Maybe when I feed cats . . . I feed my father," he finally said, "my brother, or my uncle."

Harriet closed the piece with the wry observation, "There is no more interesting place in the quarter than the Sacred Furnace of Mon War, and the nightly rendezvous of Chin's spiritual ancestors."

Photographs that accompanied the story were uncredited, but it was around this time that Harriet began learning how to use a camera. She was probably taught by her Bohemian acquaintance Arnold Genthe. Many of her subsequent articles featured remarkable pictures of places and cultures most Americans had never before seen.

In addition to contributing stories to various publications, including the *San Francisco Call* and the *San Francisco Chronicle,* Harriet also began reviewing plays for the *San Francisco Dramatic Review,* where her good friend Charlotte Thompson worked as a columnist. Before long, she scraped together enough money to do something very few women at the time could or would. She bought one of the new contraptions that had only recently become available to the public: an automobile, a yellow runabout convertible, in which she would explore the countryside. Years later, she scoffed in print at the disapproving looks and condescending comments she elicited as a woman driver. Her driving was an early sign that she would not be limited by society's expectations.

By 1903, with her writing bona fides firmly established, she decided the time was right to climb another mountain. Harriet never lacked ambition. Driven by the twin goals of creating a comfortable life for her aging parents and the desire to see just how far her talents and determination could take her, she decided San Francisco had given her everything it could. All the nation's major publications were based on the East Coast. So she filled some steamer trunks, likely cradled her best articles in a leather satchel, and, with few dollars but more than a little confidence, boarded a train pointed due east, to New York City.

PART TWO

4

COME FULL OF FAITH IN YOURSELF

IN THE EARLY 1900S, getting onto the isle of Manhattan from the mainland to its west was even more of a frustrating challenge than it is today, but for very different reasons. No bridge or tunnel yet spanned the mighty, and mighty wide, Hudson River. So travelers crowded onto aging ferries for a relatively short, often choppy, ride from Jersey City to Pier 63 and the Twenty-Third Street Ferry Terminal. With its nagging clock tower, arched windows, and dark brick facade, the terminal building was more function than form, but it welcomed thousands of visitors a day, disgorging them onto the bustling streets of lower Manhattan to shop or work or wander.

Fruit stands, piled high with grapes and apples, lined the avenues, and fishmongers positioned their slippery wares on tables of ice just so, arguing with the competition about quality and price. Hairy-lipped men sporting bowler hats and bow ties, framed by stiff white collars perched above woolen vests, ambled along, their weight shifting languidly from side to side like a tree in the wind, hands in pockets, indifferently eyeballing the merchandise. Pushcarts loaded with every imaginably salable thing sashayed between pedestrians and horse-drawn carriages, occasionally attracting the admonitions of a strolling police officer, brass coat buttons straining at his girth, who twirled his baton threateningly at anyone obstructing traffic. For in New York, traffic was the arterial flow that fed the heart of the hungry city.

Onto this sardined island alighted a young journalist of considerable talent, even more ambition, and absolutely no usable connections. Harriet might as well have landed on a distant planet, so alone was she. The boarding house she settled into was dreary and depressing, "a desert waste where each one is centered upon his or her own interests, and where one will find herself becoming critical and cynical in spite of herself; for it is in the very air and contagious as measles." Her stay in that sad domicile didn't last long. She found a little room nearby for hire, bought a gas stove burner for ten cents for brewing coffee, and charmed the housekeeper into bringing her hot rolls in the morning. "You will find [a rented room] more comfortable and homelike," she later advised young women who were hoping to follow in her footsteps, "and it will permit you to peruse your morning paper without interruption, or to thump on the typewriter between sips if you are in a hurry to finish an article." Among her many superlatives, Harriet was also one of the few writers at that time to use a Sholes and Glidden typewriter with its novel QWERTY keyboard, designed with the most-commonly used keys placed apart to prevent jams and thus speed up typing.

"If you are a journalist come to New York by all means," she later wrote in an article entitled "The Home and the Household: A California Journalist Making Her Way in New York."

> Come, but come full of faith in yourself, with some real ability, however little, and money sufficient to keep you at least three months. With a fund of humor and a wholesome but not surplus quantity of courage, you will in time rejoice that you came; for while competition is keen, it is also an incentive, and the field is better in every way than it is possible to find in a city where two or three leading papers hold sway. But do not expect to make your expenses from the very first, for the certain failure to do so will cause you no end of worry.

On that, Harriet spoke from a wealth of experience. As soon as her bags were unpacked, she began making the rounds of every publication in the city and racked up an impressive sheaf of rejections over a period of several weeks. She described her frustrations in the third person:

> The free-lance of this particular narrative, fresh from the west, landed bag and baggage one day at the foot of Twenty-Third Street, New York City. So far as she knew, there was no one in the entire city whom she had seen before. She had in stock a couple of years' experience on a hustling Western paper, a goodly batch of letters of introduction (still unused), good health, a well-developed sense of humor, and some, but not too much money.

She soon discovered, to her chagrin, that the pretty face that opened many a door in San Francisco was not as effective a weapon in the Big Apple, where attractive women were about as rare as tulips in Holland. "A writer, however good-looking, who thinks she will make an impression on a New York editor regardless of her work is making the mistake of her life."

But Harriet's luck was about to change, thanks to John A. Sleicher. A proud product of Troy, New York, John entered newspapering there at the *Morning Whig* as an accountant straight out of high school, but quickly realized he preferred words over numbers and fled to the other side of the building, where the reporters were undoubtedly having more fun. By the time Harriet showed up, sample articles in hand, he had relocated to the nation's center of publishing between the Hudson and East rivers and was editor of *Leslie's Illustrated Weekly*.

What began as a modest engraving business—whose biggest client was showman P. T. Barnum—evolved into *Frank Leslie's Illustrated Newspaper* in 1855. It wasn't until the Civil War broke out that the paper started to make money. Thousands of readers were at once revolted and mesmerized by its gory depictions of battle, incentives for them to turn the page and keep reading. It's worth noting the only reporter killed in action during the Civil War was one of *Leslie's* freelancers, James R. O'Neill.

Weeklies like *Leslie's*, *Collier's*, and *Harper's* couldn't compete in timeliness, so, as Henry Loomis Nelson, the editor of *Harper's*, noted, "They must excel in quality—especially quality of illustrations." Frank Leslie, who was born Henry Carter and was the son of a wealthy English glove maker, invested heavily in the newspaper's engraving department, ultimately hiring seventy illustrators. Teams of artists sketched out the pictures that would accompany stories. These were transferred to boxwood blocks on which engravers carved out the blank areas of the illustrations, and then converted to copper plate for printing. *Leslie's* dependence on visual imagery would eventually extend to its heavy use of photography.

Leslie's was headquartered on Park Row—also known as Newspaper Row—near New York's City Hall, where printing presses churned out copy twenty-four hours a day. It was a thriving time for journalism. Joseph Pulitzer commanded his growing newspaper empire from inside the copper-domed New York World Building at 99 Park Row, designed by famed architect George B. Post. At 309 feet, it claimed the distinction of being the tallest building on the planet for the briefest time. Hungarian-born Pulitzer, who served eight months as a cavalryman under General Philip Sheridan during the Civil War, was, by 1903, in the middle of another type of battle. He was dueling with his archrival, William Randolph Hearst, for the hearts and minds and dimes of America. Pulitzer doubled the *World's* circulation within three months of taking it over, hired groundbreaking investigative journalist Nellie Bly, and established his reputation as a supporter of courageous reporting.

During Harriet's early days in New York, skyscrapers were surpassing church spires as "the dominant feature of American urban skylines." Scott Joplin's addictive syncopated toe-tapper, "Maple Leaf Rag," could be heard emanating from every saloon. By sending its youngest children to kindergarten, a German import, the nation raised its literacy rate to 90 percent, even as Congress imposed a literacy test for immigrants in an attempt to stem the flow of new arrivals.

It was around this time corporations and government officials began to imagine there were large red bull's eyes painted on their backs, largely because publications like the *World* and *McClure's* saw subscriptions increase with every salacious article about greed, political shenanigans, and public betrayal. S. S. McClure, a mustachioed, bow-tied Irishman, took it as his mission to "lay out a comprehensive critique of American society" and decided "that the two great issues confronting the country were the growth of giant corporations, and the concomitant surge in political corruption." He instituted the revolutionary policy of editorial patience—rather than demanding immediate copy from his reporters, he gave them all the time they needed to dig into a story. He didn't have to wait long to see the impact.

On a November morning in 1903, readers who plunked down ten cents for *McClure's* were awed by the reporting of Ida Tarbell, who systematically dismantled the reputation of John D. Rockefeller's Standard Oil with a prosecutorial recitation of case after case of "bribery, treachery, fraud, coercion, and intimidation." Four years later, Judge Kenesaw Mountain Landis, who is best remembered as the Commissioner of Baseball during the 1919 Black Sox scandal, fined Standard Oil $29 million—almost $700 million today—and declared the company "no better than a common thief," largely on the basis of Tarbell's work. The story was a sensation and spawned a new commitment among journalists, magazines, and newspapers to hold the powerful accountable.

In the following nine-year period, two thousand such exposés were printed in New York City publications alone.

Among those cheering the aggressive journalism was New York's governor, Theodore Roosevelt, who, when he found himself a resident of the White House a short time later, soon regretted that position and tried to "staunch the flood of investigative reporting he'd helped unleash." His secret collusion with the powerful banker J. P. Morgan to create what in effect would become the vassal state of Panama for US business interests was one of the greatest scandals of his presidency (a scandal that Joseph Pulitzer exposed in the *World*).

Harriet would eventually contribute to the growing field of investigative reporting, much of which was conducted by female journalists who were able to access areas and situations men couldn't, that directly led to cultural changes in society. Her work included a story about the "grip of gambling on women" and an exposé about a secret investigation into widespread prostitution in Manhattan:

> Dens of infamy masked under the guise of manicure parlors, employment bureaus, massage parlors, hair-dressing establishments, French restaurants, Greek refreshment rooms and coffee parlors, and even fruit, candy and cigar stores are numerous, and they are to be found in what are supposed to be the respectable streets of the city as well as those in the parts of the city designated as the "Tenderloin." In the light of these appalling facts, unearthed by official investigation, we can no longer doubt that the social evil is rampant in New York. The investigators are specific in their statements and these statements are sworn to. They give names of streets and numbers of houses and the names and numbers of policemen, sergeants and captains who appeared to be, if not in league, at least in sympathy with the human traffic which disgraces the Tenderloin and other sections of the city

> and which affords a profitable business to hundreds of Raines law hotels [short-stay hotels usually located above saloons, designed to skirt strict liquor regulations. Many of the 1,500 in New York were *de facto* brothels].

Harriet's 1911 article exposed a blight the public assumed was long eliminated. Ten years earlier, scores of detectives organized by the Committee of Fifteen, a "high-powered group of bankers, corporate execs, Wall Street lawyers, academics, and civic leaders," descended on the gambling joints and brothels in Chinatown, Little Italy, and the Lower East Side. Vigilante groups soon followed their lead, with one led by Judge William Travers Jerome, who would burst into various dens of iniquity using an ax to splinter the door, hold up a Bible, and declare, "This is the law! The police won't enforce it. It is for the citizen to act!" "St. George of Manhattan," as the press dubbed him, is credited with shutting down forty-five brothels and sixty-nine gambling dens. He went on to become district attorney and continued his anti-prostitution campaign, but by the time Harriet began exploring the streets of lower Manhattan, his attentions, and those of the police, were drifting elsewhere. She reignited concerns about the treatment of women and criminal activities in the city, which eventually led to the resignation of New York's police commissioner.

That was in Harriet's future. But before she could join the ranks of crusading fact finders, she first had to get a job.

Journalism was thriving; journalists were not, at least not financially. *Leslie's* was among those publications notoriously miserly when it came to paying their freelance contributors—on average, five dollars for a thousand words from an unknown writer, about half-a-cent per word. The upper limit for a more famous contributor was, at the most, fifteen cents a word, but those notable bylines were rare. Jack London, who once was paid all of five dollars for an article he crafted for the *National Magazine*, sought imaginary revenge in his novel *Martin Eden*, during which the protagonist grabs a magazine's business manager by the throat, and screams, "Dig up, you venerable discourager of rising young talent! Dig up, or I'll shake it out of you, even if it's all in nickels!"

Regardless of the pathetic pay, an estimated twenty thousand aspiring writers—not unlike the young today who are ensnared by the irresistible riptide of movie and music fame—vied for publication in turn-of-the-century America. This caused the *New York Times* to lament that most were "either not successful or only apparently so." A concern echoed in the New York *Chautauquan*: "The mere itch for authorship—the *cacoethes scribendi*—has become a pestiferous epidemic against which there appears to be no adequate and practicable guarantee."

Harriet, as a determined and willing victim of that epidemic, recounted her first meeting with editor John A. Sleicher in *Leslie's* offices:

> It began in an interview with a particularly sarcastic editor of an influential weekly, who after a few questions and a hasty glance over the first paragraph of the article I had brought with me, informed me with seeming enjoyment that he did not in any way consider me a genius.

As she sat there absorbing John's insult, perhaps intended to take her obvious self-confidence down a peg or two, inwardly Harriet began to question whether he was right, and maybe she should consider washing windows or learning to cook in order to make a living. But the hard-nosed editor's next words jolted her out of the gloom; he offered to pay her for the article, and he commissioned more. Her relationship with the magazine took root, one that would last the rest of her life. The first check from *Leslie's Illustrated Weekly* became a "never-failing mascot." Harriet and John, who eventually formed a close professional bond, would often laugh about their first meeting years later.

For inspiration and subject matter, Harriet didn't have to search far. The Chinatown of New York eclipsed all others, including that of San Francisco. A Cantonese immigrant and businessman named Ha Ken first established a cigar store on Park Row in lower Manhattan in the 1850s, opening the gates to what would become the largest concentration of Asian people in the Western Hemisphere. A single step onto that three-quarters of a square mile of Manhattan metamorphic rock was an instantaneous journey of 6,824 miles to the ancient traditions, food, and languages of mainland China.

This was a place immediately familiar to Harriet, who found herself as entranced by the multi-tonal, clamorous conversations, the unfamiliar fragrances, and the foreign customs as she did inside San Francisco's Dragon's Gate. "I found the Chinese settlement of New York an inexhaustible source of copy. I poked about, enjoying the scene, rich with color and noisy with a peculiar tongue, and rarely did I come back without at least a column of copy."

That first "column of copy" was actually cribbed from her *Overland Monthly* article "The Sacred Furnaces of Mon War," with a few additional tidbits. Entitled "Curious Chinese Customs," it published in the January 22, 1903 edition of *Leslie's Illustrated Weekly*:

> The educated and the illiterate, alike, believe implicitly in the prognostications for the future. The high priests who enjoy an income from this superstition can be found in considerable numbers in the Chinese settlements. They generally hold court under a huge umbrella, with a table for a desk, on the sidewalk of the most traveled thoroughfare. To these sidewalk wizards the merchants and

> capitalists go for advice before taking any important step, in either business or love. The fortuneteller is an authority, and by all the power of magic his word is law. Various are the methods used in forecasting the future, but incense and a long prayer are the invariable accompaniment. And many of the predictions are correct, though the solution of this is not a mystery when one is told, that to see the future in a clear vision, the questions of the party wishing to know must be asked verbally. If the customer has not sufficient faith for that, then the wizard can do nothing for him.

Her initial, if somewhat self-plagiarizing, effort notwithstanding, Harriet found her niche in recounting the many interesting details of the "lower East Side, with its polyglot population," whose

> street signs, foreign customs, curb merchants, and little incidents all made copy which sold and still sells in the daily papers, and is also in demand for the voluminous Sunday supplements. One might easily invent these things and save the time, but this is easier said than done. Writers are often accused of "faking," but it is seldom that a story made up out of whole cloth passes muster. The prescience of the editors in this is something uncanny—in fact, they seem to have a sort of sixth sense in this regard. The best way to do, unless you have remarkable inventive genius, and in that case you would be writing fiction, is to find a good subject and proceed to write around it as truthfully as possible and at the same time making it entertaining.

Harriet professed a few years after writing this piece that her ultimate goal was to retire to write fiction by the age of thirty-five. That would have involved a nifty bit of time travel, considering she'd already reached thirty-seven.

What followed that introductory offering to *Leslie's* was a series of articles that, more often than not, chronicled some aspect of the richness of a multicultural city. A partial list from those early years includes "Chinese New Year's Feasts and Customs" (February 1904), "What Happens to a New Baby in Chinatown" (June 1904), "Chinese Military Brigade in New York" (August 1904), "Odd Features of an Italian Wedding" (January 1905), "The Germans in New York, and How They Celebrate the Metzel-suppe" (January 1905), and "The Spicy Hungarian Quarter of New York" (August, 1905). Her take:

> If one strays in for a Hungarian goulash he is greeted courteously, and he generally likes to remain; for the care-free atmosphere, romantic music, the lack of display, and the savory foods of foreign flavors are like a tonic to the diner who has been bored beyond measure by the inevitable sameness of the Fifth Avenue and Broadway cafés.

Harriet's freelance assignments began to increase in number and frequency, even as her paychecks from *Leslie's* and other publications usually arrived weeks late, and often only in the wake of "repeated reminders and some sass." But after six months of scrambling to cobble together a viable existence on the vibrant, confusing, fascinating streets of Gotham, Harriet finally figured out how to play the newspaper game. She was now earning between ten and two-hundred dollars a month, depending on the number of stories she sold, and found writing multiple features about various holiday seasons to be especially profitable. Her career was established in the great city that would be her home for the remainder of her life.

"Success cannot be spelled these days with a capital S," she mused, "unless one has special talent and a capacity for hard, grinding work; but the latter, with some ability and plenty of the spirit called go-aheadativeness, will after a year of discouragements mingled with occasional lightning flashes of success, more than repay one for coming to New York."

5

HANG ON FOR DEAR LIFE

ON JULY 23, 1903, a dentist in Chicago named Ernest Pfennig became the first person to buy a Ford Model A, a red two-seat convertible runabout that cost around $800. Its engine was a horizontally mounted flat-2 that produced all of 8 horsepower, with a top speed of twenty-eight miles an hour. The model became notorious for overheating and transmission problems, which were much improved in the Model C, released a year later. After burning through $28,000 of initial investment funds to build the factory and develop the prototype, the Ford Motor Company's working capital was almost exhausted, and as its founder and namesake watched his first customer drive off, he did so knowing the company had only $223.65 left in the bank.

Henry Ford gambled everything on the belief that middle-class Americans wanted affordable cars, and the only way to get them to the waiting public was to mass-produce them on an assembly line, as cheaply as possible. Like Harriet, Ford was born on a Michigan farm. A former engineer for Edison Illuminating Company of Detroit, he also shared with her a fascination with motored contraptions of all types. He even built and raced his own early models.

Harriet's appreciation for automobiles started at a young age. She was one of the only women to drive in San Francisco, and after her move to New York, she became one of the earliest licensed female drivers. It was a passion she also often mined for stories. The first appeared on August 13, 1903, the same year the Chicago dentist chugged away from the Ford factory:

> The chauffeur, his lean, sun-tanned face almost concealed behind a huge pair of spectacles, turned hastily in his seat and gave the lever a gentle touch. The motor-car, slim and graceful as a racehorse, quickly responded and backed over the edge of the high curb. There was an involuntary surge forward of the spectators, and a hundred pair of eyes were directed toward a gold watch lying with open case upon the asphalt pavement directly beneath the rubber-tired wheel. With a whir of its hidden machinery the black-painted car gave a quick lurch downward, then just as the watch vanished beneath the tire and every one listened for the faint smashing sound, there was an upward lift of the auto and the delicate watch stood revealed with its case closed. The audience applauded vigorously. "Prettiest trick I've seen anywhere," commented a stout man in a leather auto coat. "Closed the case as gently as a child could. It's wonderful how some fellows can handle a machine, isn't it?"

The article was about all the silly stunts drivers were learning to do with cars, from balancing them on large seesaws, to cracking eggs without crushing the yolks. It was lighthearted fluff to be sure, text that Harriet probably banged out in a single afternoon, but it quickly led to a more substantive and opinionated piece about automobiles and the women who drive them. She undoubtedly remembered the derision tossed her way while she weaved through the streets of San Francisco in her own little convertible.

> One of the marvels of this century is the woman with the automobile, and the avidity with which she masters the mechanism of the vehicle despite oily fingers and smudged face. The day of the helpless languid beauty has passed, and with the automobile... the alert, level headed woman who takes an interest in everything from the servant problem to astronomy is now occupying the immediate foreground.

She goes on to mock the "sensational clamor about the dangers of automobile traveling" and observes,

> It is no longer a novelty to see a sixteen-horse-power machine making its way through a crowded thoroughfare under the sole guidance of a woman. In fact, the importance of women in the field has reached a point where the manufacturers are putting out vehicles with special appointments to meet the demand of her fastidious taste. From the monogram plate and the clock, the fittings have extended to little pockets for veil, gloves, books, etc., a zinc-lined box for luncheon, and another box large enough for an extra hat should my lady be going a distance and wish to save her plumes from the ravages of the wind during a brisk run.

Eventually, Harriet took her love of motorcars to a new level, hinting at a fearlessness she would call upon in the future. Using every tool in her formidable arsenal, she charmed her way into the passenger seat of one of the most powerful automobiles of the day for a "brisk run" of one-hundred miles an hour.

On an early October morning, Harriet stood at the Vanderbilt Parkway on Long Island. The track was being prepared for the annual Gordon Bennett Cup, an early precursor to the Grand Prix and one of the "greatest races ever run in America," to be competed two days hence. The contestants were national automobile clubs, not just individuals. France, Great Britain, Germany, Austria, Switzerland, Belgium, Italy, and the United States could field three cars each with a driver and riding mechanic, each of whom was not permitted to weigh less than 132 pounds. Every competing nation paid an entry fee of three thousand francs, and together they covered the cost of the event. The winning driver was not guaranteed any prize money, but he could expect rewards from the manufacturer of his car and from his nation of up to $10,000.

That morning Harriet watched as a coating of oil was laid over the dirt track to harden it. The road bore ruts cut into it by drivers who'd been practicing for the event for weeks, getting a feel for their machines. Left behind was a daily carnage: every morning the local farmers gathered the carcasses of the unfortunate chicken or rabbit that happened to wander into a race car's path.

Next to Harriet squatted a "demon of iron and explosives and fire," a Pope-Toledo race car tuned to an unheard-of 120 horsepower. The driver, Herbert Lytle, was talking intently with the manager of the car company, A. E. Schaaf, and he didn't strike Harriet as being at all happy. As she later wrote with subtle understatement, "He thought twice before he gave his consent" for her to "hang on for dear life while...its driver put it through its pace." Herbert was undoubtedly thinking he was about to become party to a screaming farce; A. E. was undoubtedly thinking about all the free advertising for his company's automobiles an article would represent, given *Leslie's Illustrated Weekly's* three-hundred-thousand-a-week readership.

> "So you are going to ride in the racer?" says Herbert Lytle, who had reluctantly consented to take a chance at killing a journalist. "Afraid?" asked Bert Dingley, who won in the elimination race last year over the Vanderbilt course, and who will ride with Lytle this year in the race.

"No—not afraid?— stand eighty miles an hour? What—a hundred! Well, tuck your skirts well around you, and put on this duster and goggles, for the machine throws up dust and oil," a fact which you will experience later, when, after the thirty-mile spin, your face is a study in oil splashes of varying colors and sizes....

He is not nervous, for, after all, this is only a speed test, and he has entered and won two genuine races, besides winning honors at the American eliminating Vanderbilt race last year. He is not nervous, but there is a certain tension—there's no mistaking that. Through your goggles you look at him equally goggled and appearing in the darkness as uncanny as the machine he is driving sounds.

You are now going at about seventy miles an hour, and you feel the swift currents of air produced by the mad flight of the machine. Thump—what was that? "A spirit has slapped me in the face," you shout to Lytle. "Bug," he shouts back, and you think he is slangy, until you feel another and another, and still more. Thick and fast they come against you like a shower of rocks, and you find that they are really bugs which have been attracted by the headlights and have been overtaken by the flight of the car. These bugs nearly pound the life out of you during that ride. There is something ahead—merciful saints! You are going straight into it—but by the time you catch your breath you are a mile past. It was, after all, only a vegetable wagon, whose sleeping driver had allowed the horses to stray to the wrong side of the road. Again something—and with the driver you lean far forward as from the rail of a ship, vainly hoping to make out the vague object looming before you in the gloom.... You have a faint notion that you are dreaming, and that you will wake up to see the walls of your room.

It is beginning to get light, and more machines appear on the course. So far you have only been going at from sixty to eighty miles an hour, but now that it is light, Lytle says that he means to speed up a bit. You make a discovery that right before the driver's eyes, under the wheel, is the register of the speedometer, and this races back and forth, recording the varying speeds of the machine as it takes the curves and strikes the highway....

A curve and a sharp angle—there are thirteen curves on the course—you slow down to about fifty, and the car careens virtually on one wheel, and the whole machine seems lifted up in the air and comes down to earth again with a jump. You are so busy with the register, your hat, and the corner that you did not hear the lever click into fourth speed, but you feel the car leap—zip!—for the fraction of a minute you are going at a trifle over a hundred miles an hour. You think, if indeed you think at all, that if it goes much faster you will topple right over, but soon you begin to slow down, seventy, sixty, fifty. Why, you seem to actually crawl along at fifty an hour, and although every nerve in your body is quivering and you have just enough strength to hang on to the strap, you manage to shout an answer to Lytle, who asks with exquisite sarcasm, at the top of his voice, "Was that fast enough?" and you enjoy the satisfaction of seeing him nearly fall over with surprise as you fire back, "'Twasn't very fast; can't you make one hundred and twenty?"....

You are glad enough to start for home again, but you will remember for many a day how it seems to fly.

Portentous words, for the next time Harriet would reach one hundred miles an hour it would indeed be flying—in the pilot seat of an airplane. But it is the very first sentence in her article, "A Woman's Exciting Ride in a Racing Motor-car," that reveals her clever wit: "Hats off to the driver of a racing car!" Somewhere along the thirty-mile course, in the whipping wind and barrage of bugs, she had, in fact, lost hers.

6

IT'S THE SMILE THAT'S THE HARD PART OF DANCING

> As a curtain-raiser to "The Noble Spaniard," a W. Somerset Maugham comedy at the Criterion Theater, a little sketch written by James F. J. Archibald, a well-known war correspondent, was added to the program this week. Although beautifully staged as far as scenery and lighting are concerned, the piece is not only maudlin in its sentimentality, but it is wretchedly acted.

THAT SCATHING ASSESSMENT FLEW like the dark angel of death from the bulky black typewriter of *Leslie's Illustrated Weekly*'s drama critic, whose opinions carried enormous weight on and off Broadway. "Miss Harriet Quimby has the reputation for being the most entertaining writer in the theatrical world," her editor, John A. Sleicher wrote. "Those who are interested in stageland topics will find her criticisms and descriptions of current plays of more than passing interest."

As her clever turns of phrase and sly observations in covering everything from automobiles to foreign cultures to women's issues gained a steady readership, John offered Harriet the coveted position of drama critic in 1906. Her background in theater and acting, however brief, was seen as a solid foundation for reviewing the scores of shows that appeared in New York every year—230 in 1906 alone.

With the commensurate rise in income and status, Harriet could now afford to relocate to a suite in the Hotel Victoria between Broadway, Fifth Avenue, and Twenty-Seventh streets, right in the middle of the theater district. It boasted the distinction of being the only hotel in New York with entrances on two main thoroughfares. The strikingly elegant eight-story building featured "new plunger hydraulic elevators, safest and best in the world" and offered daily rates of one dollar and fifty cents and upward. After years of sharing bathing accommodations with various other tenants, Harriet was delighted to finally have her own private bathroom. She was also making enough money to send for her aging parents. It's not clear exactly when William and Ursula joined their daughter in New York, but they had to have been exceedingly proud that her reality was now competing with the family fiction.

Among the newly minted theater critic's first scoops was a refreshingly frank interview with arguably the most popular actress of the day, Rose Stahl, whose work in *The Chorus Lady* was almost universally heralded. From the moment the actress opened the door to her apartment until the columnist found herself strolling back home, Harriet could not stop laughing.

> The first thing that impresses the visitor to Miss Stahl is the absence of perfume. The windows are open, the curtains up, and there is no attempt toward a stage setting. There are no poodles or other dogs, no parrots, and there is also an absence of the inevitable maid. Miss Stahl is a comedienne to her finger-tips, and as irrepressible as the ripple of an ocean wave.

Like Harriet, Rose managed to keep her background somewhat of a mystery. Theatergoers wondered whether the slender, curly-headed woman with "beautiful soft hair with glints and plenty of them" was

William and Ursula Quimby with their daughter.

German or French, when in fact she was Canadian by way of New Jersey, the daughter of a newspaperman. To her stage-door autographs she added a signature phrase, a line from *The Chorus Lady*, "It's the smile that's the hard part of dancing."

In her interview with Harriet, Rose shared her secret desire to play Juliet someday (there's no indication Harriet told her about her own turn as Romeo) and confessed that she once considered becoming a nun. The conversation turned serious when Rose offered advice to anyone wanting to become an actress, betraying no small amount of bitterness over what her success had cost.

> "What is my hobby?" echoed Miss Stahl. "To have everybody like me. I want them to like my acting, too, if they can, but rather than that, if I am to have but one, I want them to like me."
>
> "As [my character in *The Chorus Lady*] would say, it is easy to be good when our brownstone front is situated in the Eden of the earth, Riverside Drive or the West End, as the case may be, and our tables are laden with the pomegranates of the land; but how about the other side of a great city? Advise a girl to go on the stage? Not if she can earn her three meals a day and a place to sleep in any other way. Why? Haven't you seen *The Chorus Lady*? Because only one girl in a thousand has the strength and the patience to stand the heart-breaks and the knocks that every successful actor or actress on the stage to-day has gone through from beginning to end before they saw the light of even moderate success. There is no such thing as hand-made success."

The hours melted away. Before Harriet saw herself out, Rose offered a parting comment that stayed with the journalist for the remainder of her life, when her privacy was harder to protect, and fame and fans became inexorable parts of her day-to-day existence: "The less the public knows of your private life the better it likes you.... At the peril of being found out, don't be too much on exhibition."

With the newfound power of her words and the reach of her columns, Harriet herself often handed out advice to those struggling to find their way in the world. In an article entitled "Chances of the Homely Girl on the Stage," she included an account of a telling moment between an acting teacher and an aspiring actress of less-than-gorgeous looks:

> "Not long ago a young woman came to me with a request that I hear her recite and give her a professional opinion," Mr. Sargent recalled. "I looked up from the desk and met the eyes of one of the homeliest women that I have ever seen....
>
> "Without any of the embarrassment attendant upon such occasions, the girl rose, announced her subject as an old Greek poem, and began. The transformation was remarkable. Her voice took on qualities which had seemed impossible from her speaking tones, the homely face lighted up, the stooped and angular body became as graceful as a reed. She seemed another person, so much is the body under the influence of the mind....
>
> "The result of the interview was that, without a request from her, I broke a cast-iron rule and gave her a letter to one of our greatest managers with a request that he hear her. Before long the world will hear of her. She is a genius, but what possible chance would she have had in an agency, where managers are on the lookout for attractive leading women? The fate of the average plain girl is character parts—the fate of the unusual one is fame."

As for Harriet's fate, it was about to take yet another unforeseen turn. At 5:12 A.M. on April 18, 1906, two enormous tectonic plates off the coast of California shifted along 296 miles of fault line, grinding together like the teeth of a gigantic leviathan. Twenty seconds later, when the vibrations reached San Francisco, glassware began falling from shelves, bricks from buildings, and sleeping residents from their beds. Local witness Peter Bacigalupi recalled,

> I was awakened from a sound slumber by a terrific trembling, which acted in the same manner as would a bucking broncho. I sat up in bed with a start. My bed was going up and down in all four directions at once, while all about me I heard screams, wails, and crashing of breaking china-ware and nick-nacks. I was very quietly watching the clock on the mantel, which was doing a fancy stunt, while the ornaments in the parlor could be heard crashing to the floor. A great portion of plaster right over the head of my bed fell all around me, and caused a cloud of dust, which was very hard to breathe through.

"I was within a stone's throw of that city hall when the hand of an avenging God fell upon San Francisco," wrote Fred J. Hewitt, "The ground rose and fell like an ocean at ebb tide. Then came the crash. Tons upon tons of that mighty pile slid away from the steel framework and destructiveness of that effort was terrific."

And said Emma Burke, who lived on Waller Street within site of Golden Gate Park,

> We never knew when the chimney came tearing through; we never knew when a great marine picture weighing one hundred and twenty-five pounds crashed down, not eight feet away from us; we were frequently shaken loose from our hold on the door, and only kept our feet by mutual help and our utmost efforts, the floor moved like short, choppy waves of the sea, crisscrossed by a tide as mighty as

> themselves. The ceiling responded to all the angles of the floor. I never expected to come out alive. I looked across the reception-room at the white face of our son, and thought to see the floors give way with him momentarily. How a building could stand such motion and keep its frame intact is still a mystery to me.

It was arguably the most terrifying sixty seconds any humans ever endured. The great tenor Enrico Caruso, who was in San Francisco to perform in *The Queen of Sheba,* was discovered minutes later by his orchestra conductor in suite 580 of the Plaza Hotel, still in bed, weeping hysterically, surrounded by jumbled piles of his forty pairs of boots and silk shirts, and the crystalline shards of a French chandelier. Seeking to calm the panicked singer, Alfred Hertz motioned for him to come to the window, assuring him that the earthquake was over.

> As they watched, a woman in a nightgown ran down the street, carrying a baby by its legs—"as if it were a trussed turkey." Several men stood around with shaving lather on their faces. A couple were carrying a large painting out of a tenement block across the street. Everybody seemed to be talking, "as if it was all too much to take in," and hoping that by talking they could make some sense of what had happened.

Alfred opened the window. Turning back to Enrico, he commanded him to sing. The tenor was incredulous at first, but the conductor insisted, somehow instinctively knowing the proud Italian needed to regain his grip on reality, his courage, and thus, and perhaps most important of all, his public image. Enrico hesitated, then, to the amazement of the stunned people stumbling around the street beneath them, leaned over the sill and unleashed one of the greatest voices of all time.

It was a brief reprieve for a very few from the horrors of the morning. But then came the fire, which consumed some 28,000 buildings. Almost 500 people perished, and 225,000 out of a total population of 400,000 found themselves instantly homeless. Arnold Genthe, Harriet's friend and photography mentor, stood at the top of Sacramento Street, taking pictures of the wall of flames and smoke as it marched inexorably closer, like a Dantean army from hell. People in the foreground of his photos are seen standing on sidewalks amid the rubble, gawking in disbelief. A few blocks south, in the brick building where weaving spiders were warned away and writers expounded on grand ideas, the portrait of Harriet that Arnold took years earlier was reduced to ash, like the sacred papers of Chinatown.

Among the multitudes who suddenly found themselves without a place to live were Harriet's close friends Charlotte Thompson, Linda Arvidson, and Linda's new husband, David Wark Griffith. All three decided it was time to move east.

David was in New England on business at the time, but Linda found herself in a long refugee line at the train station with nothing but Red Cross–donated clothes on her back. "Where to?" the clerk asked when she finally made it to the window. "Boston," she replied. "What is your occupation?" "Actress." He nodded and handed her "a yard of ticket." On May 9, she boarded a train with a box lunch of fried chicken, raw potatoes, and two small bottles of California claret, kindly provided by friends. Along the way east, she cried herself to sleep every night.

Months later, to Harriet's delight, Charlotte showed up at the Hotel Victoria and proceeded to rent a room. Newlyweds Linda and David, who at some point decided he would prefer to be called D. W., moved into a more modest flat downtown. The change of venue proved immediately beneficial to Charlotte, the former San Francisco drama critic turned struggling playwright, as *Leslie's* star theater writer was now in the perfect position to introduce her to the movers and shakers of Broadway as well as return an old favor. Harriet did so with a glowing review of Charlotte's *The Awakening of Helena Richie* that virtually guaranteed her dear friend future billings:

> Margaret Anglin's return to America, after reaping honors before critical audiences in Australia, has been signaled by unqualified triumph in a part which affords her the best opportunity that she has ever had and which lifts her to the foremost rank of America's emotional actresses. Who but Margaret Anglin could play Helena Richie? Is the query which hovers on the lips of those who attend the performances of "The Awakening of Helena Richie," Charlotte Thompson's dramatized version of Margaret Deland's novel, which, because of its problem, has been one of the most-discussed books of recent years. Who, indeed?...audiences have become so accustomed to sex problems that it requires something very unusual in both character and interpretation to wring so much as a sigh of sympathy for one. That Miss Anglin and Miss Thompson have succeeded in compelling genuine tears for Helena from an always more or less blasé Broadway audience speaks more for their combined efforts than anything that can be written.

The Griffiths would end up forging an even closer working relationship with Harriet, in a very different medium. It took some time, however, for D. W. to find employment in the new city, and jealousy gnawed at him when their old friend came to visit. Linda recalled,

> Harriet Quimby was now writing a weekly article for *Leslie's,* and summering gratis at the old Oriental Hotel at Manhattan Beach as payment for publicizing the social activities of the place. Beach-bound one day, she called at our modest ménage, beautifully dressed,

> with wealthy guests in their expensive car. As the car drove off, Mr. Griffith gazing sadly below from our window five flights up, as sadly said, "She's a success."

D. W. viewed Harriet's triumphs as an inverse reflection of his own lack thereof.

> What Miss Quimby—and others—had achieved with apparent ease weighed heavily on him. One can detect no direction in his career to this point, no movement that would have imparted to him a sense of progress toward a well-defined goal. Indeed, he seems to have had none, beyond a generalized desire for economic well-being derived from a career in one art or another.

Weeks later, a five-dollar bill changed his fortunes and the entertainment industry forever. An old friend D. W. knew since his Louisville summer-stock days mentioned in passing that he'd been "going down to a place on 11 East 14th Street and doing some kind of weird acting before a camera." The money wasn't great, he explained, but a buck in hand… He said,

> "I work in them during the summer; make five dollars some days when I play a leading part, but usually it's three. Keeps you going, and you get time to call on managers too. Now you could write the little stories for the pictures. They pay fifteen dollars sometimes for good ones. Don't feel offended at the suggestion. It's not half bad, really."
>
> "Ye gods," said the temped one [Griffith], "some of my friends might see me. Then I would be done for. Where do they show these pictures? I'll go see one first."
>
> "Oh, nobody'll ever see you—don't worry about that."

The next day, D. W. walked into the offices of American Mutoscope and Biograph Company and asked for an acting job. The man at the desk barely looked up. Motioning to the stairs, he told Griffith to go below and put on some makeup. After a short rehearsal and some rudimentary stage directions, the camera began noisily grinding through twenty feet of film. When the scene was finished, the director handed D. W. his pay for the day and asked him to return tomorrow, when they would be filming outside "and there were to be horses!"

"It's not so bad, you know," an amused D. W. told his wife later, "five dollars for simply riding a horse in the wilds of Fort Lee on a cool spring day. I think it wouldn't be a bad idea for you to go down and see what you can do."

The couple never returned to a theater stage. D. W. Griffith went on to become among the most inventive, prolific, and ultimately controversial directors of the silent-film era, and Linda Arvidson starred in many of his movies.

Motion pictures weren't much more than a novelty until 1895, when the Lumière brothers, Auguste and Louis, hired a pianist to accompany the first public projection, in Paris, of their film about the Lyon fire department. They shot with a camera of their own invention, named a *Cinématographe,* from which the word *cinema* derives. Within a few years a handful of visionaries cranked away with their heavy cameras and nitrate film stock, designing the angles, lighting, and visual storytelling the world now takes for granted.

As there were few movie theaters and even fewer investors, D. W. and Linda worked with minuscule budgets, requiring their actors to build props, make their own costumes, supply their own makeup, and sometimes pen their own scripts. They often recruited family members, friends, and even people they happened to meet on the street, as actors. Experience was no requirement for an industry in which no one had any.

But even given those limitations, the couple found that by working fast and hard, they could make a good living.

Harriet wrote several scripts for D. W.'s nascent production company, including *The Fisherfolk*, in which she had a small walk-on part and, more significantly, for which she became the first credited female screenwriter. "True love is born of the soul, hence it is stable, but love induced by personal appearance is as transitory as winds, changing with each new attraction," reads the handbill promoting the film. "In this Biograph subject the line is clearly drawn comparing the two, with fate a controlling power."

Over a period of twelve months in 1911, sitting at her Sholes and Glidden typewriter in her hotel suite, Harriet proceeded to write six more:

> *The Broken Cross*—A country boy on leaving his little sweetheart on his departure for the city to seek his fortune plights his troth [betrothed]. The girl breaks in two a cross giving him one half as a love token agreeing that if either wishes to break the engagement he or she will send back the piece. In the city a manicure girl becomes impressed with him and tries to win him for herself by sending him a piece of broken cross purporting to come from his country girl sweetheart. Her scheme at first seems to be successful, but he discovers the parts do not match and so, disgusted with the falseness of city living, goes back to the country and his little sweetheart.
>
> *His Mother's Scarf*—The moral of this Biograph subject is the power of a mother's love. Two brothers out in the wilds of the Western hills, meet and fall in love with a young girl, who was the sole survivor of an Indian outrage. Through jealousy one brother is about to annihilate the other when the sight of a scarf, the present from their mother, now

dead, awakens his better self. The scenic beauty of this production has never been equaled.

In the Days of '49—During that exciting period men were wont to rush from place to place in their mad lust for gold, and Bill Weston was one of these, who, after locating with his wife in one settlement, goes off to another where the chances seem better, intending to send for her if he strikes luck. He hits it fairly well and so sends a letter telling his wife to take the first coach out, which she does. On the way she meets handsome Jack, the gambler, who, riding on the same coach, deeply impresses her with his attentions. When she meets her husband, who is but a plain honest fellow, she compares the two, and Jack finds it easy to induce her to meet him later and go away. Bill feels his wife's coolness towards him and is grief stricken, telling the boys of the camp that his wife does not love him. Jack sees his plight and realizes what a great wrong he is working so he goes away leaving a note advising the wife, "Don't be a fool. Appreciate a good man's love while you have it. Go back to your husband who loves you with a better love." The wife at this is also awakened.

A Smile of a Child—The innocent smile of a child has more influence than any other power in the world. It can change the cloudy into sunshine as will be seen in this Biograph subject. An ill-tempered Prince is met by a little child who is wandering through his grounds, and his entire nature is changed into one of excessive good nature. Later, while out on a lark, he meets for the first time a very pretty peasant woman, to whom he, by virtue of his rank, makes sinister advances. It happens that she is the mother of the same child and it enters in time to arouse the Prince to his better self with its sunny smile and saucy wink, which wink is really infectious of good nature.

The Blind Princess and the Poet—The blind princess upon consulting the soothsayer is told that upon the first kiss of unselfish love she receives she will see. All the great lords assemble to pay her court and bestow kisses in hopes of restoring her sight. There are Lords Gold, Selfish, Folly, Presumption and their ilk, but their attentions are in vain. A poor Poet has humbly loved the Princess, but considers himself unworthy until the Child Equality argues differently. Lord Good in rage kills the Child Equality and the Poet loses hope. However, when the Princess sleeps the poor Poet steals a kiss. The Princess sees, and through the Poet's kiss. Lord Selfish would kill the Poet but he is thwarted by Justice, as the Poet goes singing to his apparent death. Justice takes him to the Princess's side.

Sunshine through the Dark—The poor little housemaid, with her tired hands incessantly toiling, despairs of ever experiencing a kindness, for although she reproves herself for complaining, having what she deems a good job, still her life is that of one driven like a beast of burden. Even the spoiled child of the household orders her about and treats her with absolute disdain. The child wears a bright ribbon sash, which to the poor eyes of the slavey is overwhelmingly beautiful; so much so that she is tempted to steal it. She has it in her possession but a few minutes, when she reproaches herself and starts to return it. But, meanwhile, her act has been discovered and she is denounced as a thief. This is done in the presence of her sweetheart, the stable boy, who at first turns from her, but finally realizing the act was one of impulsiveness, forgives her and takes her to his heart.

The question is, did Harriet take D. W. to *her* heart? He had soulful, dark eyes, a creative mind, and a dimpled world-weary smile, which he might flash during their long evenings crafting screenplays, dining and wining, and admiring each other's climb to the top of their respective careers. Were these enticing enough for Harriet to betray one of her closest friends? D. W.'s biographer, Richard Schickel, implied so:

> We do know, from an interview with a former Biograph employee, that at some point in this period he was wearing a ring presented to him by Harriet Quimby, the aviatrix-journalist whom he had met through his wife. We also know that he betrayed no outward sign of strain when his marriage broke up.

The director already had a reputation as a ladies' man when he and Linda separated in 1911, with no reason ever made public. They continued to work together for many more years. He went on to become arguably the nation's single most important filmmaker, producing five hundred movies. He forged an art and industry that carries his mark to this day, despite the stain of his unapologetically racist magnum opus, *Birth of a Nation,* the world's first blockbuster, which earned an estimated $10 million ($254 million today). He died a resentful man, ostracized by the Hollywood he created, alone in the lobby of the Knickerbocker Hotel in Los Angeles in 1948. He had completed his last film, *The Struggle,* more than a decade earlier. In recalling D. W. Griffith, Charlie Chaplin once shrugged and declared, he was "the teacher of us all."

Harriet never spoke of him in her many interviews, and she and Linda Arvidson remained the best of friends for the rest of her life.

7

WE MUST SEE THE SPHINX BY MOONLIGHT

HE POSSESSED A SWOOP of brown hair that leaned over the right side of his forehead like a fallen tree branch, wide-set, kindly eyes, and a right arm stolen from the god of thunder. Christy Mathewson was born to play baseball. From the age of fourteen he played it professionally, when not kicking footballs on a gridiron, and by the end of his career he amassed 2,507 strikeouts and an ERA of 2.13. He strolled into the Baseball Hall of Fame as one of the first five initiates. In the 1905 World Series, he carried the New York Giants to victory over the Philadelphia Athletics on the strength of his three shutout games. Over that period of six days, Christy allowed not a single run, and he gave up only fourteen hits.

On an autumn day in 1911, the "Big Six"—so named for his six-foot-plus height—stood on a pitcher's mound in Havana, Cuba, to face down an aggressive base-running local team. "They are as fast as lightning on the bases," manager John McGraw declared, "and they can throw to beat the band. They have picked all the knacks of fielding, but they cannot bat." Initially billed as a good-will cultural exhibition, the series turned out to be a hard-fought affair for the Giants and the other visiting American team, the Philadelphia Phillies, who dropped four games against the upstart Cubans and limped home with only one win.

The Giants, however, fielded not only Christy Mathewson, but also slugger "Laughing" Larry Doyle, who was riding into town on a .310

batting average. The Giants had a 99–54 win/loss record against the very best the United States could field that year. But the formidable Giants had not yet seen the fastball and "snapping curve" of Cuban ace José Méndez. The team that "cannot bat" split the series with the New York team 2–2. From that moment on, Cuba announced its presence in the baseball world, and the baseball world was forever better for it.

Even before the series, Cuba held a deep fascination for Americans. Closer to the mainland than Los Angeles is to Las Vegas, New York to Boston, or Chicago to Denver, Cuba was romanticized by travel writers as a friendly, relaxing, and tropical destination. One of those was Harriet Quimby, who ventured to the island nation as early as 1906 on holiday. Ever the frugal opportunist, she parlayed the trip into a paid vacation by submitting dozens of photographs to *Leslie's Illustrated Weekly.* These showed the rural life of Cubans, ponies laden with peddlers' wares, hat makers toiling in a thatched-roof hut, farmers carving their fields with a plow made of tree branches, and an early automobile race on the outskirts of Havana. Harriet was also able to cobble together no fewer than six articles from the week she spent there, including a discussion of the Americanization of the island nation:

> To one wandering along and enjoying the quaint charm of the narrow streets, scarcely wider than an aisle in a New York department store, and the sidewalks which admit passage of only one pedestrian at a time, it is not a little startling to suddenly face a sign which proclaims the principal business thoroughfare in this most Spanish of cities as O'Reilly Street.

That curiosity and eye for unusual detail once again caught the attention of *Leslie's* editor, John A. Sleicher, who, in 1907, promoted Harriet to foreign correspondent and sent her on an unprecedented and expensive around-the-world journey to Africa, Europe, South America, and the West Indies.

Over the past decade, ocean travel had dramatically improved for tourists of means. No longer would they be forced to endure what Harriet called a "stuffy cabin and coffin-like berth." They could now spread out in a five- or six-room suite, complete with a private bath, a food warmer, and a personal attendant. Between January and June of 1906, 118,000 people settled into first- and second-class cabins for the six-day journey from New York to Europe.

That following spring, Harriet embarked on the "lavishly decorated" *Amerika*, an enormous eight-deck ocean liner of the Hamburg America Line. The largest and most luxurious of its day, it featured the novelties of an electric passenger elevator and an à la carte restaurant. Some days she rose late and made her way to the deck, where she settled into a steamer chair, a gauzy, thin veil securing her hat against the ocean breeze. As she gazed out at sea or caught up on the news of the day transmitted to the ship via wireless, a deck steward served her a small cup of bouillon and "an array of dainty sandwiches of thin brown and white bread and Westphalian ham or cheese." She spent her evenings socializing in the main dining hall while listening to the resident band. It was a relaxing precursor to what became a grueling, but fascinating, twelve months. "It was tea-time," began one of her many dispatches,

> and Shepheard's porch was filled to overflowing with tourists. Everybody goes to Shepheard's at least once while they are in Cairo. The wicker chairs were filled with them—young and old, thin and stout—all doing Egypt. The waiters flew gently about—they were English waiters—carrying trays filled with the inevitable jam pots, plates of thin bread and butter, and other little plates filled with cakes. Ours had come, and the Englishman with me had assumed the duties

> of pouring, while I looked and listened. At an adjoining table a stout woman with two rosy-cheeked daughters, all three in deep mourning, talked across the table to a jolly-faced Western type who was traveling alone with her niece.
>
> "Yes," cooed the stout woman, "we've visited every mosque in Cairo and we've been to the pyramids twice—the girls did so enjoy having tea and the Mena House that we just had to go out there again. I'd like to see the Assuan [*sic*] dam, but it takes the better part of the week on the train to get there and back. And then, after all, it would scarcely pay, for there's nothing but temples and tombs between here and there, and when you've seen one temple and one tomb you've seen 'em all."

Harriet held no such view of the temples and tombs and people of Egypt; rather she was obviously enamored with the culture and its history, concluding one of the nine articles of her wanderings there with the enthusiastic declaration, "We must see the sphinx by moonlight." In another story she mused about "The Mysterious Women of Egypt":

> Mystery, together with a veil which conceals every feature, compels one and all unconsciously to accredit an Egyptian lady with dazzling beauty and immeasurable charm. In the light of this universal disposition of mankind to consider the veiled daughters of the Nile fair to look upon, the few who have seen them, minus veil and mystery, commend them at once for keeping covered.
>
> Egyptian eyes, masculine or feminine, are beautiful—beautiful in a varied way—and their charm is considerably heightened by the concealment of the other features... And because the rest of her face is hidden, the Egyptian woman early learns to use to the best advantage that part which peeps over the veil.

> To see an Egyptian woman on a donkey is a most curious sight. She always rides astride and never at a gallop, but either at a jog-trot or a walk, and she is always accompanied by some male relative or a servant. The Egyptian woman is inconsistent, in that while on the street she has little fear that her feet and a portion of her ankles will show just so long as her face is covered, but, once perched up on a donkey, it is extremely vulgar, according to her notion, to allow her feet to hang down as nature intended. This train, which sends up little cyclones of dust as the wearer glides along, is designed to cover her tracks, so that susceptible men who may pass along the same road may not see the footprints in the sand and become infatuated with the woman who made them. This notion of the Orient may sound a trifle foolish, but we cannot be too severe with the Egyptians in this belief when we recall the fact that only last summer some New York ministers recommended, and almost commanded, that women who attended service wear hats because the beauty of their hair distracted the attention of the masculine worshipers from the sermon.

While Harriet came from a fairly religious family and eventually refused to fly on Sundays at her parents' request, she couldn't resist this little dig at oppressive, even sexist restrictions. The article also hints at her feminist leanings, which she assiduously kept to herself. What bothered her more than chauvinism, though, was the poor behavior of Americans on the world stage. Prior to her yearlong adventure, she had denounced British writers who criticized her fellow countrymen when abroad as "prigs ignorant of their subject." Her perspective changed somewhat after she endured the full-voiced, spoiled demands of a child in the tight confines of a transport ship and the embarrassing "vulgarity" of a young woman who felt the rules of acceptable behavior were different in Europe. While conceding the cliché of "loud-voiced, strenuously-inclined" Yankee tourists, she added, somewhat kindly, that Americans could also be "generous to a fault, good-natured, easy-mannered" and "appreciated by the hotel-keepers and catered to by all that have anything to do with the tourist business, because they are far the best paying of all the travelers."

In London, she watched in amusement as a "young and good-looking French woman" pampered her little dog with more tender care than "the majority of women do upon their firstborn." It was fed out of its own special basket, wrapped up against the chill air, and sported a "gay collar with a huge bow." The former farm girl laughed out loud when the French woman pulled out a bottle of mineral water and a tiny folding traveling cup and gave a drink to her pet. In Nice Harriet noted, "Everybody... is young, apparently, and everybody is cheerful." And evidently, everybody shares the same views as the French woman on pet care: "Apparently every woman and girl in Nice either buys, begs, or borrows a dog of some kind for no other purpose than to put a big bow on his neck and to show him off on the promenade, where he tows the owner along like a disabled yacht."

The native divers of St. Thomas caught her appreciative eye, as "unusually splendid specimens anatomically, and their brown bodies, bare except for an abbreviated hip girdle, glisten in the sun as they poise on the edge of their tilting craft." When she stood on top of Ancon Hill in Panama, Harriet marveled how it was possible to look upon the Atlantic and Pacific oceans at the same time. She felt "appreciation of the gigantic size of the channel which has been cut through the mountains at the cost of thousands of human lives and hundreds of millions of dollars, and which is easily the most important public work being carried on in the world to-day."

Given her affection for automobiles, it should come as no surprise that Harriet spent much of her time motoring around various countries.

Once back from the journey, she published an article giving her fellow drivers a warning:

> It is in Paris that stories are circulated concerning some of the French garages which have a neat trick of emptying, by means of suction pumps, the gasoline and cylinder oil tanks of the cars that have been run in for the night, leaving just enough fuel to get the machine well underway before the loss is discovered.
>
> Again it is in Paris that one hears all about the watered and dirty gasoline that is sold in Italy, and which, bad as it is, costs all sorts of prices, sometimes reaching as high as a dollar and a quarter a gallon. The dirty gasoline, which even the straining through chamois will not clarify, is one of the principal causes for engine trouble in Italy.
>
> It is on these foreign trips that the American becomes patriotic and longs for the clean gasoline produced by the much-abused Standard Oil Company. The matter of gasoline is the most serious financial proposition with which automobilists abroad have to contend.

The article is accompanied by one of the many photographs Harriet took during her travels—that of a "country woman en route to the market... on the back of a hat-wearing donkey." While her words and descriptions amused, educated, and opened up the world to her readers, her photographs intrigued and perhaps even shocked them. The National Geographic Society began featuring pictures in its groundbreaking magazine in 1905, only two years before Harriet's 1907 trip, and in those early years Harriet's contributions to *Leslie's Illustrated Weekly* were every bit as novel. Her photographs introduced Americans, often for the first time, to piñatas in Mexico, sponge-trimming in Nassau, a Hindu priest in the West Indies, and a family's stone-and-thatch hovel in Ireland. She photographed donkey drivers bathing in the Nile; mental hospital patients tending a garden in Central Islip, New York; a Romani family pulling a Punch and Judy–themed hurdy-gurdy cart in London; and Laplanders passing time in front of their earthen yurt. In other photographs she shows a legendary Florida fisherman fight a thirty-pound grouper onto a rickety skiff, and a lovely young Trinidadian girl smile shyly, ankles crossed, arms beckoning, as if initiating a dance.

Many of her best photos were included in a series of books the *Leslie's* company published from 1910 to 1919. Harriet's ear for a good story was evenly matched by her unerring eye for interesting, often strikingly beautiful images. Sadly, she has never received full credit for this talent.

8

A PRETTY WOMAN IS PRETTY WHATEVER HER DRESSES MAY BE

SHE WOULD'VE TAKEN A little more time in front of the mirror preparing for an evening out than for a day at work, but not too much more. Harriet never wore a lot of makeup. Perhaps this was her way of moving in and out of the world more freely and easily, and another way for her to detach from the cultural expectations of her day.

By 1908, women's clothing took a turn toward the more fitted tailored blouses and skirts. *Démodé* were the cumbersome bell-shaped dresses of the earlier decades, embellished with frills and laces, and Mme. Gâches-Sarraute's masochistic corsets, although the new "health corsets" that forced women into an unnatural S-shaped bosom-forward-bottom-out posture were still in vogue.

Harriet gave serious consideration to her raiment, even though her wardrobe closet was anything but overflowing, as evidenced by the fact she was often photographed in the same few ensembles. She was rarely seen without a hat, usually one that dipped low around the sides, framing her face. She had a slightly chipped front tooth, which, when she smiled, reinforced the impression of her mischief and youth. Even though she was earning a good salary now, enough to support William and Ursula who had recently moved to New York from California, Harriet was far from wealthy. She complained that maintaining a respectable appearance took a great deal of money and effort.

When Eve plucked a fig leaf in the Garden of Eden and converted it into a costume, there began a tragedy which has ever since been attached to the problem of clothes. The desire for personal adornment is universal. To shine in the splendor of beads and feathers and broadcloth and fine linen is an ambition which stirs in the breast of every rational and irrational man, woman, and child....

To get enough to eat is a comparatively simple matter; but to earn enough to dress respectably and somewhere near the prevailing mode, and to house and care for the garments after they are once procured, is without doubt one of the most serious problems of everyday life confronting the great majority of the less prosperous wage earners. To be in the height of fashion is not imperative, but to keep somewhere within a year or two of the pace set by the austere *Dame la Mode* is necessary if one lives in a city and works for a livelihood. The working woman cannot afford to be conspicuous with something extremely old-fashioned or a costume constructed in a makeshift manner, because her dress is apt to be regarded by her employer and her associates as a significant expression of character and sustaining an intimate relation with manners and morals. A pretty woman is pretty whatever her dresses may be, it is argued, and there is more or less truth in the assertion; but the fact remains that a pretty woman is ten times prettier when she is well and harmoniously garmented, and many a woman who has no claim whatever to beauty has gained the reputation of being beautiful because she thoroughly understands the intricacies of gowning and the wonderful effects of harmony of color.

Harriet managed to maintain enough energy to work during the day and attend shows or social events several nights a week, yet, in later interviews, she admitted strenuous exercise wasn't how she kept fit.

> I don't think I could be classified as an "athletic woman" at all. I don't care for golf, and I don't like tennis, nor am I very fond of walking. It may be because I'm inherently lazy. I'm exceedingly fond of horseback riding (you know I'm a Californian), and I thoroughly enjoy running a motor, if you call that a form of sport.

She'd taken to wearing various trinkets—scarabs from Egypt or clay figures from South America—picked up on her overseas trips as jewelry, and she joked that they were her good luck charms. (The scarab ring she gave D. W. Griffith was the only piece of jewelry he wore.) Those decorations were likely the last things she would place around her neck and wrists before bidding her parents goodnight and sweeping out the door.

Outside, the doorman would hail a ride for her, or whoever was accompanying her for the evening would be waiting on the sidewalk, perhaps with a corsage in hand as was the fashion. In those days taxis were the easiest way to get around New York, largely because of a man named Harry N. Allen. In 1907, the thirty-year-old grew so angry after paying five dollars—one hundred and forty dollars today—for a horse-drawn hansom cab ride of less than a mile that he shipped sixty-five gasoline-powered automobiles from France and founded the New York Taxicab Company. "I got to brooding over this nighthawk," he said. "I made up my mind to start a service in New York and charge so-much per mile." He painted them a bright yellow so they could be spotted by potential customers from far away. Within a year, seven hundred taxis were chugging around Manhattan.

On Harriet's night out, perhaps the couple, or a trio or so of friends, caught the latest spectacular at the "gargantuan" Hippodrome, where an audience of between five and eight thousand could watch everything from "onstage auto races or naval engagements fought in the humongous eight-thousand gallon water tank." Or they took in the senior Oscar

Hammerstein's production of *Salome* at the Manhattan Opera House in the area of town he helped transform from unimpressively named Longacre Square to the Times Square of today. Maybe Harriet found herself in the dark, at one of the six hundred nickelodeons that sprung up seemingly overnight in the city, alternately laughing and marveling at Georges Méliès's "fantastical fourteen-minute film *A Trip to the Moon*" that had been pirated and distributed around the US by none other than Thomas Edison. She likely attended New York's first appearance of famed prima ballerina Anna Pavlova, as the Russian star spun and swirled on stage to Mikhail Fokine's *The Dying Swan*.

If it was a working night, she would be seated near the front of any number of theaters, taking notes about "the delightful revival of that old Gilbert and Sullivan favorite, 'The Pirates of Penzance,' at the Casino," or fashioning a particularly brutal assessment of a less-than-competent player:

> With the opening of the autumn theatrical season, another star is scheduled to rise on the horizon. Laura Crews, who for years has played in inconspicuous parts in the supporting company of some star, is, so a press agent says. I have nothing in the world against Miss Crews. She is a pleasing and altogether likable little person, but I cannot see any reason whatsoever for thrusting another mediocre actress upon the public in the guise of a star.

Afterward, Harriet and her entourage would have gone to one of the dozens of fine restaurants in Midtown such as Rector's, which featured the city's first revolving door and 175 tables to accommodate the theater crowds. With an interior modeled on other, more famous restaurants—Delmonico's and Sherry's, for example—Rector's attracted anyone and everyone who wanted to see and be seen. Entering the enormous main room, millionaires, politicians, producers, actresses, and actors paraded through an "opulent stage set," with "their reflections ricocheting in the floor-to-ceiling gilded mirrors."

For a more intimate experience, Harriet and her consort might have dined on *potage mongol* followed by *paupiettes de bass, sauce aux crevettes*, and a *sorbet de fantaisie* under the stars on the roof of the Waldorf Astoria Hotel, or on the excellent prime rib at Keens Chophouse, beneath the world's largest collection of churchwarden pipes, smoked by the likes of John Barrymore, Theodore Roosevelt, and, of course, Sir Arthur Conan Doyle's Sherlock Holmes. Despite the best efforts of the Woman's Christian Temperance Union, dinner would be served with alcohol, probably champagne, the drink most favored by trendy ladies of the day. Harriet was known to smoke cigarettes, although discreetly, as a 1908 law banned women from doing so in public. A Manhattanite by the name of Katie Mulcahey was arrested for smoking, fined five dollars, and thrown in jail the week the law went into effect. She bears the distinction of being the only person punished under the quickly rescinded stricture. While at dinner or clubs, Harriet would have regaled her company with stories about her world travels. She maybe even told a joke or two, like this groaner she included at the end of a column: "'Say, the Bell Company charges for phoning!' a miserly customer complained. 'So I've been tolled,' grumbled the other."

But the last forkful of cake, or last effervescent sip of Veuve Clicquot, did not necessarily spell the end of the evening. With the speed of a Blitzen-Benz race car, new sexual mores overtook Victorian ideals of behavior after the turn of the century, especially in the big cities. And the engine for that change was music.

Bands everywhere were learning Irving Berlin's "Everybody's Doin' It Now," Harry Williams's "Naughty, Naughty, Naughty," and George Botsford's "Honeysuckle Rag." African American composers along Tin

Pan Alley on West Twenty-Eighth Street, so named for the dissonant sound of badly tuned pianos emanating from almost every open window, were churning out as many sheets of ragtime music as they could create.

What eventually became known as the "dance craze" hit New York sometime around 1910. For the first time in American history, unchaperoned women, from secretaries to socialites, began flocking to public music halls in Times Square and Coney Island, dressed in "gaudy eye-catching outfits" where they would "twist, shake, and leap about shamelessly in public, as if they had contracted a virus." They had no interest in waltzes or folk dances. The Turkey Trot, Bunny Hug, Grizzly Bear, and Texas Tommy—dances imported from southern African American jook joints—all reigned supreme and were seen by some as little more than energetic excuses to "press their loins together in mock intercourse." As historian Mike Wallace notes,

> Nor was all the intercourse mock. Women made dates, and sometimes had sex, with men they met on the dance floor. Yet they weren't prostitutes and indeed were known as "charity girls" for refusing to accept money. They coupled for pleasure, or in exchange for being treated to evenings on the town.

Were Harriet and her girlfriends ever among the gyrating masses, "looking for fun, romance, a husband?" Of that we have no clear record. But we do know she took a dim view of women who advanced these chance encounters a little farther and then claimed they were forced into compromising situations out of economic necessity.

In "The Girls That Do NOT Go Wrong!" Harriet wrote an uncharacteristically scathing rebuke of Reginald Wright Kauffman's *The House of Bondage*. This popular but controversial book claimed to expose the root cause of prostitution as "white slavery"—young women seeking an end to financial hardship by selling their bodies. As someone who grew up in poverty, Harriet took personal affront to that theory, arguing that there are always other means for putting food on one's table and clothes on one's back than degrading one's "dignity."

> White slavery does exist. It is the canker worm of this country. The way Mr. Kauffman would remedy the evil, according to his own words, is to do away with poverty. His theory stands just about as firmly upon its feet as do his stories on theirs. The girls who voluntarily exchange their honor for pretty clothes and luxury are not white slaves. The definition of slavery is "held in bondage."
>
> There are at least one hundred girls employed in the office of LESLIE'S WEEKLY, where I am now writing. I can see a number of them from my desk, working happily away. Nearly every one of these girls has at some time been in just the situation in which Nan [one of the examples cited in Kauffman's book] found herself. Every girl or woman who ever set out to earn her living has at some time found herself "out of a job," so this in itself does not constitute anything but a commonplace. Nor was there anything remarkable in the fact that, because of her inexperience, Nan failed to find work immediately upon seeking it. That, too, has happened to thousands of girls. Finally Nan became hungry. She did not have her breakfast and could not find work. Mr. Kauffman did not say whether Nan was looking for work entirely beyond her ability. He intimates that she could not place herself even as a housemaid, which in these days is very much to be doubted. However, this has nothing to do with the case. Upon finding herself hungry and still out of work, Nan turned easily and almost naturally to the disgraceful life which demands an indiscriminate association with men and for which she received money. How any thinking

> man or woman, after reading this story, could look upon Nan as a real flesh-and-blood girl is a puzzle to me.
>
> A real girl in Nan's predicament, upon failing to find employment, would have had her sister to call upon or she would have been helped out by any one of the number of friends with which the story-writer supplied her at the beginning of his story. If she had been a real girl in earnest search of work, she would have found something to do, with sufficient compensation to keep her from deliberately selling her soul. It is only the exception that falls into the life of habitual lax morals.
>
> Much as I regret to write it, I am forced to a realization of the truth that members of my sex are by no means blameless. It is only too true that many women as well as girls are constantly on the *qui vive* for temptation. Some of them find temptation in the lightest word or the first merry compliment paid them by a man. Men are by no means angels. On the other hand, we cannot call them fiends. Physicians of repute will testify that women as well as men are born with a natural inclination to go wrong.

This opinion piece is atypical for Harriet. In the hundreds of interviews she sat for and articles she wrote, Harriet rarely expressed her opinions about women's issues such as suffrage and the equality of the sexes, choosing instead to demonstrate that equality through her actions, not her words. Time and again she deflected questions about her political views, perhaps out of deference to her growing legion of admirers, many of whom were not as progressive as she. Or she may have desired to avoid controversy in accordance with actress Rose Stahl's early advice to "not be too much on exhibition." Yet in "The Girls That Do NOT Go Wrong!" she made it absolutely clear whom she thought might be better at solving society's problems:

The solution will come, in my judgment, when those who believe in better things take the matter into their own hands and give us a better government—not only of the State and nation, but of municipalities, where vice prevails and white slavery is encouraged by official sanction and under a system of blackmail as revolting as it is indescribable.

Men have had the right to vote, and what has been the result? If the women had the right to vote, would things be different? That must be left for the arbitrament of the future. Why not give the women a chance? Certainly the men thus far have failed.

9

AN EPOCH-MAKING EVENT

THEIR EYES STRAINED UPWARD, blinking through the drizzling rain, past cigarette advertisements and the soot-smudged windows of Midtown Manhattan, searching for a sign that their hopes would be realized. It was the morning of October 22, 1910. The focus of their earnest stares was a 395-foot-tall building on Forty-Second Street.

First a murmur ran through the crowd, then scattered shouts, followed by sustained cheers and a headlong rush in the direction of Pennsylvania Station, the enormous Beaux-Arts building ten blocks away that was completed barely a year earlier. What sent them on their frenzied way was a large white rectangle of cloth flapping damply in the wind at the top of the Times Tower. It was not a flag of surrender, but rather a message that announced encouraging, if not exactly perfect, weather conditions for the largest air show the US had ever hosted. Allan Ryan, the general manager of the Belmont Park Aviation Meet, had requested the owners of the Times building hoist one of three banners to the awaiting spectators: blue if the weather was too bad for any airplanes to take off, red if the winds were calm and the rain allayed so much so that pilots were already flying, and white if conditions were promising enough that flights were probable. Allan's call to fly the white flag may have been a bit optimistic. Most of the potential spectators that first day took one look at the low-hanging clouds and steady rain and opted to stay home. "The wires have been kept hot," said one of Allan's assistants, "replying to ticket holders asking if the meet would go on as scheduled. In view of the fact that rain does not in any way interfere with the flights our answer was that the contests would be held." No refunds were offered.

Within minutes of seeing the white flag, hundreds of men, women, and children crowded aboard train cars for the roughly thirty-minute trip east. The Long Island and Pennsylvania Railroad companies had already canceled most of the planned additional trains due to the forecast. As they neared the town of Elmont, young faces pressed against the rain-mottled windows, hoping to catch a glimpse of one of the magical flying machines. The first of the special trains arrived at Belmont Park around noon, disgorging a surging sea of umbrellas that moved forward toward the famed racetrack as a single, organic being.

Hundreds more New Yorkers took to the roads when the weather began to clear later in the day, lining up along Hempstead Turnpike in a traffic jam that stretched for miles. The best parking places at the track were quickly filled with row upon row of mud-splattered automobiles—Pierce-Arrow Broughams, Whiting Runabouts, Overlands, Bergs, an exquisite Premier Four-Door Touring Car (posing in the field, a rose among daisies), and of course, Fords. Hundreds of Fords. Five thousand parking spots were reserved ahead of time, far fewer than needed. Anyone living nearby quickly realized a financial windfall was afoot, and signs appeared in front lawns offering parking for one dollar a spot.

"What astonished you most at the aviation meet?" an attendee was later asked. "The automobiles! They were parked in masses, hundreds of them, possibly not far from a thousand!" He speculated the total value was well over $3 million. A columnist who wrote under the pseudonym "The Spectator" for *Outlook* magazine described the miserable scene later in the day as the throngs left the area:

> At night, returning to New York, a closed grade-crossing held up the line, and in a few minutes perhaps three hundred cars, in four parallel rows, with lights blazing and horns tooting, filled the highway as far back as the eye could see—a strange spectacle not soon to be forgotten. When, one wondered, would the sky-pilots be supplanting the chauffeurs? Not more marvelous would the establishing of passenger air-routes seem to us than did this mass of chugging, restless cars seem to those who remembered the quiet of the Long Island roads ten years ago.

Organizers hoped for an attendance of one hundred thousand. Unfortunately, because of the dreary weather, receipts showed only a fraction of that entered the gates on day one of the eight-day event. The *New York Times* estimated barely two thousand. Thousands more who eschewed the one-dollar entrance fee were perched on blankets and chairs outside the race grounds, despite the best efforts of Belmont Park managers, who erected large canvas screens to discourage such free-loading, evidently not realizing "that flying is not a sport to be easily fenced in." Unlike baseball fans who had to get onto the bleachers to watch the game, these fledgling fans of flight had

> a larger choice, for aviation is a supremely public sport. Any one within a mile of a meet, with a good pair of field-glasses, or even with an ordinarily acute pair of eyes, can see the flights of the bird-men most satisfactorily. Therefore the early comers, picking out good banks by the roadside or comfortable spots on the beach, needed no admission fee.

Both inside and outside the gates, spectators "were enthusiastic, with that sort of enjoyment which shows itself, not in wild shouting, but in gazing as if they could gaze forever."

Although in operation for only five years, Belmont Park—"the world's greatest inclosed [*sic*] race course"—already possessed a reputation as an exciting destination for horse-racing fans. It was also easily accessible, owing to the political *cadeau* of a Long Island Rail Road extension built specifically for its founders, August Belmont Jr. and William Collins Whitney. During its first fifteen years of operation, it featured the odd characteristic of running races the British way, clockwise, "like you deal cards," as sportswriter Ring Lardner put it. This must have been a challenge for horses used to taking a left lead into the corners. Airplanes would have no such constraints.

Track managers took pains to make Belmont Park as aviation friendly as possible. Gone were the inside fences, timer's stand, infield jumps, and jockey board. Across from the grandstand, in full view of the spectators, they placed an enormous scoreboard, "fifty feet long and thirty feet high," on which events and the names of competing pilots were posted.

Due to its location near the tempestuous Atlantic, the track was sometimes cursed with windy, wet, sloppy conditions. The *New York Times* dubbed it the "breeziest race track now in use, a veritable cave of the winds." Such was the case that first Saturday of the air show. The *Times* went on to declare the weather conditions "impossible," with "a wind-driven fog, which hung low over the field and through which descended a steady drizzle of cold rain."

More than thirty aviators traveled to Hempstead for the meet, most by train. The event attracted the biggest names in the aviation world, among them Americans Eugene Ely, Walter Brookins (who held the altitude record of 6,175 feet), and J. Armstrong Drexel (of the Philadelphia Drexels), as well as Arch Hoxsey and Ralph Johnstone (Wright biplane fliers who were dubbed the Heavenly Twins). The inventors Orville and Wilbur Wright were on hand to oversee any technical issues with their planes and keep hawks' eyes on any possible patent infringements, as was the American Glenn Curtiss, the inventor of another style of biplane there to compete.

Tall, handsome Britisher Claude Grahame-White—stylishly sporting a double-breasted suit and woolen flat cap, which he turned front to back whenever he flew—made it in time for the first day's events. He had just come from Washington, DC, where a week prior, he'd flown his Farman biplane across the Potomac River, circled the Washington Monument, and then landed on West Executive Avenue next to the White House. President William Howard Taft was away for the day, but Claude's feat garnered him a handshake with Admiral George Dewey and lunch at the US State Department, as a large crowd of gawkers surrounded his plane, still parked in the middle of the street. Far from happenstance, the flight was actually a brilliantly executed publicity stunt and marketing ploy orchestrated by the Brit's airplane company with the cooperation of the local police.

Regardless of these noteworthy aviators, it can safely be said that most of the spectators at Belmont Park were there to see an upstart American by the name of John Moisant. At 5'3" and 135 pounds, with "keen brown eyes," and a hairline at low tide, he was a small man in size alone. His exploits as a fearless young mercenary in Central America only added to his luster. A very brief two months before the Belmont meet he became the first pilot to fly with a passenger across the English Channel, beginning on the outskirts of Paris. Just hours after landing at Tilmanstone, six miles from Dover, he vowed to pack up his passenger again and fly to London in time for dinner. Instead he embarked on a near-disastrous "series of glorious failures" (maintenance fiascoes and rough landings) as he hopscotched seventy miles to the capital. He finally set down on a cricket field at Beckenham outside of London, three weeks after the wheels of his airplane left the ground near Paris.

Inexplicably, given his almost comedic struggles to make good his boast, the former architecture student became at that moment a global phenomenon. Photos of his chiseled features graced many of the major newspapers, even as some misspelled his last name or misidentified the Chicagoan's place of birth as somewhere in Europe. His renown grew only larger when he told an astounded covey of reporters with characteristic sangfroid, "I took up flying as a hobby eight or nine months ago, and this is the sixth time I have been in the air, and the machine I'm using is the only one I have ever flown in." The next day's headline in London's *Daily Chronicle* read, "Remarkable Flight by Unknown Man."

A chance meeting with the now anything-but "unknown man" at Belmont Park would change Harriet Quimby's life forever. She had motored out to Long Island in her bright yellow car, a convertible runabout, on the last day of the meet with the blessing of her editor at *Leslie's*. Twenty-four months had passed since she first showed interest in aviation, and an impressive grasp of its physics, with the article she wrote about a scientist studying buzzards near Miami.

> For the past two years a bright, cultured, and refined young man, giving the name of Pierre La Montaine, but bearing every evidence of Japanese lineage, has been a sojourner throughout the winter season at Biscayne Bay. He has made a study of the very industrious scavenger, the buzzard. He has spent weeks at a time with his cameras, photographing buzzards at rest and in flight. He made numerous offers to fishermen and boys of generous rewards if they would secure for him live specimens of the buzzard family.

Pierre, an ill-considered nom de guerre if ever there was one, turned out to be an agent of the Japanese government and member of that nation's military. He was in America posing as an ornithologist in order

to study the flight of the large scavenger birds. Japanese scientists rejected the concept of multiple wings and straight angles as the best designs for human flight and instead were looking to nature for inspiration. Pierre recruited a local boy named Abico to trap a live buzzard for him to study more closely. This was against the law, as scavengers served a public-health purpose by consuming rotting trash and dead animals. How Harriet stumbled onto the story was never disclosed, but she made the most of her discovery.

> This young man captured a buzzard and took it home to deliver to his Japanese employer. His mother, fearing her son's arrest for violation of the law, insisted on freeing the bird, but, at the urgent solicitation of the boy, did not do so until the Japanese had been notified as to the capture, as he had promised the lad a special and liberal bounty if he would secure the prize unharmed.

Pierre evidently grew fond of the boy and began explaining to him the concepts of flight.

> Abico says that his instructor pointed out to him that the four essentials of a successful flying machine were: First, lightness of construction; second, breadth of lateral extension; third, a longitudinal deflecting steering plane, like a tail, placed at right angles to the laterals and covering a much larger area than the aeroplanes of flying machines as now constructed; fourth, he insisted that the extremities of the laterals and the steering aeroplanes must be constituted as the wings of the buzzard are, with lines of curves terminating in a spreading device with great mobility, so that, like the outstretched feathers of a wing or tail, the wings of a flying machine could be spread out or contracted so as to preserve its balance when meeting wind waves of varying velocities.

That detailed description from 1909 predicted the exact attributes of the airplanes that crisscross today's skies: strong but light materials; an empennage, known today as the tail; flaps and ailerons for steering and altitude control; and long, curved wings that reduce drag and induce lift. These concepts were years, even decades, ahead of their time.

Accompanying the article was a photograph of a graceful buzzard soaring above the waves, with the caption, "Perfect Aeroplane in Flight"; a declarative statement, not a question. The bird in the photo clearly had more in common with a Blériot monoplane than a Wright Flyer: two wings, not four; maneuverable, graceful, and streamlined; not angular, not ungainly. Perhaps that's why Harriet was drawn to the monoplanes at the meet. And to one monoplane pilot in particular.

John Moisant, soon after his historic landing in London, was recruited by Cortlandt Field Bishop, president of the Aero Club of America, to return to the US and compete at Belmont Park. With his mysterious background, flying prowess, and devil-may-care attitude, John quickly became America's Claude Grahame-White—glamorous, witty, good-looking, courageous, and seemingly unstoppable. On his first visit to Belmont Park, the week prior to the meet, he declared it would be "the greatest air show ever seen." And on the subject of whether aviation was simply a fad or a pastime for the well-to-do, the thirty-five-year-old replied, "The next generation will use airplanes as we use automobiles." The assembled reporters were aghast. It was one of several stunning predictions John stated before leaving England:

> In five years time an aeroplane will be flying across the Atlantic in twenty-four hours. In less than two years time we will produce a monoplane with a 200-horsepower engine that will thrust the machine through the air at one hundred miles per hour. Air stations will be great open flat places, surrounded by sheds and repair depots.

> Aircraft will be constantly rising from them and arriving at them after long aerial journeys.

His conjectures were remarkably prescient, if off in their timing by fifty or so years.

When one reporter asked how John was able to fly across the English Channel with so little experience, he raised a few more eyebrows: "There is no great mystery or great difficulty about operating an airplane. Learning to guide an airplane is about as easy as learning to ride a bicycle." That was a disingenuous claim at best. John was incredibly fortunate to have survived his early attempts at aviation. Twenty other pilots had already met their ends that year alone, with many more doomed to die in the years to come. Given that there were perhaps only a few hundred people attempting to fly powered aircraft at the time, that is a fatality rate unmatched by any other human endeavor except war. One can only guess at Claude Grahame-White's reaction when he read that comment in the newspaper, considering he had only a day earlier declared flying so demanding that "not one man in a thousand can master it."

The jewel of the air show was the second annual International Aviation Cup, a time-trial competition established by James Gordon Bennett Jr., the multimillionaire son of the publisher of the *New York Herald* newspaper, whose eponymous auto race was the site of Harriet's hundred-miles-an-hour "brisk ride" in 1906. The air race's elaborate trophy, designed by French sculptor André Auroc and featuring an androgynous winged figure supporting a Wright Flyer biplane, was first claimed by Glenn Curtiss in the air over Reims, France in 1909 with a time of 15 minutes and 50.4 seconds, besting Louis Blériot himself by a mere 5.8 seconds. The American victory not only established Glenn's celebrity but also ensured that the second competition would be waged in the United States in 1910, with $75,000 in prize money.

Early pilots at the meet were still learning the fledgling science of flight, lift, and the vagaries of maneuvering in winds and weather. They were figuring out how to do all of that under racing conditions, trial and error, where seconds meant the difference between financial profit and loss. Aviators were literally making it up as they went along, not unlike the explorers of old who squinted at the ocean's horizon, unsure of what lay ahead, imagining sea monsters and waterfalls at world's end, but venturing forth regardless.

In the 1909 race, Glenn was an underdog to Europe's finest flyers. But he managed to press his Golden Flyer, a sturdy pusher biplane with yellow oiled silk wings and an engine mounted above and just behind the pilot, to the limits of its mechanical abilities through little more than creativity and courage.

> I climbed as high as I thought I might without protest, before crossing the starting line—probably five hundred feet—so that I might take advantage of a gradual descent throughout the race, and thus gain additional speed. I cut corners as close as I dared and banked the machine high on the turns. I remember I caused great commotion among a big flock of birds which did not seem to be able to get out of the wash of my propeller. In front of the tribune the machine flew steadily, but when I got around on the back stretch... the air seemed fairly to boil. The machine pitched considerably and when I passed over the "graveyard," where so many machines had gone down and were smashed during the previous days of the meet, that air seemed literally to drop from under me.

Despite the turbulence, he kept the engine roaring at full power and set a speed mark no one could match.

The machines may have been constructed of simple materials, but early aviation was an expensive prospect. Inventors were often their own financiers, mechanics, and test pilots. Houses were mortgaged, credit lines maxed out, contributions sought from friends and families, all to pay for yet another engine or pile of parts only to see the aircraft obliterated into worthless debris. Louis Blériot spent much of his own fortune on a series of disastrous designs before he was forced to seek prize money at various competitions to keep his endeavors afloat. Such competitions were usually financed by newspapers and wealthy patrons who were acolytes in the church of the new science.

Authoritarian and vain, with pale blue eyes, a bushy walrus mustache, and a razor-straight part that cleaved his dark hair down the center of his skull, James Gordon Bennett Jr. (who went by "Gordon") was also a generous visionary and one of the most extraordinary characters of his time, marshaling his riches to finance yacht, motorcar, and balloon races around the world, and enlisting drivers to deliver his newspapers to remote areas. He introduced competitive polo and tennis to the American shores and captained the first winner of a transoceanic yacht race. It was Gordon who sent Henry Morton Stanley on his quixotic journey to Africa in search of the missing explorer David Livingstone, and he backed the development of dirigibles and the Demoiselle airplane. His boorish behavior by New York society's standards—he drunkenly relieved himself in the fireplace of his fiancée in front of her parents and guests—got him exiled to France in 1877, where he was embraced as a charmingly colorful playboy. When he turned his attention to heavier-than-air flying machines and established the International Aviation Cup, he created the single most coveted prize in all of flying.

Gordon's air race was the Super Bowl, Olympics, and World Series of 1910 combined, capturing the imagination of millions and rousing nationalistic fervor. The age of the celebrity athlete was emerging, and

Americans saw those brave young men in their flying machines as nothing less. Inside one of the thirty hangars assembled at the track sat John Moisant's new, powerful Blériot plane, specifically designed for racing. On the afternoon of October 19, John and his mechanic, Albert Fileux, were busily tightening bolts and trusses when Claude Grahame-White approached. The British aviator was, per usual, dressed to the nines—three-piece suit, bow tie, impeccably shiny brogues. John wore grease-stained overalls and a heavy sweater. The two men reportedly shook hands and chatted amiably. Physically, they couldn't have been more different: Claude towered over the little American. But John figured he had the better of it mentally. He was an aggressive gambler and fearless risk taker, whereas the Brit was known for his extreme caution. "I can buy a new airplane, ladies and gentlemen," he once told an angry crowd disappointed that he refused to fly in dangerous crosswinds, "but I can't buy a new life." Claude may have been a darling of the American public and press, but at least one columnist was having none of it. The Brit, he wrote, "delights to bask in the full glare of the calcium and wants all that there is in the game" whereas John "is painfully modest and self-deprecating in his manner, avoiding the lime-light whenever possible."

When Claude bid his farewell, John turned back to finishing the prep work on his plane. Since he had not yet tested the new machine, he and his crew pushed it out onto the field, cranked up the engine, and took off into the low skies. The clock on the grandstand wall showed 4 P.M.

The inner track of the raceway sported a series of thirty-foot-high pylons, evenly spaced, that would be the slalom course for the meet's first event. John eased his monoplane up to two hundred feet and leveled off, then began carving slow circles around the infield. Barely five minutes into his flight, something went wrong. The plane bucked, almost flipping completely over onto its back, and plunged to the ground nose first.

A cloud of dust and smoke obscured the crash scene. As John's ground crew and family rushed over, they were surprised to see a grime-covered specter rise from the crumpled aircraft and brush himself off, miraculously unhurt. The Blériot plane, however, didn't fare nearly as well. The wooden frame was splintered and right wing broken. The motor shaft was bent. The propeller a twisted heap of wooden shards.

As Claude, who had just taken off, flew low over the crash site, John waved to him that he was okay, then turned to his sisters, Matilde and Louise. His embarrassment visible on his oil- and dirt-smudged face, he admitted, "I simply forgot to have my oil tank turned on and when I was trying to do it, my foot slipped from the control. When you lose control, it's all off." Later he told reporters,

> It was sheer carelessness and lack of forethought on my part. These Gnôme rotary motors grip when the oil ceases to flow, and I realized I would have trouble unless I got my oil flowing at once. Of course, I might have come to the ground, but I thought that I could attend so simple a thing in the air. I lifted my foot to kick open the oil cock, but the moment I let go of the rudder control, my machine wobbled badly, almost turned turtle, and threw me completely out of my course.

When asked if he was injured, he replied with a laugh, "Why, nobody ever gets hurt flying!"

The other competitors assumed the popular young American's participation in the meet was all off. But they were wrong. The former daredevil and soldier of fortune planned for any eventuality, lugging along with him to Long Island not only four sets of parts for the new Blériot, but also his old plane, the one that carried him across the twenty-two miles of open water two months earlier. John sent the twisted remains of the racer to the Lovelace-Thompson aircraft plant at Fort George for repairs, and he set about registering his other plane for the week's competitions.

Three days later, on opening day, with the stadium crowds thin and the clouds thick, only seven of the twenty-eight registered pilots braved the miserable conditions: among them was John Moisant. Evidently the editors of the *New York Herald* didn't bother to glance outside the windows of their Newspaper Row offices, for the front-page story began, "At the dawn of the opening day of the great International aviation tournament at Belmont Park auspicious weather is all there is now needed to make the Meet an epoch-making event."

New York's aristocracy was not about to be discouraged by a little rain and wind.

> The grand stand and concourse very much resembled a rainy-day scene at an English race course, for long ulsters, cravenettes, furs, and felt hats prevailed, and no attempt was made to display new gowns. There was much visiting between the occupants of the boxes between flights, and when the machines were in the air the aviation "gaze" was cultivated. One woman in the boxes, whose name could not be learned, amused herself between flights by knitting.

Viola Johnson, who wrote a society column for the *New York Evening Mail*, allowed herself a bit of snark when she commented about New York's elite families, "The Four Hundred had at last discovered a new sensation and a new expression... a human thrilled look of intense, absorbing interest... faces that have become so hardened from years of immobility that they look like plaster casts relaxed and wrinkled." She went on to describe a new phenomenon—the airplane stare: "Straining lines of necks and double chins... faces so foreshortened and out of perspective that only the tips of teeth were visible to those directly under the boxes."

John, Claude, and J. Armstrong Drexel, the millionaire playboy with a doughy face and perpetually bemused expression, took to the air for the first event of the air show, a distance race wherein the airplanes would fly around the oval racetrack. The three pilots were not trying to pass one another as they would in a car race, rather they simply wanted to stay aloft as long as they possibly could while flying within the prescribed course. J. Armstrong scratched after the ninth lap with engine trouble. Due to the gusty conditions, John found it difficult to keep his aircraft within the race's boundaries marked by the tall pylons. He was disqualified twice by the judges for cutting corners, and so took his revenge upon the "workman like" Claude, who was slogging around the tall pylons like a train on a track, by "rising and falling, turning and dipping, as easily and gracefully as a swallow." He brought the audience to its feet when he dove down to the infield and zoomed along a few feet above the grass. Chalk up two wins for the Brit, but it was the American who was conquering the hearts of the masses.

Next came the altitude contest. The man who held the record in his Wright Flyer, Arch Hoxsey, managed only a fraction of his previous best, 742 feet, because the fog was so thick. Arch, a bespectacled instructor at the Wright brothers' flight school in Montgomery, Alabama, had a week earlier incurred the wrath of his employers when he took former president Theodore Roosevelt for an unauthorized ride in his biplane. The Wrights were incensed that he would so impudently risk bad publicity for the company in the event his adventure ended up in disaster. Arch would get another try at the record later in the week. Two other contestants simply got lost in the clouds and were forced to land their planes elsewhere.

The final event of the day was a twenty-mile dash over the Hempstead Plains to a balloon marker and back. But with the rising wind and thickening fog, six of the seven competitors bowed out, leaving John as the only pilot willing to give it a try. The others thought him daft at best, but what they didn't know was the American had a secret weapon that had aided his flight across the channel—a compass. Aviators distrusted the device because the engine's vibrations tended to whap its sensitive needle back and forth, thus rendering it worse than useless, but John was using a new type of compass filled with liquid glycerin, which deadened the shaking.

At 4:17 P.M., he bounded down the makeshift runway and lifted into the gray, dwindling light, disappearing almost instantly from the view of the spectators. "They waited until it was out of sight and then there was a rush for café and restaurant," the *New York Times* reported,

> Hot tea and coffee and other drinks entertained the crowd for the next fifteen minutes. They knew Moisant couldn't get back in that time, but presently they began to grow restless. Man after man and woman after woman stepped out again into the rain to peer down the track for a sight of the aviator. Minutes passed, and it got to be 4:30 P.M. Then it became 4:45, but still there was no sight of Moisant. "He must be down somewhere," was the remark most generally heard. "He may be hurt."

Flying blind as the rain pelted his face like miniature daggers, John could only get his bearings by descending to one hundred feet time and again, a dangerous tactic that he was keenly aware might cause him to "knock down a church steeple or get caught in a tangle of telegraph wires." He glanced down at the compass, carefully keeping his heading east by one-eighth south. When he reached what he figured was ten miles out, he leaned forward on the wooden controller stick, eased the monoplane below the clouds, and began scanning for the balloon that marked the turnaround point. But no balloon came into sight. After a few minutes of squinting along the low horizon, John finally discerned a clump of trees that fit the description relayed to him for landmarks at the end of the required distance, and so he banked his Blériot and headed back to Belmont Park, depending once again on the compass that lay on the floor between his feet to keep him on course.

The spectators heard the sputter and growl of the rotary engine long before they saw the monoplane, but that was enough encouragement for the band to begin playing. John approached the field at a high rate of speed, "flying with the wind," and managed to set down gracefully in the racetrack infield. The drenched, shivering American was lifted from his seat because he was so cold his muscles weren't working properly. A check for $850 was shoved in his hands to raucous cheers from the audience. For saving the soggy first day from disaster, John earned the gratitude of the meet organizers and inch upon inch of slavering ink. "A mariner's feat in midair!" wrote one breathless reporter, "The most marvelous aviator in the world!" declared another.

Not everyone was impressed. Many of the pilots who decided not to compete that day grumbled that John was a reckless showman. When asked why he didn't take to the air, English aviator James Radley said,

> I think the easiest reply is to the reverse of that question: namely, why were any aeroplanes flying at all in such bad weather conditions? A short time ago no one would have flown in such bad conditions as unfortunately prevailed at Belmont Park to-day. Among other reasons are the rain soaking into the canvas and the woodwork loosens the planes and these cannot be tightened without rebuilding. This considerably lessens the speed of the machine.

When not gazing up at the airplanes in flight or chatting with the privileged class she had come to befriend through her theater column,

Harriet spent much of her day at Belmont Park wandering the grounds, taking pictures. One of her images captures the Demoiselle, the smallest and one of the fastest flying machines, streaking past a pylon. Another pictures Arch Hoxsey beginning to climb while attempting yet another altitude record. An image she took from the top row of the grandstand, with spectators milling about like ants on a dirt field, shows three biplanes lined up on the racetrack at the start of a ten-mile race. And in yet another of her photos a Blériot monoplane, perhaps John's, appears tiny in the distance.

For some unknown reason, Harriet's articles and photographs were sometimes published under a pseudonym. Perhaps it was at the preference of her editor, who might have been slightly embarrassed that his star drama critic, investigative journalist, women's issues editor, and sometime foreign correspondent was also out on places like Long Island covering regular news or, in this case, the biggest sporting event of the year. He did, after all, have other capable reporters on his staff. Or possibly, she already posted a story in that week's edition and it would appear unseemly for a single reporter to get so many column inches.

At any rate, one such article published shortly after the Belmont Park meet is entitled "How to Learn to Fly: What the Sky Chauffeurs Say, A Remarkable Interview with the Noted Birdmen." The byline is one Arthur H. Gleason, but a search of *Leslie's Illustrated Weekly*'s archives turns up no other works by this name. It's also highly unlikely that *Leslie's* would invest the resources to send two correspondents to the event. And by Harriet's own admission, the charming, irresistible journalist finagled at least one chat with the dashing new American celebrity at Belmont Park. She writes,

> John B. Moisant, who has dared winds, heights, darkness, fog and unknown territory, still retains an aversion for land heights and will

reach out for a chimney or piece of coping when he stands on the top of a building. He has no love of precipices and would not make a success in mountain climbing. But seated in the car, with the motor chugging and the wide-extended wings at his armpits, he is at home. That, briefly, is "the instinct for the air," which is the phrase dearly beloved of flyers.

The sense of relationship to the machine the flying men describe in pretty much the following terms: Every moment the pilot is in action, his body alive and flowing, his hands at the levers and wheels, his shoulders squirming about to shift the steel tubing frame which governs the balancing planes. With each new position of the machine, so sensitive to the wind pressures, his body takes a new position to meet the demand, a vital dynamic ballast, guiding, manipulating, balancing. He fits in as part of the flexible machine. At his shoulders he sprouts wings, with clever wires his hands stretch out to the trailing rudder—he is no alien body in the wood and wire structure. Erect, but flowing, he thrusts out of the winged creature like the brain-laden head of the bird.

Like most practical men, working in concrete things, the flyers are full of figures of speech. They describe their performance variously as balancing on a bicycle, where every instant, unconsciously, or, better, instinctively, you establish new equilibriums. Again, they speak of flying through air as like the act of skating over thin ice or cakes of floating ice, where no single layer will bear the weight, but where the speed diffuses the pressure. It is like tight-rope walking in the intense concentration of mind and muscle to a constantly changing position. It is like automobile racing in the focusing of attention to the route just ahead and the violent new conditions which will spring up out of the unknown. Moisant calls the air a river, with strong main currents, and now and again unexpected eddies and whirlpools, where, going slow, you will be spun around like a chip or upset like a cockleshell, but where with momentum you will cut through the swirl of trouble.

The Belmont Park meet was indeed shaping up to be "epoch-making"—in ways the organizers could never have foreseen. With no small amount of trouble and drama, including a wing-crumpling accident that nearly ended his participation for the week, Claude Grahame-White took the Gordon Bennett Aviation Trophy that Saturday, October 29, 1910. The Britisher willed his just-arrived 100-horsepower Blériot to sixty-one miles an hour over the sixty-two mile course and claimed the $5,000 reward. John Moisant, limping along in a less powerful craft, came in a distant second.

The International Aviation Cup may have been the most prestigious event in all of aviation, but it was not the most remunerative. That title belonged to the newly created Statue of Liberty Race, dreamed up by New York businessman Thomas Ryan, who suggested the planes dash from the Belmont racetrack to Lady Liberty and back in a winner-take-all speed contest for a $10,000 ($273,000 today) prize. Claude, with his muscular monoplane, was immediately the odds-on favorite. But the confident and debonair aviator with the Broadway-star looks failed to take into account the determination and cunning of "the daring Mr. Moisant."

10

KING OF THE AIR

"ABANDON SHIP!" THE CAPTAIN shouted in Spanish, as gale-force winds and towering waves forced his tramp steamer closer to shore. Aboard was an estimated $100,000 worth of cargo, but the ship's crew wasn't concerned about that at the moment. They simply wanted to survive. One by one, the men clambered over the sides of the boat and into the dinghies, leaving all of their belongings behind. The steamer, now unguided by human hands, bucked and listed before grinding its belly into the rocky coastline of Honduras.

Within hours after hearing of the mishap, and with the storm still raging, a man made his way alone to the ship and took possession of it. As the *New York Times* recounted, "In the morning the storm abated, and the ship's captain, accompanied by members of the crew, and an agent of the line, rowed out to the ship, which had withstood the pounding of sea and wind, but which was held fast on a sunken reef in the outer harbor." Before they could climb onboard, however, a shot rang out—from the gun of John Moisant.

> There was some parlaying, and the ship's skipper rowed back to shore to inform the American Consul and the authorities that Moisant claimed the ship and her cargo as salvage, and had threatened to "blow the head off the first man who tries to come aboard." There was

a second expedition to the ship, this time with the American Consul and some native soldiery, but Moisant refused to be impressed, and to show his sincerity of purpose shot a hole through the sombrero of the native commandant.

Before the captain could return with more reinforcements, a second storm slammed into the coast and the hobbled ship, finishing the work of the first. The steamer settled down onto the reef, its hull breached and taking on water. When the weather cleared the next day, the ship's skipper, the American Consul, and the military entourage came to survey the damage. They found John lashed to the top of the ship's rigging, clinging to his now sunken treasure, with his sopping-wet boots dangling just a few feet above the water.

By that time, John Moisant was already known throughout Central America as a wealthy, fearless adventurer and sometime mercenary with a reputation "which is nothing short of legendary. No hero of romance ever had so many extraordinary exploits attributed to him."

His older brother Alfred established a successful plantation and banking business in El Salvador, and much of the Moisant clan relocated there from California in the late 1890s to help run a hacienda named Santa Emilia. One reporter described it as

> a beautiful and very fertile irrigated estate producing hard timber, sugar cane, cattle for beef and dairy purposes, corn, rice, etc. About 150 workmen are there employed and many reside on the place, this being encouraged by the Moisants. There are two American employees on the place, the engineer and sub-manager; all the remainder are natives. The profits annually average 100,000 silver and are increasing.

The six-thousand-acre plantation was so expansive it would take a horseman from sunup to sundown to ride across it.

The Moisants, by all accounts, enjoyed good relations with their employees and the villagers, albeit one tainted, in retrospect, by colonialist and even racist undertones. But those affections were not shared by government officials. In 1907, the two eldest Moisant brothers, Edward and George, were arrested on charges of plotting a coup to overthrow El Salvador's incendiary president, Fernando Figueroa. The trumped-up charges were likely made in response to the family's refusal to pay bribes, but Fernando also made no secret of his desire to take over the Banco Nacional, founded by Alfred, as well as the Moisant plantation. He demanded the Americans leave El Salvador altogether.

It didn't help relations that, while traveling through the region, John became close friends with Fernando's archenemy, Nicaraguan President José Santos Zelaya. The president's impressive mustache boasted almost as much follicular glory as the rest of his head. His ultimate dream was to reinstate and oversee the former Central American federation of Costa Rica, Honduras, Nicaragua, Guatemala, and El Salvador. With so much North American interest in the region, "the Moisant affair" was becoming a political embarrassment. To resolve it, the US dispatched the USS *Yorktown* and envoy William Lawrence Merry, who implored the Salvadorian government to release the brothers, even threatening a US Navy blockade. But as negotiations slogged along, the youngest brother grew impatient and set about taking matters into his own hands.

On June 11, 1907, John Moisant and a sizable invasion force of eight hundred troops and volunteers, including fifty convicted felons whose sentences would be commuted if the coup succeeded, landed on the beach at the port town of Acajutla, El Salvador, with the support and blessing of the Nicaraguan president. When they commandeered two trains and started toward the city of Sonsonate, the US emissary pleaded that the Moisant brothers be released, fearing they could be killed if the fighting reached the capital of San Salvador, where they were being held in prison. Fernando Figueroa, wary of such a public-relations nightmare and likely unaware that John was leading the assault, agreed.

The ensuing battle killed and wounded an estimated 150 Salvadorian soldiers who engaged the invaders. But by midnight, the rag-tag revolutionaries grew weary. There came a point when John and his fighters "pushed right up to a force of several thousand troops under the flag of Salvador, and was preparing to attack when his 'army,' thinking the jails of Nicaragua safer than a battle field in Salvador, deserted and high-tailed it back to prison." John and his remaining fighters climbed back onto the trains, returned to Acajutla, and sailed south aboard the gunship *Momotombo*. When John showed up at his sister's house in San Francisco a few weeks later sporting his signature large diamond ring, suit and tie, devil-may-care grin, and a flattering tan, he insouciantly explained he had "backtracked north by burro, over the mountains of El Salvador and through the jungles of Honduras, to the Atlantic where he boarded a ship for New York, then took a train to San Francisco."

But Saint John the Rebel wasn't quite finished sailing so close to the wind. He soon returned to Central America and continued harassing the Salvadorian president. In July, he stormed aboard the Pacific Mail steamship *San Jose*, pistol in his waistband, riding whip in hand, possibly hoping to kidnap President Fernando Figueroa's chief of staff, who managed to flee the ship. Then in December John paid $1,000 in Panama for a gasoline barge big enough to smuggle an army into El Salvador. Somehow a California newspaper got a whiff of the plan and exclaimed "Moisant Buys Himself a Navy: Alameda Admiral Bravely Plans to Invade Salvador." That invasion happened two months later, when the American and about one thousand volunteers, consisting mainly of natives and freed convicts, made landfall at the Gulf of Fonseca. It wasn't exactly a well-kept secret. Fernando Figueroa capitalized on a tip about the plot, and his army regulars captured or killed two hundred of Moisant's militia. Ducking away under cover of night, John escaped almost certain public execution at the hands of the enraged Salvadorian president.

As for the American president, Theodore Roosevelt, he and his diplomatic corps were growing weary of the dramatics and Nicaragua's regional ambitions, which were interfering with multiple trade deals and the development of the Panama Canal. When John tried to launch yet another assault on the Salvadorian government the following spring, the US Navy was waiting. The USS *Colorado*, the *Albany*, and the Mexican naval vessel *Guerrero* surrounded the gunship on which John was manning a rapid-fire machinegun. His rebel-laden barge loitered nearby. Commander William S. Benson announced in no uncertain terms that should the rebels attempt to land in El Salvador, the full might and wrath of the United States would descend upon them. John took him at his word.

Yet again, the daring but diminutive Yank was forced to retreat. He booked passage to New York, all the while mentally gnawing through plot after plot to exact his revenge. It became his all-consuming obsession. Then, at some point in 1909, John Moisant read a newspaper article about the new science of aviation. A thought percolated; perhaps he could someday return to El Salvador with a fleet of armed airplanes and finally finish his revolution. He later mused about the prospect to a reporter: "People talk of shooting at flying machines from the ground and warding off an attack that way. [Airplanes] can travel seventy miles an hour, more than that soon, and can go up 5,000 feet or more. Can they [be hit] under those conditions?"

With the financial backing of his brother Alfred and perhaps the encouragement of Nicaragua's President Zelaya, John made his way to France. The country was, at the time, the center of the aviation world largely because of Louis Blériot, who on July 25, 1909, for the first time ever, piloted an airplane across the English Channel. John happened to be on the streets of Paris that momentous day to watch the crowds cheer their new national hero. The adulation of the masses affected him deeply.

In spite of the fact that he, to that point, had not received a moment's instruction, John decided to design, build, and ultimately fly his own aircraft. Given to extraordinary self-confidence sprinkled with delusions of immortality, he was also indisputably intelligent, with a background in architecture and engineering and a mastery of three languages. But the "crazy American kid," as one Frenchman labeled him, still had much to learn. He just didn't know it yet. Or, as the French would say, *Il ne sait pas ce qu'il ne sait pas.*

At the airfield of Issy-les-Moulineaux, about forty miles outside of Paris, John gathered a team of balloon makers to help him build his Aluminoplane, an all-metal biplane with a 50-horsepower Gnôme engine and boat-shaped body, "as much at home in the water as in the air," he boasted. When the gleaming contraption was finished, John climbed aboard, ordered the engine cranked, and gestured at the six men holding the plane to the ground to let go. It was his first time sitting in a flying machine, with exactly zero minutes of instruction.

The plane shot straight up at eighty miles an hour. The sheer velocity slammed the amateur pilot back into his seat. Perhaps for the first time in his thirty-five years, John Moisant panicked. He did exactly the wrong thing: he cut the engine.

The Aluminoplane was approaching a height of ninety feet. It took only a few seconds for gravity to return it that distance to earth, slamming into the ground tail first. John was miraculously unharmed, but his creation now resembled the business end of an accordion. After crawling out from under the debris, he shoved his hands into his pockets and shrugged, "I had the fun of getting off the ground anyhow, didn't I?" But he added with apparently no sense of irony, "No man should build an aeroplane and then try to fly it unless he has had experience in the air." That admission notwithstanding, the impetuous American wasn't done. He and his band of merry tinkerers cobbled together a monoplane from the Aluminoplane's tangled leftovers just days after the mishap. It was a Frankenstein creature that could barely stay upright when on the ground, and never left the earth.

Humbled but not defeated and certainly not discouraged, John made his way to Paris and paid four hundred dollars for thirty days of flying lessons at Louis Blériot's new monoplane factory, where 150 workers were already cranking out hundreds of airplanes to sell to enthusiastic buyers. By all accounts John was an excellent student. At the end of July 1910, he passed all the tests required for certification and became the thirteenth American to receive a pilot's license. That, however, was in no way the pinnacle of his ambitions. When he confided in Alfred Leblanc, the director of the Blériot aviation school, that he intended to fly from Paris to London, something that had never been done, the shocked instructor declared, "Mais vous êtes fou, Monsieur!"—*But you are crazy, sir!*

By the time John successfully flew across the channel from France to England and was preparing to embark on his "series of glorious failures"—his three-week-long odyssey to London—he had shed his revolutionary past and all thoughts of aerial bombardments of the Presidential Palace in San Salvador. He now kept his compass firmly pointed toward a future of aviation glory.

During one of his many setbacks, as his Blériot plane was stranded at the bottom of a brick pit near Upchurch, England, a group of Royal Engineers gathered to help pull the damaged monoplane back to level

Aviator and adventurer John Moisant and the kitten that accompanied him across the English Channel, Mademoiselle Fifi.

ground. While his passenger-*cum*-mechanic, Albert Fileux, was attaching a replacement propeller, one of the British soldiers handed John a placid handful of soft fur and whiskers—a little Maltese kitten. He adopted the feline immediately and, in honor of the moment, named him (or her) Paree-Londres. The gender of the cat is somewhat in question; some newspaper accounts give its name as Mademoiselle Fifi. John put the blue-gray cat into a paper bag—a contented second passenger in the Blériot for the rest of the odyssey. "You ought to have seen this kitten," John told a gathering of reporters during yet another repair stop just outside of London. "He enjoyed himself immensely and wasn't a bit afraid. He was still curled up in the bag, his bright eyes peeping up at me when the crash came, and even the noise of breaking wood did not disturb him." The cat was his constant companion for the remainder of John's life.

The long journey took a toll on the usually elegant American's appearance:

> During the trip he slept beneath the wings of the plane. When he arrived at Upchurch, England, he was black from head to foot, his clothes were covered with dirt, his hair was matted with oil and his hands and face were covered with grease; a diamond ring and tiepin gave an incongruous touch to the whole.

When John Moisant, Albert Fileux, and Paree-Londres (or Fifi) finally made it to London, the brash American's biggest detractors—pilots Hubert Latham and Claude Grahame-White among them, who had been certain of his imminent death—became reluctant admirers of the historic feat. "What an airman he is," Hubert declared. But how it must have galled those experienced and legendary aviators to see the novice flier celebrated in the world's newspapers, including the *Chicago*

Daily Tribune, which declared in banner headlines, "John Moisant KING OF THE AIR."

The three men would meet in person a few months later, on the wind-swept, foggy tournament field in the skies over the New York Bay.

11

INDEED, AT THAT TIME IT WAS A MIRACLE

ON SUNDAY, OCTOBER 30, 1910, the sun finally decided to make an appearance over Belmont Park, and the wind, which tormented fliers and fans alike all week long, settled down to a gentle breeze. "Fleecy clouds moved lazily through a blue sky with almost no wind to hasten their pace." A late-fall chill set a sharp edge to the air. Special trains out of New York's Penn Station delivered throngs of bundled-up eager spectators, and by one o'clock, the parking lots and neighboring yards were teeming with automobiles. Seventy-five thousand people paid one dollar apiece for standing-only tickets or two dollars for grandstand seats. They funneled through the entrance gates at the racetrack under the watchful eyes of Pinkerton detectives, who were charged with apprehending turnstile jumpers and pickpockets. Box seats were occupied by the bold-print names of the era: Drexels, Vanderbilts, Biddles, and Belmonts, the men attired in "silk hats and frock coats, the women suits of satin and velvet with skirts cut in the narrow 'hobble' style of the time and furs of sable, silver fox, and lamb." An estimated one million more moved chairs, pillows, and wooden boxes onto Manhattan rooftops, Queens parks, and Brooklyn stoops to witness what was destined to become one of the most exciting races in aviation history. Inside the grounds, eighteen dollars would buy one a heavy black coat, part of Macy's "Aeronautic Age" promotion, which also included Macy's gauntlet gloves like those worn by the pilots, Macy's aviation-luncheon baskets, Macy's cameras, and Macy's toy airplanes—monoplane or biplane, depending on a child's preference.

The event they all came to see was the inaugural Statue of Liberty Race. It was as exciting an idea as it was controversial, with at least part of its thirty-five-mile route over densely populated areas. *Aircraft* magazine demanded that the "most dangerous aviation contest" be outlawed immediately "before a bad accident makes it a necessity." Wilbur Wright announced he was "strongly opposed to flying over cities.... While it is an aviator's own business whether he decides or not to risk his own neck, he has no right to endanger the lives of others." Also, in consideration of the fact the race was happening on a Sunday, he and his equally devout brother forbade any of their pilots from participating.

Most of the pilots shared the view that the race was inherently dangerous. That—coupled with the attrition from the week-long International Aviation Cup, fraught with accidents—left only three of the nearly thirty registered pilots to enter the competition: the French aristocrat Count Jacques de Lesseps, Claude Grahame-White, and John Moisant. Claude lodged a formal protest when the meet organizers changed the qualifying rules at the eleventh hour, which allowed John to compete. It was ignored by the race officials.

Once again, with his rakishly perched cap and his beastly machine, Claude held the horsepower advantage, but John figured he knew a way to level the playing field. It didn't take an engineering genius to realize his 50-horsepower Blériot plane was no match in an all-out speed slugfest; he would have to dare a more direct path over the heart of Brooklyn. Having never encountered the eddies and currents buildings can cause, he sought the advice of fellow pilots Arch Hoxsey and Ralph Johnstone. The men dubbed the Heavenly Twins, whose battles for the altitude record were legendary, urged him to climb high, away from the capricious winds and dips surging around the skyline and avenues. "Just be careful John," Ralph admonished. "There's no point in getting yourself killed. No amount of publicity's worth that."

The planes were to take off in staggered starts. As he shrugged on two layers of flying suits, two sweaters, and a knit cap to protect him against the frigid temperatures he would face at altitude, John watched the Brit and the Frenchman roll down the field and part ways with the earth in close succession. He sensed someone move close to his ear. "You're going to win," his little sister, Matilde, whispered to him. "I can feel it in my bones." Claude and Jacques were soon buzzing at top speed toward Coney Island, swinging wide of downtown Brooklyn. The Englishman chose a northern route to the target, the Frenchman headed south.

John's mechanic Albert Fileux and his assistants rolled his monoplane out to the track. John climbed aboard, settling into the metal seat, and signaled to Albert to pull the propeller. The Gnôme engine sputtered and caught, sending a fine spray of castor oil onto his goggles. But rather than taxiing out onto the field, the Blériot suddenly began to violently spin in a half-circle like a rodeo bull freed from the gate. John quickly realized the rudder was jammed. He struggled with the control stick but knew there was no way to steer the wheels, which, unlike those on today's airplanes, were fixed in place. The plane lurched forward, out of control, and violently smashed into the wreckage of a biplane that an inconsiderate pilot had abandoned next to the hangars.

Alfred rushed to the Blériot and asked his younger brother if he was okay. "Not a scratch, Fred," John replied, standing and brushing off his pants. "But I'm out of the race now." Without hesitation the wealthy banker who was given to wearing "a gold nugget as big as an egg and a long string of gold nuggets as big as filberts for a watch chain" shook his head and immediately declared, "I'll buy you another machine." The two brothers hopped into a car and raced down the row of hangars to the one marked number 7. Inside, two planes squatted amid gas cans and spare parts: one, the hopeless wreckage of a 100-horsepower racer Alfred Leblanc crashed the day before, and the other the French pilot's new Blériot, which was in perfect condition but which possessed a much smaller engine than that of the mangled plane. It was partially disassembled for the journey back to France. "Can you drive it all right?" Alfred Moisant asked. "Sure I can drive it," John responded. It was a model similar to his own. The hefty older brother turned to the assembled mechanics and declared, "I am now the owner of that machine, put it together as fast as you can and there'll be extra dollars in it for you," and trundled as fast as his considerable bulk would allow across the field to the nearest telephone.

"Grahame-White was the first of the airmen to delight the eyes of the impatient watchers at the Statue of Liberty," the *New York Times* reporter observed.

> A shout of "Here he comes" hailed his approach, for the news had gone out that he had left the aviation field. Far in the dim horizon of Brooklyn he looked like a swallow winging its flight. He was sighted at 3:27, flying at an altitude of 2,000 feet.

At the clubhouse, Alfred Moisant quickly found that Alfred Leblanc was ensconced in the Knickerbocker Hotel in Manhattan, nursing his injuries. "He's in bed?" the banker shouted to the operator. "Get him up!" When the drowsy pilot answered, he spoke to him in fluent French, "I want to buy your craft." Without missing a beat, the disconsolate aviator, who had been leading the International Aviation Cup before his accident, spitballed a response: "It will cost you ten thousand dollars." That was five times what the machine was worth; the banker instantly agreed. "But... you know..." the pilot continued, his brain now fully functioning and working all the financial angles, "it was admitted without duty merely for exhibition purposes. If you want to keep it in this country, you'll have to pay the duty." Again, Alfred Moisant offered his approval. "*Oui. Bien sûr.*"

"[Grahame-White] thinks he's safer from those Brooklyn spires and chimneys in the higher air planes," said a representative of the Aero Club to the *Times* reporter, who continued his account of the airplanes approaching Lady Liberty.

> He took the air above the East River a little north of the Brooklyn Bridge and made for the statue in a direct course. As he approached the statue the propellers of his little craft could be seen revolving rapidly, and the exhaust of his motor was spitting out a great volume of smoke. He appeared to be making great speed.
>
> The airman circled the statue at 3:30, passing directly over the hand that holds the torch. To the surprise of everybody he flew south as far as the Narrows before he finally turned and sped on the return leg via Brooklyn and Coney Island. Scarcely had Grahame-White circled the Statue when a second airman was sighted. It was De Lesseps.

Head shrouded in bandages and limping stiffly, Alfred Leblanc made it from Manhattan to the racetrack by car in just under an hour. He took a few moments to peer closely at the $15,000 check Alfred Moisant presented him. Neither of the brothers had thought to bring any checks with them from New York, so Alfred begged a blank one off a bystander and scribbled in his own account information and number. The wounded pilot eventually tilted a nod, his classically Gallic lip curling into a smile under his bushy handlebar mustache. The unexpected lucre offered a salve of sorts to the pain of his loss and injuries.

With Claude Grahame-White fading into the distance at 3:31, the spotters at the Statue of Liberty watched Jacques de Lesseps make a wide turn at a thousand feet, barely a minute behind the Englishman's pace. "After circling the statue he headed for Governors Island, thence he flew over Brooklyn, and disappeared in the direction of Coney Island."

Long minutes passed. Then, as the Moisants' new monoplane was being prepped for flight, a huge cheer went up from the grandstands. Word came that the other competitors had landed. Jacques completed the course in forty-one minutes; Claude in thirty-four minutes and thirty-eight seconds. It looked to all observers like the debonair Brit would be victorious yet again. He settled into the clubhouse, enjoying the congratulations of those gathered around him. From the grandstand, a young girl cried out, "Oh, but it's a shame! Why couldn't America have won just one event?"

In Hangar 7 the Blériot was tightened and oiled and fueled and ready. "Roll her out, boys!" shouted John.

On the rooftops and avenues and the bridges and parks, on the waterfronts and beaches and balconies of Queens and Long Island, Brooklyn and Midtown, Chinatown and the Battery, a million pairs of eyes peered upward into the blue October sky. "They came in automobiles, crested carriages, by bicycle, on foot, and in streetcars, the rich standing alongside the poor. The decks of the Staten Island and Brooklyn ferries were packed." This was more than a battle of man and machine; it was a high-stakes race among nations, each vying for a claim it had the steeliest grasp of the future. France and England just passed the final furlong, and America, young America, had twenty lengths to close.

In a craft half as powerful as his opponents', John Moisant knew his only chance at victory was to set a course as straight as the flight of an arrow, one that placed him directly above the dangerous church spires and apartment buildings of Brooklyn. This route was, in the words of one reporter, "regarded by aviators as almost beyond the bounds of recklessness. A fall means almost certain death." John pushed the throttle wide open and barely taxied at all before he was soaring almost straight up, his dark eyes fixed on the western horizon, the muscles of his jaw clenched in determination.

"Miss Liberty was at home to them all yesterday," recounted the *New York Tribune*,

> but she saved her most alluring smiles for her last visitor, the only American aviator to call, John B. Moisant. The man from home gave her time to arrange her hair and see that her skirt hung all right in the back, and although she was short of breath she assumed the honors of the occasion with fine dignity when Moisant, who is a little fast in his ways, could not stop for tea at 4:28 o'clock because fifty thousand visitors were waiting for him out at Belmont Park.

John's Blériot roared into view of the watchers on the statue as he crossed the East River near the Brooklyn Bridge, then passed over Manhattan above the Battery.

> Moisant made a very sharp turn at the island, and it looked to some of the spectators as if he had turned on the outside of the captive balloon that, strung to the statue by a rope, was used as a stake for the airmen. Otto Luyters, however, the representative of the Aero Club, who was stationed at the statue to see that the airmen observed the rules of the race, was looking at Moisant through his glasses, and he said that the airman had passed on the inside of the balloon. Moisant seemed to realize that he was in a fair way to win the prize. He put on

additional power, and taking a straight course over the housetops of Brooklyn, he sped back toward the starting point.

"How does an aeroplane, going a mile a minute, grow out of the sky into the vision?" a writer pondered.

> You are looking in the direction the airmen are to come from. The sky is clear. Between your eye and the illumitable [*sic*] reaches of space there is nothing but a tremendous pile of blue air. Now you see nothing—now there is a black mote before the vision. Maybe it is one of the minute dead cells that float around in the eye, crossing occasionally the stream of light coming in through the pupil and falling on the optic nerve. It isn't that, because the motes clear away in an instant. Maybe it is a sea gull. No, this black speck is too high for a sea gull. Besides, look how the thing is growing. Now...a shape is making itself apparent.

The crowds at Belmont Park stood transfixed, squinting into the low sun stained red by the chimney smoke of the city. A photograph of that instant shows every head at the racetrack tilted back, mouths pulled into grimaces from the strain of trying to see that which had not yet revealed itself. Slowly, the silhouetted shape sprouted wings, and an engine was heard roaring in agony at top revolutions, and a figure became discernible, head perched just above the body of the apparition, leaning forward as would a jockey on a charging thoroughbred. If John had had a whip, he would undoubtedly have been striping the sides of his Blériot.

One of the timers shouted, "He's got two minutes to beat Grahame-White!" A woman, tears running down her face with excitement, was shredding her lace handkerchief. A pair of men tipped over a barrel of gasoline in the infield and set it aflame as a beacon to the pilot. When the monoplane swooped down to just above ground level and howled across the finish line in a rush of wind, pandemonium erupted. "He's won! He's won!" shouted his sisters and brother, leaping up and down and hugging each other. Wilbur Wright, who up until that moment was an outspoken critic of John, yelled with elation at the top of his lungs. "I don't care!" an excited elderly man declared as he pummeled his expensive silk hat into a rag of indistinguishable shape against the backs of fellow celebrants. "It is worth a hundred silk hats to show them that Uncle Sam has a boy to hold his end up." The scoreboard showed John had beaten Claude's time by forty-three seconds.

Up until, perhaps, 1909, the American public refused to accept human flight was possible. The Wright brothers' historic accomplishment on a North Carolina beach barely received any coverage at first from major newspapers, because it was simply assumed to be fake. When people did finally begin to believe, they did so rapturously, with almost a religious fervor. In his reflective years, Igor Sikorsky, the famed Russian pilot and helicopter designer, tried to explain the exuberance of the crowds at those early events. "Aeronautics was neither an industry nor even a science," he wrote.

> Both were yet to come. It was an "art" and, I might say, a "passion." Indeed, at that time it was a miracle. It meant the realization of legends and dreams that had existed for millenniums and that had been repeatedly pronounced by scientific authorities to be impossible. Therefore even the brief and unsteady flights of that period were deeply impressive. Many times I observed expressions of exultation and tears in the eyes of witnesses who, for the first time, watched a flying machine carry a man in the air.

Stiff and numb from the cold, the American climbed slowly down from his smoking and hissing aircraft and into an awaiting car, which wove through the deliriously jubilant throng to the judge's stand. The meet manager, Allan Ryan, and the other judges abandoned all pretense of objectivity as they pounded on the weary flyer's back and pumped his hand in congratulations. "They tossed him on to their shoulders, shoved an American flag into his hands and shouted their exultation in his ears." With a wave of his baton, the bandleader signaled his musicians to launch into "The Star-Spangled Banner," followed by "Yankee Doodle" and "Dixie." The thousands of spectators, surging forward from the stands, were hysterical with joy.

> There were tears in the cheers and there were sobs in the shouts of every man, woman, and child who had seen Moisant's return, for something was welling up that made them want to cry for sheer happiness. When a victor had been so greeted before none who watched could tell.

Forgotten for the moment was the Gordon Bennett trophy and all the record-breaking achievements of the prior week: a gutsy American had defeated the world's best in a race to the national symbol of liberty. The *New York World* declared it "the greatest race of modern times." "He doesn't fly to land," Matilde Moisant told another reporter, "he flies to win." John was hoisted yet again onto the shoulders of his admirers and carried into the clubhouse, where Claude sat fuming.

> Almost as soon as the announcement was made, Grahame-White let out a roar like a stabbed tiger. He demanded that the race be run over again. The Aero Club officials said he could run it over again for the record if he wanted to, but Moisant had won the prize. Grahame-White challenged Moisant to race him over the course again for a $10,000 bet. Moisant declined to do it in a 50-horsepower plane.

Legendary British pilot Claude Grahame-White. He lost the 1910 Statue of Liberty Race to John Moisant.

With the crush of bodies there was barely enough room to breathe, yet cheers and shouts of "Moisant! Moisant!" resounded again and again. The aviator asked to be lowered to the floor and stood with raised glass until the crowd quieted down. "To America!" he bellowed. The response shook the windows.

Looking on was a woman who knew what it was to take risks, to ignore fear, to shrug off the faint-hearted warnings of those who would limit what can and should and must be achieved. In John Moisant and his victory, against all odds, against all expectations and assumptions, Harriet Quimby saw a fellow spirit—someone who refused to cower in the face of the impossible.

She later confided to her closest friends that at that moment, then and there, she knew she wanted to become an aviator. "I said, I believe I could do that." A thoughtful pause, a characteristic tilt of the head, the flash of a dazzling smile, and the declaration: "And I will!"

That evening, as the Moisant family enjoyed a dinner at the Hotel Astor, Harriet approached their table. She wasn't there by happenstance—she had used her reporter's skills to discover where they were dining. Like John, who planned a winning route over the dangerous rooftops of Brooklyn, Harriet was beginning to design a direct line from the impoverished farm girl, to the fearless adventurer, to the accomplished journalist, to the... next. An unknown future. She didn't know it then, but the key to her ultimate destiny was sitting at that dinner table in New York. "I went directly over to him and told him I wished to learn to fly."

Likely amused if not impressed by the obviously confident young woman standing before him, John told her yes, he'd be happy to teach her. As good fortune would have it, he and his brother were planning to open a flight school on Long Island in the coming spring. Notably not mentioned was her gender. Notably not questioned were her abilities, or intelligence, or physical strength. Instead John simply apologized—the season for flying in the Northeast was ending, he explained, and he had some air shows to attend down South. There was money to be made.

That was the last time John Moisant and Harriet Quimby spoke.

PART THREE

12

THERE'S ANOTHER GOOD MAN GONE

IN THE YEAR 1911, *Leslie's Illustrated Weekly*'s 320,000 readers saw an article signed by its celebrity columnist, Harriet Quimby, every week. She expounded on the opera, or theater, female drivers, and zoos, animals performing on stage. For the first six months of that year the columns were typical Harriet fare: fluff and gossip and critiques, humor and unique observations, with the occasional slap in the face of harsh, and often hidden, reality. But on May 25 a different kind of headline appeared in *Leslie's*—six words that shocked the world: "How a Woman Learns to Fly."

> Americans are called an inquisitive race. I am satisfied that this is true. I am also satisfied that curiosity is not confined to the men. Here I am, a novice with a fortnight's experience in the Moisant School of Aviation, at Hempstead Plains, Long Island, and yet I have forty-seven letters, thirty of them from women, eagerly asking how to learn to fly.

Harriet had been taking lessons for barely two weeks, but by the time the article appeared in *Leslie's,* she had already been outed. A slight mishap on one of her training runs attracted the attention of a *New York Times* reporter. When a tire blew on her monoplane, causing the undercarriage to collapse, journalists who were gathered nearby ran over. Before Harriet could duck into a hangar, they recognized her.

"Woman in Trousers Daring Aviator" trumpeted the head. "Long Island Folk Discover that Miss Harriet Quimby Is Making Flights at Garden City. SHE DRIVES A MONOPLANE. Thinks Sky Scraping Hardly More Dangerous than Riding in a High-Power Automobile."

> Rumors that there was a young woman aviator at the Moisant Aviation School here who made daily flights at 4:30 A.M. have brought many Garden City folk and townspeople from Hempstead and Mineola to the flying grounds here on several mornings. These early risers have seen a slender, youthful figure in aviation jacket and trousers of wool-backed satin, with leather puttees, heavy goggles, and a big aviation cap, mount a Moisant monoplane, glide over the ground after the motor had been started, and then rise for flight after flight around the field at an average height of 50 feet.
>
> The young aviator has attracted attention as much because of the heavy veil which hung from the helmet brim as for any other reason. There was a wind this morning, however, and as the aviator crossed the field towards the hangars the breeze lifted this veil long enough for an onlooker who knew her well to recognize the features of Miss Harriet Quimby, a young magazine editor of Manhattan and the daughter of San Francisco parents, now resident with her at the Hotel Victoria, in Manhattan.
>
> Miss Quimby laughed when she found she was discovered for, in the two weeks that she has been here making daily morning flights under the direction of André Houpert, chief instructor in the Moisant school, she has managed to keep her identity a secret. For more than a week it was not even suspected that she was not a man, for her costume, in every detail, is that of any expert aviator.
>
> "Do I like flying?" Miss Quimby repeated in response to a question. "Well, I'm out here at 4 o'clock every morning. That ought to be

> answer enough. I took up the sport just because I thought I should enjoy the sensation, and I haven't regretted it. Motoring is all right, and I have done a lot of that, but after seeing monoplanes in the air, I couldn't resist the desire to try the air lanes, where there are neither speed laws nor traffic policemen, and where one needn't go all the way around Central Park to get across Times Square. Why shouldn't we have some good American women air pilots?"

Despite the concerns of her parents and friends, Harriet's dinner-table request of John Moisant would ultimately be fulfilled. Three days after the Statue of Liberty Race, John's brother Alfred, fully convinced that aviation was a tremendous business opportunity, incorporated the Moisant International Aviators with an initial capitalization of $250,000. His vast wealth ensured an additional $500,000 for equipment and staff. It would also cover travel to exhibitions and air shows around the world, for which Alfred chartered seven yellow and green railroad cars, including a diner and two luxurious Pullman coaches. The trains would carry not only the Moisants and various pilots, but also mechanics, roustabouts, eight airplanes, and a Fiat speedster for use in races between planes and cars. Company offices were opened in the Times building on Forty-Second Street in Manhattan, and vacant land was acquired on the vast flatlands of Hempstead, Long Island, for the future site of a flying school into which, seven months hence, Harriet would enroll. In the meantime, Alfred was eager to capitalize on his brother's popularity and the spectacular interest in aviation generated by the Belmont Park air show. There were paying audiences to entertain throughout the South.

The word "international" in Moisant International Aviators was more than a marketing ploy. Most of the great flyers of the day were from Europe, so John quickly recruited three Frenchmen he grew fond of at

Moisant School of Aviation, Hempstead, New York.

Belmont—René Barrier, René Simon, and Roland Garros, the future national hero of France and WWI ace—for his company.

He was known to sit down at the piano and quiet a noisy room with his musical talent. All of twenty-five with a ready smile, heavy brows, and a signature bushy mustache he habitually twirled like a silent-movie villain, Roland Garros was one of the most popular pilots of the day. The former law student, champion bicycle racer, and son of a diplomat had instructed John Moisant at the Blériot aviation school.

Not long before, Roland watched the world's smallest plane, the Demoiselle, being flown by a Swiss pilot, Edmond Audemars, and bought it on the spot, before it even came back to earth. The twelfth time he took it up, a wind grabbed the plane and tossed it to the ground. The Frenchman, thrown clear, landed forty feet away. He stood, walked over to the crumpled wreck, kicked it, shouted a colorful Gallic curse, and promptly demanded a replacement.

Shortly after John earned his pilot's license, he took his instructor and new friend up for a flight over the center of Paris to the suburb of Issy-les-Moulineaux, a first for aviation. Passing by the Eiffel Tower, the Frenchman grew so excited he stood up in the rear of the monoplane, nearly turning it over. John, the student but ten years Roland's senior, desperately groped behind his seat to pull the impetuous passenger back down.

Dubbed "the Cloud Kisser" by Alfred due to his altitude record of 1,500 feet, Roland was almost as small as John. It is perhaps fitting that he was most closely associated with an airplane as endearingly undersized as its pilot. For some the Demoiselle, made of bamboo and silk, had the affectionate nickname the Hummingbird. Others were not so kind. "Nothing so excruciatingly funny as the action of this machine has ever been seen," wrote *Aero* magazine.

> The little two-cylinder engine pops away with a sound like the frantic drawing of ginger beer corks; the machine scuttles along the ground with its tail well up; then down comes the tail suddenly and seems to slap the ground while the front jumps up, and all the spectators rock with laughter. The whole attitude and jerky action of the machine suggest a grasshopper in a furious rage.

At the Belmont Park meet, the Demoiselle became a comedic diversion, which meet organizer Allan Ryan planned all along. Roland climbed into his Lilliputian airplane, which the *New York Sun* snickered resembled

> a good-size umbrella. When she first leaves the ground one is minded of a rubber ball. She bounces back to brush the grass blades for just a moment and then she is off for good.

But once Roland and the speedy little Demoiselle took to the air, the crowd erupted in cheers as the plane streaked around the pylons. It was as maneuverable as a rodeo barrel racer.

Joining the three Frenchmen in the Moisant International traveling team were Swiss pilot Edmond "Tiny" Audemars, all of one hundred pounds soaking wet, who held his country's speed and altitude records, and four Americans: Charles K. Hamilton, a red-headed, hard-drinking firebrand who was scarred "head to foot" from countless accidents; John J. Frisbie, an experienced balloonist and skydiver; expert automobile driver Joseph Seymour, who was recruited to race the Fiat against the airplanes; and, of course, John Moisant. Their salaries varied from $500 to $2,000, with annual bonuses of $10,000 to the star flyers. Unlike members of the Orville and Wilbur Wright and Glenn Curtiss exhibition teams, the Moisant pilots were allowed to keep whatever prize money they won as an extra incentive.

It was Roland who made the company's first exhibition flight on a dreary November day in Richmond, Virginia. Buzzing a large crowd gathered for a presidential speech by William Howard Taft, the Frenchman made dozens of new fans with his acrobatic stunts. Having been drowned out by the roar of the Gnôme engine, the president reportedly wasn't one of them.

Poor weather plagued the team's swing through the South. When his pilots couldn't take to the air in search of records to be broken, Alfred sent Joseph off in the Fiat to zoom around the track at breakneck speed, at least once with Matilde Moisant in the passenger seat, to Alfred's displeasure. Or he invited ticketholders into the tents to examine the airplanes up close—anything to keep the paying public happy. But Richmond proved a financial disappointment, Chattanooga was worse, and when the dejected troupe rolled into Memphis, they stepped out of the train cars to blowing snow and freezing temperatures.

Concerned the company was losing vast sums of money, John was determined to turn things around. In dangerous conditions he took his monoplane to fifteen hundred feet on an eighteen-minute flight, despite the thirty-five-mile-an-hour winds "standing his Blériot nearly on end." René Simon followed with a thrilling series of acrobatic tricks, and Roland proceeded to set a new American record for sustained flight. The next day, Charles Hamilton energized the appreciative audience by setting another record, this one for reaching 79.2 miles an hour, which René Barrier promptly exceeded with an 87.93-mile-an-hour run, winning himself a $5,000 prize put up by the *Memphis Commercial Appeal*. John Moisant then cemented the adoration of the standing-room-only crowd by climbing to 9,264 feet in a frigid temperature with ice forming on his plane. He found his way back down to the fairgrounds in the dimming light only by spotting a bonfire his team lit. Almost before his Blériot stopped rolling, an ecstatic mob nearly succeeded in pulling him from the pilot's seat.

Though the team's aviation efforts were historic, its Memphis leg was costly. John J. Frisbie's motor stopped as he was taking off, causing the plane to smash into the ground from twenty-five feet. He walked away uninjured. The Curtiss biplane was not so lucky. Roland Garros broke his nose and suffered a badly cut eye when the steering wire on his Blériot broke and sent his plane hurtling downward. He managed to avoid more serious harm to himself only by lifting his feet away from the rudder pedals at the last possible second, which prevented them from being crushed under the front of the fuselage. It was a two-day, stormy and freezing stint in Tupelo, however, that became a defining moment for the Moisant International Aviators. The pilots flirted with injury and death to entertain thousands of spectators, most of whom had never before seen a flying machine in person. The team realized that regardless of the risks, the only key to financial success, for better or for worse, was to fly.

"There is a deeply rooted belief with the majority of flyers that when called upon to take out his machine and go into the air, one must do so regardless of his own judgment as to his safety," Harriet later observed.

> The one great fear of the flyer is that he may gain a reputation for being what is known as a "ground hog," or of having lost his nerve. For that reason many will venture into a wind with their frail crafts when they know they may imperil their lives by doing so. Every new invention of note has to go through its own trying experience. Some would not ride on the first steamboat because they were sure the boiler would explode. Some bitterly opposed the construction of the first railroad because they said it would be deadly to run trains at full speed.
>
> As to aviation, is it dangerous? Yes; so is swimming, if one is to try to swim through Niagara or across a turbulent stream or in the ocean

> with its perilous undertow. As is skating where the ice is thin, bicycling, motor-cycling, motor-driving, and a lot of other things in which we constantly indulge are perilous unless conditions are made comparatively safe. Over a good flying ground on a calm day, driving an aeroplane is as safe as driving an automobile in a crowded city. Over a ground filled with holes and ruts which send up gusty whirlpools and cause treacherous "air pockets," aeroplaning becomes hazardous. Yet with a clear-headed pilot, it need not necessarily be dangerous.

On the morning of New Year's Eve 1910, frost dusted the tupelos and bald cypress trees of the bayous near New Orleans. The drowsy little suburb of Harahan, Louisiana, named after the Illinois Central Railroad's president, who still held the job, sat positioned between the Mississippi River to its south and Lake Pontchartrain to the north. Those residents who were hoping to sleep in late on that Saturday were about to be awakened by a sound that had never before reverberated over the swamps—that of an airplane in flight.

John Moisant stood next to his brother Alfred at City Park and began donning his flight ensemble: flannel underwear, two coveralls, and two sweaters, with a layer of newspaper between them for additional insulation. He bent over to pull on three pairs of socks and canvas shoes, again with alternating layers of paper. He then wrapped wool blankets around his legs with more paper inserts and tied them in place. It was all he could do to hobble over to his awaiting plane like a knight in full armor. The pilot hastily slurped down a cup of hot bouillon before climbing aboard the Blériot and waving at his ground crew to pull the prop.

His plan was to take a practice run at the course laid out two days earlier for the Michelin Cup, a contest of endurance and distance that offered a $4,000 prize. It would be the perfect capper to the

Moisant International Aviators' Louisiana stop. In order to maintain a record-breaking sustained flight, John's monoplane was equipped with an extra thirty-five-gallon gas tank, mounted below and slightly forward of the engine. A few days earlier, when his business manager, Albert Levino, expressed concern about the risks of flying with modified equipment, John calmly told him, "I think there is no danger in making an aeroplane flight if the machine is properly adjusted before the ascent is made. I do not expect to die in an aeroplane flight."

After making two circuits of the field, John pushed forward on the control stick, lowered his altitude to two hundred feet, and started to bank the plane on approach to his landing spot. According to the *New York Times*, "He waved his hand to the watchers, swerved the machine to the left, so as to get in line with the landing place, but went too far, and made the hazardous 'right turn' he had invented and used by himself almost exclusively." With that move, the wind was behind him, which made landing under the best of conditions "one of the most dangerous experiments," in Moisant's own words. This was not the best of conditions.

"The wind, which was blowing about twenty miles an hour at the City Park track when he left there, and increased in velocity, and from being steady had turned gusty, tossing his little machine about like a gull in a storm." Spectators watched as it began pitching and lurching. "Suddenly, when the machine was within fifty feet of the earth, a squall came hurrying across the rice fields. It caught the tail of the monoplane, tilted it heavenward, and hurled the driver from his seat."

Other witnesses described the aviator as being propelled through the air "as if he had been shot from a gun." This was the era before safety restraints were in common use. The pilot sat in an open cockpit with no windshield, exposed to the cold and the rain in a seat that was little more than a metal lawn chair. In the event of turbulence, fliers like John could only hold more tightly to the rudimentary control yoke, which was little more than the tiller of an airship, and ride it out. The leading cause of death among pilots, then and now, is gravity.

"With arms abreast, Moisant fell. Half way the spectators saw his body turn over, and fall head downward into the mud of the marsh. O. M. Sutter, a civil engineer, was the first to reach the aviator's side. Moisant's lips were shivering and he was breathing faintly." There were no visible bruises or injuries save for a red mark on his nose from his goggles. He appeared almost peaceful, as if he was resting from a mildly unpleasant experience. Those who read of his many prior accidents were skeptical that he was badly injured. "Dead! Bah!" declared one such man who dashed upon the scene. "That dear boy Moisant has more lives than a flock of kittens! Lift up his head and I'll bet you he'll smile." But no smile was forthcoming. His glassy eyes remained unfocused. He offered forth no witty rejoinder, no matter how desperately the men gathering around him prayed for it. They bent forward and slid hands underneath his body, lifting him as delicately as one would the most precious treasure in the world.

No road was yet built through the swamplands nearby; only a train track was there. John was carried to a flat car and carefully placed on it, a pillow laid under his head, a pile of coats over his body for warmth. A locomotive chugged slowly over and coupled with the car, and, after a hasty telephone call from the switch house, the railway was cleared all the way to New Orleans.

Alfred Moisant was nowhere near the scene at the time. He was hustling up some extra gas cans. On the way to the makeshift airfield, a passing rail worker told him, "They don't need that," not recognizing whom he was talking to. "Why?" the elder Moisant asked. "The machine is wrecked and the aviator killed." Alfred's knees buckled. The next time he saw his brother was at the McMahon Funeral Home.

Moisant's fatal accident, 1910.

The coroner declared John Moisant's death was instantaneous—the cause, a broken neck. His face bore no expression of pain or fear, more like that "of a sleeping man." Alfred and the rest of the flying team gathered at the funeral home and wept. "Everybody who knew him loved him," fellow pilot Charles K. Hamilton said. Stanlie Moisant, John's fifteen-year-old son, was quoted as saying, "I have not seen my father for five years and now he is dead." The *Times* reported the young boy fainted at the news. Most of the world was unaware John even had a child or was once married.

Moments after hearing of the accident, Arch Hoxsey, who was about to attempt to break an altitude record in Los Angeles, said, "There's another good man gone." But, he added, Moisant "was awfully reckless, and a reckless man and a Blériot do not go together. He took more chances than any man I know." Monoplanes like Moisant's were considered capricious and difficult to hold steady in less-than-ideal conditions—a wild-minded colt as compared to the plodding draft horse of a biplane. But one can be forgiven for wondering if Arch's harsh words angered the aviation gods, for just minutes after speaking to reporters, he, too, lost his life, when his Wright Flyer biplane inexplicably plummeted to the ground.

The Aero Club of America issued an official statement explaining its theory of what happened to Moisant—an unlucky combination of a lower center of gravity due to the temporary gas tank coupled with a sudden gust of wind threw the Blériot into a dive. "Not only his country but the whole world lost a man destined to pre-eminence in the development of the art [of flight]," the club's statement read. "He did more than any man to arouse the enthusiasm in aviation which will bring this science into its own," Roland Garros declared. "Moisant was ahead of his time. He saw farther than any of us and realized better than all of us how aviation would benefit and improve mankind." But it was Edmond

"Tiny" Audemars who most eloquently summed up the feelings of the assembled flyers: "He was really king of the air, as much ahead of all of us as the great soaring birds are ahead of the aeroplane."

13

TO BECOME A COMPANION OF THE BIRDS

> Four o'clock in the morning! The light is just dawning as the telephone at the Garden City Hotel summons me to rise. The birds are chirping. The air is heavy with the odor of the fields, the trees and the flowers. It is the time when nature seems to be at rest, and is, therefore, especially adapted for a lesson in flying. This is the reason why the students at the Moisant Aviation School must submit to the penalty of an early contemplation of nature, whether they appreciate it or not.

DESPITE HARRIET'S BUCOLIC MUSINGS in her article "How a Woman Learns to Fly," her dreams of flying must have been affected by John Moisant's death. And not just his—pilots were falling from the skies at a horrific rate in the early years of aviation. But in May 1911 she plunked down $750 of *Leslie's Illustrated Weekly* money and began the process of learning to fly. Students were liable for, in addition to tuition, any damage to the school's airplanes, but they received a discounted price for a new Moisant-built monoplane upon graduation. A June 1911 advertisement in *Aircraft Magazine* assured potential students that "French Pilot-Aviators Are the Instructors" and that "Flying Is a Fine Sport, a Splendid Science and a Rich Livelihood."

Harriet continued,

> The student of aviation must be the earliest riser of all students in search of knowledge, for the lessons can be given only while the air is still and while the little signal flag on the field clings close to its mast. Dressing in a hurry and waiting for a moment to enjoy the healthful precaution of a cup of hot coffee poured from a faithful vacuum bottle, the student is soon on the way across the field to the hangars, where the aeroplanes, with expanding white wings, are silently awaiting their flights. The activity of instructors and students here is in striking contrast with the quiet of the sleepy hotel just left. Even the little white dog with a black spot on his forehead, the much petted mascot of the school, is alert and seems thoroughly interested in the goings on. An anxious look is directed from time to time to a little red flag on the end of a tall bamboo pole, placed in the middle of the aviation field, and there is considerable misgiving as the light piece of bunting flutters from its mast. Each one hazards a guess as to the possibility of a flying lesson. All hope that the wind is not too strong or too puffy, but all fear that it may be, for this is not an unusual experience. Professor Houpert, the instructor, settles that matter by walking out into the open with an anemometer and measuring the velocity of the breeze, which he may report as blowing four or five miles an hour. If it is over this, the school is called off for the day, for a student of aviation who ventures into anything more than a six-mile wind, especially with a low-powered school machine, is almost certain to come to grief.

The Moisant School of Aviation was the culmination of hours and hours of talks between brothers Albert and John. These took place late at night, on endless train rides, and over countless dinners and tumblers of whiskey. If the younger Moisant was the reckless visionary, the older was his enabler and financier, yet also a true believer. In the days after "Johnny" was laid to rest at Metairie Cemetery in New Orleans, a still-grieving Alfred ushered his depleted crew onward to Dallas for more exhibitions. He was determined to prove his brother's theories about the future of aviation correct, as well as preserve his memory.

Perversely, John's and Arch Hoxsey's deaths within minutes of each other only whetted the public's appetite for flying exhibitions. At Fort Worth, two weeks after the tragedy, the Moisant International Aviators were greeted by thousands of spectators who came from as far away as the Texas Panhandle. "They arrived in automobiles, on horseback, on trains, in buggies and rigs, and on foot. Children were let out of school at noon while stores and factories released half their workforces on alternate days to allow them all to attend the two-day engagement." After one close call in which Roland Garros was forced to land at a dangerously high rate of speed, a woman told him, "Mr. Garros, I thought that you were going to kill yourself!" To which he sardonically replied, "Madam, I could not do that for you today; maybe tomorrow."

While the team of pilots continued to travel as aviation's star emissaries, Alfred prepared to execute the second part of his and his brother's plan: the airplane factory and flight school on Long Island. A heavy-set man with a large mustache and even larger sense of self, which he honed in the jungles and plantations of Central America, Alfred had an approach to business that more closely resembled the military philosophy of Carl von Clausewitz than the economic theories of Adam Smith. He often used bluster, money, and exaggeration to bend his opponents to his will, and he rarely accepted "no" as an answer. He was also not above deception, especially where his shareholders were concerned.

By spring 1911, Alfred's newly incorporated Hempstead Plains Aviation Company was under construction on 1,600 sandy acres of desolate, flat grassland between Mineola and Garden City, New York, "the only natural prairie east of the Allegheny Mountains," where no trees or buildings could prove a hindrance. Two runways were planned, as well as a hundred hangars with electric lights, running water, and gasoline storage tanks; a large grandstand; and a clubhouse that included a restaurant and hotel. A gold-embossed brochure, featuring John's Blériot rounding the Statue of Liberty on its cover, touted it as the best aviation center in the world, with a half-dozen instructors and seven Moisant-designed monoplanes ready to take legions of eager students into the air. In one press release, Alfred fictitiously claimed he already had forty-two applicants for the school. He fed a tip that appeared in the *New York Times* in June:

> A new factory, capable of an output of 500 aeroplanes annually, will be established to take the place of the present factory in this city. It is hoped, that before the end of the year, there will be at least six schools running.

In fact, the class Harriet joined in mid-May comprised a grand total of six students, one flyable plane and one for ground practice, and a single instructor, André Houpert, late of the Blériot flight school in France. Lessons were held at a leased facility at nearby Mineola, since the Moisant hangars and runways were not yet completed. The 4 A.M. lesson time suited Harriet because "it didn't interfere with her job, the air was unusually calm then, and her unorthodox activity could be kept a secret, or so she thought."

By 1910, 27 percent of New York State's workforce was female. Young women especially were spending more time outside the home, enjoying the freedoms that independent sources of income could afford them. They could now experience all that New York City had to offer without the permission or accompaniment of a man. An archetype took root of the New Woman characterized by Daisy Miller, Henry James's protagonist in his eponymous novella, who declared, "I've never allowed a gentleman to dictate to me or to interfere with anything I do." Indeed, more and more young American women were embracing the concept of independence both professionally and financially. These included former President Theodore Roosevelt's own daughter, Alice, who broke with the stereotypes of the "good mother, good wife, good daughter."

But in a society still mired in conservative Victorian mores, the backlash was vicious. Leaders of the Catholic Church, for example, spoke out against the New Woman as a threat to traditional womanhood and society's natural order. Females expressing freedom from the judgment and influences of men were shocking to many. President Roosevelt excoriated the idea of women "self-indulgently pursuing careers and failing to breed enough babies." His racist and frothing speeches contended that white women were committing "race suicide" and being outbred by "fecund ethnics." The status quo of male dominance over all things female was perceived as suddenly under attack, and any American woman who hoped to balance a successful career and enjoyable life with societal tranquility was painfully aware that, to do so, she had to toe as delicate a line as that of an Anna Pavlova pirouette.

Politics took these societal paroxysms to even higher levels. Any push at the constraints of gender inequality carried a risk, but the mention of voting rights could invite rage if not outright violence. The suffrage movement was as polarizing as anything the nation experienced in decades, and not just among men. Many of the anti-suffrage groups comprised women who believed politics should be left to men because women had enough responsibilities running the day-to-day operations of their households and families. "Children, kitchen, and church" became a common motto. In contrast to that mindset were the thousands of women around the world who had been campaigning for political equality since the mid-1800s. In the US, Elizabeth Cady Stanton and Susan B. Anthony began fighting for a universal suffrage amendment to the Constitution as far back as 1869. Their work brought the issue to the front pages of most of the nation's newspapers and into conversations at many a dinner table or social gathering.

So suggesting that women could fly airplanes—an activity seen as not only somewhat insane, given the high risk, but also inherently male—was rife with peril, literally and figuratively. Both the Wright brothers and Glenn Curtiss adamantly refused to allow women into their flight schools, and Claude Grahame-White declared the female gender "temperamentally unfitted for the sport"—a sport limited in their minds to only the manliest of men.

Acutely aware of the social climate in which she lived and thrived, Harriet was convinced that in order to enter the virulently masculine world of aviation without raising the ire of politicians and clergymen, as well as lose any of her devoted readers, she would have to obscure her femininity, at least until she could prove that women were as capable as men of flying. She turned to one of her society friends for help.

> If a woman wants to fly, first of all she must, of course, abandon skirts and don a knickerbocker uniform. I speak of this particularly, because so many have asked me about my flying costume. It may seem strange, but I could not find an aviation suit of any description in the great city of New York—and I tried hard. In my perplexity it occurred to me that the president of the American Tailors Association, Alexander M. Grean, might be a good adviser; and he was, for it did not take him long to design a suit which has no doubt established the aviation costume for women in this country, if not for all the world, since the French women still continue to wear the clumsy and uncomfortable harem skirt as a flying costume.
>
> My suit is made of thick, wool-back satin, without lining. It is all in one piece, including the hood. By an ingenious combination it can be

> converted instantly into a conventional-appearing walking skirt when not in use in knickerbocker form. The speed with which the aviator flies and the strong currents created by the rapidly revolving propeller directly in front of the driver compel the latter to be warmly clad. There must be no flapping ends to catch in the multitudinous wires surrounding the driver's seat. The feet and legs must be free, so that one can readily manipulate the steering apparatus; for the steering on a monoplane is not done by a wheel guided by the hand, as in an automobile.

Harriet would not accept wearing some kind of boxy, unattractive sack. She knew it was inevitable that her ruse would eventually be discovered, and she was very image conscious. Her form-fitting uniform was plum-colored satin with a flattering hood and tapered legs that flowed into calf-high boots. She could pull a cord to release the trousers and convert their fabric into an elegant skirt. A photograph of her in this stylish outfit was featured in "How a Woman Learns to Fly," the first of a series of articles she wrote about her experiences at the Moisant School of Aviation.

Within a few weeks of Harriet's preliminary lesson, she was no longer the only woman enrolled in the flight school. The youngest Moisant, Matilde—described as a slip of a girl, barely five feet tall, attractive but unassuming—had been harboring a secret wish to learn. But she feared, after her brother's death, the possibility would never materialize. When Alfred told her he would honor John's promise to teach Harriet, his baby sister insisted she be allowed in as well. She later recounted saying to her brother, "Fred, I want to fly."

> He looked at me very seriously. If he had said, "You can't," that would have ended it, but he looked at me and said, "What do you want to fly

for?" "Just for fun," I said. He said, "Well, if you promise you will not fly commercially, I'll let you go."

The two women students quickly bonded. Matilde's fashion sense tilted toward large-feathered hats and pince-nez glasses, but she immediately adopted Harriet's flying-costume design, although hers was made of more modest brown wool and she preferred a snug helmet over Harriet's flowing hood. She looked ten years younger than her actual age of thirty-three, and she never corrected anyone who guessed wrong.

On days when the weather cooperated, Matilde walked to the airfield from the adjacent Atlantic City Hotel, where Alfred had rented her a room, while Harriet caught the 3:45 A.M. train from New York to Hempstead Plains. Classes started at 4:30 sharp. "The first lesson of the beginner in an aeroplane," *Leslie's* new aviation correspondent wrote,

> is intended to accustom her to the noisy and jarring vibration of the engine. Before the student climbs into her seat, she will discover why it is well to cover her natty costume with washable jumpers or overalls. Not only the chassis of the machine, but all the fixtures are slippery with lubricating oil, and when the engine is speeded a shower of this oil is also thrown back directly into the driver's face. It is interesting to know that castor oil is used as a lubricant for high-tensioned engines, like the Gnôme.

As she climbed aboard the airplane and settled into the metal seat, Harriet's first lessons were focused on safety. André Houpert, the school's chief flight instructor, demonstrated the function of the ignition switch and when to flip it on so as not to injure the mechanic who would be heaving on the propeller to get the Gnôme engine started.

The timing of the switch was crucial to prevent a sudden reversal of the propeller that could easily break a wrist or even an arm.

The quiet of the morning was soon shattered by the roar of the engine as it fired up. Four other assistants clung to the aircraft to keep it in place as Harriet eased the throttle lever forward. Once her teacher was satisfied the engine was turning at enough revolutions, he ordered the assistants to let go of the airplane.

The monoplane bounded forward, hopping along the uneven ground. Harriet recalled how challenging it was to keep the airplane headed in a straight line, even on the ground:

> This looks very easy, until you discover that an aeroplane possesses the perversity common to all inanimate objects. It always wants to go the other way, instead of the straight way that you seek to direct. Your first dash across the field and back takes two minutes, if no mishap occurs. After two dashes of this description, a discreet teacher will dismiss you for the day. You have had all that your nerves ought to be asked to stand. In the best schools of France—a land famous for its aviators—no pupil, however apt, is permitted to have a longer daily lesson than five minutes at the outset of his course; and Monsieur Houpert, who is a graduate of a leading French school of aviation, follows this plan. When we read about Grahame-White or some other noted aviator learning to fly to altitudinous heights after only three days' lessons, we must bear in mind that these three days do not represent all the time required in training, but simply the aggregate of hours devoted on many consecutive days to short lessons. Though I have been a student at the Moisant school for almost two weeks, my actual time in the monoplane would not exceed half an hour—yet I am already called a flyer!

Once the students got the hang of making a straight line on the ground and, briefly, in the air, they were then taught how to maintain the airplane's balance while flying. This involved "warping" the wings by manipulating the control lever rising between their knees. Harriet and her fellow novices often gathered around André in front of the hangars for instruction on reacting to emergency situations as well as caring and maintaining an airplane. As she told her readers:

> You are not yet prepared to make an application for a pilot's license, but you are well on the way to reach your goal. Like learning to swim, the first requisite of one who would learn to fly is confidence and the knowledge that you can do it. The future mastery of the swimmer's art depends upon himself and how much time he can give to the recreation. The same may be said of the would be flyer.

The aircraft used at the flight school was essentially a down-to-the-bolt copy of the Blériot XI, the monoplane John once favored. Unlike the Wright brothers, Louis Blériot did not send teams of lawyers out to competing factories in search of patent infringements, although he did hold several patents, including for ailerons and a primitive form of a joystick with coordinated flight controls. Variations of his initial plane design could be seen at almost every air show. His aircraft, the first monoplane to be successfully flown, was a study in aeronautic elegance and aesthetics, qualities that the American public appreciated. In 1912, an aviation aficionado named John Hayward published a book that contained intricate step-by-step instructions on how to build a Blériot:

> Like most monoplanes, the Bleriot has a long central body, usually termed "fuselage," to which the wings, running gear, and controls are all attached. It consists of four long beams united by 35 crosspieces.

> The beams are of ash, 1 3/16 inches square for the first third of their length and tapering to 7/8 inch square at the rear ends. Owing to the difficulty of securing good pieces of wood the full length, and also to facilitate packing for shipment, the beams are made in halves, the abutting ends being joined by sleeves of 1 1/8 inch, 20-guage steel tubing, each held on by two 1/8 inch bolts. Although the length of the fuselage is 21 feet 11 1/4 inches, the beams must be made of two 11-foot halves to allow for the curve at the rear ends.

The directions and diagrams continue for thirty-three more pages. Another instruction pamphlet from the era describes in excruciating detail how specific the airplane's setup must be before flight:

> TRUEING UP FUSELAGE. Place machine in flying position, i.e. with lower front longerons in pilots bay and wing tube level. VERTICAL MONTANTS [upright pieces of framework]. Stretch lines from centre of rudder post to marks measured 280 m.m.s. up number 1 montants; Adjust side cross bracing wires until these lines cut No. 2 & 3 montants 285 m.m.s. above bottom longerons and cut the centre points of the remaining montants. TRANSVERSE MONTANTS: Adjust top and bottom cross bracing wires until the centre points of all transverse montants are in line. DIHEDRAL [the upward angle of an aircraft's wing, which enables airplanes to fly level] = 4 percent (i.e. a rise of 1 in 25). Tighten landing wires until correct dihedral of front spar is obtained. Check dihedral for being balanced by measuring from a central point of undercarriage to corresponding points on either wing," etc., etc., etc.

As more airplane designs took to the air, or failed to, more data were being collected. Aviation was moving beyond the "on a wing and a prayer" stage and into that of determinable physics. While there was still considerable debate about the number of wings a safe and effective plane should have, the size of the engine, and whether the propeller should be in front or behind the pilot, strides were being made in understanding how particulars like the shape of the wings and the amount of thrust affected flight. As early as 1912, engineers calculated the ideal lift-drift ratio for the area of wings as

$$S = \frac{W}{K_y V^2}$$

in which W is the weight of the machine fully loaded; K_y is the highest lift coefficient; V is the minimum speed expected in miles an hour; and S is the surface, or area, sought. Science was trying to catch up with those magnificent men and their flying machines, but there were still enormous gaps in knowledge.

The Blériot XI measured twenty-seven feet long with a wingspan of thirty-four feet. Its framework was a combination of ash and Oregon pine reinforced with piano-wire trusses, and it had two wheels mounted to the undercarriage on rubber-cord shock absorbers.

> The body of the bird consists of a central portion which contains the motor and the aeronaut's seat in the front part, followed by a tail-like appendix which, like the rest, consists of a covered skeletal frame. The tail has the form of a quadrangular pyramid, tapering to a rather sharp point.

With a lever that came straight up from the cockpit floor, pilots controlled their airplanes and preserved their lateral balance by warping the semiflexible wings (not unlike how birds twist their wings in flight—a technique eventually replaced by ailerons) and raising and lowering the elevator at the tail. They turned the rudder with foot pedals. A round attachment not unlike the steering wheel of an automobile perched atop the controller stick, but it did not rotate, and instead was used to pull the lever back and forth and for ease of grip.

The Blériot monoplane had a graceful design, compared to the boxy biplanes, that was years in the making. "*J'ai été à la peine, je suis fière d'être à l'honneur,*" Alice Blériot sighed, "I have gone through the bad days with my husband, when he toiled and struggled, and I am now proud to share the honours showered upon him. Believe me," she added, "the domestic side of an aviator's wife's life is not a bed of roses."

While still studying engineering, Louis Blériot spotted an attractive young woman at a restaurant and vowed to his mother "I will marry her, or I will marry no one." On that July evening nine years later, Alice was the self-professed "happiest woman in France." Her husband was being celebrated by the Aero Club of Europe as the first person to fly an airplane across the English Channel on July 25, 1909. The *Daily Mail* presented him with a silver cup and £1,000. "I hope that France and England," Louis said in his acceptance speech, "already united by water—by the Channel that was below me during my flight—may now be still closer united by air."

The aircraft in which he achieved that momentous feat was the result of an almost comical parade of failure after failure. In 1901, he built a monoplane with flapping wings that couldn't clear a fence. A glider design followed, then a biplane with elliptical wings and dual engines, both without success. But revenues from his invention of the first practical acetylene headlamp for cars kept his dreams, at least, aloft, and in 1907 the Blériot VII monoplane took flight. The stocky, hawk-nosed man from Cambrai knew he was onto something. Two years later, he lifted off from Calais, France en route to Dover, England.

As Louis Blériot was trying to become the first person to fly across the English Channel in a powered machine, he was in a race against a formidable and popular opponent. Hubert Latham strode through life as if he were writing the script; a dashing, chain-smoking, big game hunter born in Paris to British and French parents, he was fluent in three languages, graduated from Oxford in 1904, and had crossed the English Channel in a hot air balloon a year later. Both England and France claimed him as their own national hero. When his interests evolved to airplanes, he chose the elegant Antoinette as his flying machine of choice, considered by many to be the most gorgeous man-made creation to ever take to the air. But as with many beautiful creatures, the Antoinette could be difficult. At an English air show, Hubert hung on as his monoplane was "smote by the wind... it hung poised in mid-air like some bird of prey while Latham calmly fought to control his plunging, reeling aircraft."

When newspaper magnate Alfred Charles William Harmsworth, the first Viscount Northcliffe, announced a $5,000 cash prize to the first human to pilot an aircraft across the English Channel, Hubert leapt at the chance. He was one of five men who immediately notified Lord Northcliffe of their intentions to challenge for the honor.

On July 19, 1909, his Antoinette lifted off from a beach near Calais. "Latham is coming!" went up the cry among the thousands of people who traveled to Dover to witness the momentous event. Their eyes scanned the skies for any sight of the flyer, but the lovely monoplane never came into view. Only eight miles into the flight, the plane's engine sputtered and died. Hubert managed to glide gently to the channel's uncharacteristically calm waters and set the Antoinette down without injury to himself or his aircraft. The crew of the French destroyer *Harpon* found him sitting on the floating plane, casually smoking a cigarette. He was already planning his second attempt.

Although the English Channel was, in the words of one historian, "A seemingly insignificant little stretch of water," it was cursed by constant foul weather; fog, rain, and swirling winds chopped up the waves and churning currents. Those very elements that made the twenty-two-mile-wide stretch of water so dangerous are also what kept the Island Kingdom safe. "It was the downfall of the Spanish Armada. It stymied Napoleon's dream of a conquest of England. It even frustrated Hitler's plans to crush 'that nation of shopkeepers.'"

The infamous weather kept the dueling aviators waiting for six days, until it was clear enough for Louis to make his attempt. He was acutely aware that Hubert's Antoinette replacement had recently arrived and the "man of the world" was ready to have another go, with a much more powerful airplane than his own. It was a classic example of the tortoise and the hare. Louis got the jump on his opponent when the latter overslept on the first morning of fair weather. His little Anzani 25-horsepower engine sputtered to life and he rolled toward the cliffs, plunging off the edge like the descent of a roller coaster, before his plane swept upward into the air at 4:41 A.M. Hubert, sleeping nearby, was awakened by the sound of the monoplane heading out over open water. Bursting out of his hotel room, he sprinted to the makeshift airfield. But before his plane could be readied, a sudden squall blew in from the North Sea, and his chances were crushed. When he finally made his second attempt two days later, his engine failed yet again, and he splashed into the channel within sight of the White Cliffs of Dover. Three years later, Hubert Latham, already suffering the fatal effects of tuberculosis, was gored to death by a buffalo while on a hunt. He was twenty-nine.

As for Louis, once his wheels left the ground that July morning he could relax. "As soon as I am over the cliff I reduce speed," he later told the *Daily Mail*. "There is now no need to force my engine. I begin my flight sure and steady towards the coast of England. I have no apprehensions, no sensations, *pas du tout*."

Meanwhile, Alice Blériot, on board the destroyer *Escopette*, watched her husband disappear overhead. She was about to endure the longest half-hour of her life.

"Below me is the sea, the surface disturbed by the breeze," the pilot continued, "which is freshening. The motion of the waves beneath me is not pleasant. For more than 10 minutes I was alone, isolated, lost in the midst of the immense sea, and I did not see anything on the horizon or a single ship." Then he spotted the English coast and the small figures of two men, journalists, waving a large French flag as a signal.

Those thirty-six minutes propelled him into the stratosphere of French national pride and put the world, specifically England, on notice that "there are no islands anymore." A hundred thousand of his countrymen greeted him on the streets of Paris with delirious cheers. In their midst stood John Moisant, who at the time had no way of knowing he was seeing his own future.

With the success of his design and technological advances, Louis Blériot eventually became the father of modern airplanes, and the Wright brothers' biplane Flyer was relegated to a historical artifact. Years of frustration, crashes, and injuries, "without benefit of textbook or teacher," finally paid off. "How could I help believing in him?" Alice asked. "His confidence in himself and his work was so absolute and so contagious that I had to share his hopes."

Those hopes formed the soil in which took root the aspirations of thousands of others around the world—young men and women who pictured themselves soaring among the clouds. Flight schools couldn't open up fast enough. One advertised for bold students who wished

> to become a companion of the birds; to search the skies and from great heights to look down upon the flattened earth while his monoplane bears him where his whim directs; to realize, to the throbbing of the motor and the song of the propeller, the dream of men throughout the centuries; all of these and more are what flying means. And there is none, except the mentally or the physically unfit, who may not taste its delights.

Harriet and Matilde spent their first week of class in ground school learning about the machine itself, including the rotary engine. Matilde evidently skipped a large portion of that instruction:

> They'd go and get classes on the motor and the carburetor and all that. But I didn't—if I had I wouldn't have known what they were talking about. To me, all I wanted to do was fly. I felt, my brother flew, and he had never had a lesson when he designed those machines and just started to fly and went up in that corrugated one there [presumably the Aluminoplane].

The second week saw the students take turns in the airplane, learning a technique called "grass cutting" or "trimming the daisies" intended to familiarize the novice in the basic controls of the airplane before the potentially troublesome element of altitude was added to the mix. Harriet writes

> If Professor Houpert's [weather conditions] verdict is favorable, there is a general scurrying toward the dressing-rooms, where the students cover their natty aviation costumes with homely, one-piece mechanic suits, calculated to withstand any kind of wear and tear as well as oil. Each student picks up a chair and drags it from the hangar to the field,

> so as to rest comfortably until his or her turn comes to take a lesson. The beginner takes his first lesson in grass cutting. This means that he mounts the machine, the motor is started and he attempts to guide it as it moves swiftly on its wheels over the long stretch of grass to the far end of the aerodrome. Here a mechanic is posted to await the student's arrival, turn his machine around and start him back again over the course. He is, indeed, a promising student if he has made anything like a straight line in his grass cutting. If he succeeds in doing this five or six times without mishap, he is permitted to take short jumps of two or three feet in height in the air as he rushes across the field. An irreverent newspaper man termed this feat kangarooing, which name seems to fit the performance pretty well. It is at the kangarooing stage that the fascination of flying begins.

Harriet was enthralled. Day after day, week after week, she would rise early and make her way to the airfield by train or by car, take her lesson, weather permitting, and then return to the city for her work with *Leslie's*. It was a grueling schedule. During these months, she published a handful of non-aviation articles, including an indictment of America's horrific infant mortality rate: "There is no doubt that the excessive mortality is due primarily to ignorance and improper feeding and care. The mothers of our crowded districts lack nothing in affection, but they cannot practice what they do not know." And another calling for government action to protect endangered bird species: "I am trying to do my part in sounding a general alarm and in sending CQD [now known as SOS] messages to about eighty millions of apathetic and easygoing people before it is entirely too late. The time to send in a fire alarm is before your house is entirely consumed, and not after." But it takes only a brief glance at the list of the Quimby bylines to see that, for the first half of 1911, Harriet's mind wandered endlessly skyward.

There is no exaggeration regarding the much reported sense of fascination which accompanies a flight, however low, through the air. The feel of the first freedom experienced as the wheels leave the ground makes the student eager for a longer flight. It is not surprising that sometimes a fledgling will forget what the instructor says and elevate his planes, which, of course, like a flash, shoots the machine into the air. Finding himself much higher than he expected to go, he is more than apt to seek a sudden descent, involving both a breakage and humiliation....

It is, indeed, a time for rejoicing in the school when Professor Houpert informs the student that he has graduated from the rather clumsy kindergarten machine and is to take his first flight in a lighter and more powerful machine fitted with a sensitive control. This means that he is really going to fly. The humor of the aviation school differs from any other. The students are invariably a light-hearted and a jolly crowd, seeing and enjoying the funny sides of things. A great deal of good-natured banter is exchanged between those who return from a flight and the students who have watched them. Although one young fledgling reached a height of only ten feet or so and that only one fraction of a minute, he returned with an exciting tale of having fallen into an air hole and a laughable explanation of how he dexterously straightened his machine and returned to earth with safety. Another created a roar of laughter, when he returned from a kangarooing trip, by his account of being attacked by a vicious sparrow on the way. M. Vedrine, who crossed the Alps and startled the world by reporting that in transit he had been attacked by an enormous eagle, has nothing on the students of the Moisant school.

The early morning activities at the school began to attract spectators, who wandered over from the nearby towns of Garden City or

Mineola regardless of the hour. Sometimes they would pull their automobiles together in spontaneous watch-parties. Harriet noticed that, more times than not, most in the audience were women.

Matilde, whom Harriet and her family called "Tild" or "Tilly," shared Harriet's belief that piloting airplanes was not a gender-specific skill.

> Why shouldn't a woman fly if she wants to? Now, I'm not a suffragette and I'm not of the opinion that just because a man does this that a woman has a right to also, but I do believe a woman is entitled to enjoy good sport as well as her brother. There is tremendous exhilaration in an early morning flight. The grass is cool and wet with dew. The air is clean and sharp and the speed at which one flies gives one an appetite for breakfast that must be experienced rather than described. I have never felt so well in my life as since I have been taking my early morning flights.

The two friends firmly believed in their own abilities. They would soon have the opportunity to prove them to the world.

14

ONLY A CAUTIOUS PERSON SHOULD FLY

AFTER WEEKS OF KANGAROOING over the Hempstead plains, Harriet and Matilde finally graduated to actual flying.

> It was a happy day for me when Professor Houpert told me that my grass-cutting days were over and that I was ready for a flight in the air. It was the day I had longed for with an expectancy that I cannot describe, the fascination of flying had such a hold upon me.... The second machine in which I was to take my first flight in the air differed in essentials from the first one, known as the grass cutter. The latter is equipped with three wheels, so that it can roll over the ground smoothly, while the former has two wheels in front and a skid instead of a wheel behind. The student must, therefore, rise above the ground promptly or run the risk of injuring the dragging skid. The chassis of the flyer is lighter than that of the grass cutter and the power of the former is considerably increased. The student who takes his first real flight is instructed to fly straight across the field and to alight near where a mechanic stands waiting to turn him around for his return trip. His first lesson as a freshman is intended to teach him to manage his machine while running over the ground. His first lesson as a graduate is to learn how to cut his pathway through the air. While grass cutting, the freshman learns how to steer. While air cutting, the graduate

> must not only steer, but he must learn the more difficult task of warping his wings and of manipulating his elevating and lowering planes. The warping is done by a wheel resembling the steering wheel of an automobile and which rests directly in front of the pilot. This wheel, by a movement back and forth, elevates or lowers the plane. After one successful straight-away flight, I was instructed by my pleased instructor to fly across the field and to turn around and come back without alighting at the other end. The fundamental requirements of a good student are that he shall be able to make a good ascent and a safe landing. These are the most difficult accomplishments of a flyer. When he has mastered them he has learned his lesson pretty well. After learning to make a circuit of the aerodome, the student is asked to do what is considered difficult—a right-hand turn. After having done this without mishap, he is then capable of attempting to make a flight in the form of a figure eight, which is the essential requirement before he can secure the much coveted pilot's license from the Aero Club of America.

They might not have realized it at the time, but Harriet and the other students were in exceptionally good hands. André Houpert was the first man to fly over Mexico City. When he landed, the locals, thinking he was a god descended from the heavens, tore his plane to pieces and ripped off every shred of his clothing for souvenirs. He escaped martyrdom by jumping on a passing train. The native Parisian wore an effortless smile shrouded by a slim mustache, but his eyes were distinctively guarded and evaluative as the chief instructor at the Moisants' Hempstead Plains Aviation Company.

André, who learned to fly under the tutelage of Louis Blériot himself, was initially skeptical about women pilots. But as months went by and he observed his two female students' progress, he grumpily conceded with a shrug that "an aircraft was probably safer in the hands of a woman than most men." Still, he was protective of all his students, most especially Harriet and Matilde, stubbornly never budging from his rules about not flying in winds over five miles an hour and not exceeding five minutes in the air at a time.

One day in mid-summer, André was testing a new Blériot that had just arrived at the Mineola airfield. He took it up for a few moments and then landed to make some adjustments to the engine and tail mechanism. The instructor then committed a sin he would've roasted one of his students for; he tried to start the plane by himself.

Typically, a pilot would sit in the cockpit and flip the starter switch, which would then open a circuit allowing electric current to flow to the spark plugs inside the cylinders, as a mechanic or assistant then pulled hard on the propeller to create a spark that ignited the gasoline and started the engine. Between two and four other assistants would be hanging on to the airplane to keep it still—since the early planes had no brakes—until the pilot signaled for them to release it and took to the air. That day, André couldn't be bothered to wait for any such help.

As he heaved on the propeller, the engine immediately caught and the plane lurched forward, trundling down the field, with the Frenchman in frantic pursuit. As the plane picked up speed, he managed to grab onto the wires and pull himself partially into the pilot's seat. In doing so, he bumped open the throttle, and the Gnôme engine responded in kind, accelerating to thirty miles an hour. With the Blériot now gleefully skipping over ruts and small hillocks, André slid backward but was able to find a handhold on the side of the plane, stopping his fall, until the wheels hit a clump of ground, which caused him to swing underneath the fuselage, lose his grip, and be run over. Even so, he refused to declare defeat. He bounded up and raced after the machine, somehow grabbing onto the tail and, while being dragged like a fallen water-skier who refuses to let go of the rope, bellowed for help.

Three mechanics came dashing across the field at an acute angle to intercept the runaway plane. They were summarily tossed away by the rampaging monoplane, much as a rodeo bull rids himself of a pesky rider. André, still somehow hanging on, reached up and yanked on the rudder, which sent the plane into a jarring spin. He was thrown clear and the machine plowed into a hill, instantly converting its propeller into fractals of wood.

All the while Harriet looked on from a safe spot behind a tree. Whether or not she was laughing at the spectacle is lost to history.

There is reason to believe André and Harriet had a closer relationship than just that of instructor and student. Houpert family legend has it the two were lovers, at least for a short time. Six feet four, handsome, with an elegant mustache and dark eyes, André was Parisian born but spoke English with a Scottish accent, acquired from years spent there as a mechanic's apprentice starting at the age of twelve. He was quiet and dignified, never known to brag about his historic flying accomplishments or his service in WWI as a bomber pilot, although he evidently enjoyed wryly recounting his many accidents and adventures. Up until his death in 1963 at the age of seventy-seven, he discreetly avoided any discussion defining his friendship with Harriet, sensitive to the fact that his wife, Emma, hated the rumors.

One tantalizing clue about the depth of André and Harriet's relationship remains, however—a gold locket. It was given to the instructor by the student in August 1911 and engraved with the date and his name. When opened it reveals a photograph of Harriet, flying goggles pulled up onto her forehead, a brilliant smile on her face. Whether it was simply a token of gratitude or of true affection, one may never know. Harriet kept the secrets of her heart to herself.

André's prize student was not without her mishaps. During a practice takeoff, the wheel of Harriet's plane caught a gopher hole, severing

André Houpert. Early pilot and flight instructor and, to Harriet, perhaps more.

the struts that held it to the undercarriage and sending it spinning into a wing, shredding it. The amateur "aviatrix"—an awkward term that was eventually replaced with the gender-neutral "aviator"—calmly shut off the motor and returned to the hangar on foot, where she asked André if there was another airplane she could use. The cost of repairs was deducted from her $1,500 "breakage" deposit, which all students were required to post.

"Everyone," she wrote, "asks me how it feels to fly. It feels like riding in a high-powered automobile, minus bumping over the rough roads, continually signaling to clear the way and keeping a watchful eye on the speedometer to see that you do not exceed the limit and provoke the wrath of the bicycle policeman or the covetous constable."

Despite her growing friendship with Matilde, Harriet rarely mentioned John Moisant, the inspiration for her desire to fly, and his historic race to the Statue of Liberty. But in June, *Leslie's Illustrated Weekly* featured an article by Harriet in which his presence was palpable as she discussed air lanes and wind conditions with Roland Garros.

> Roland B. Garros, before his departure for Europe, told me that, during the aviation meet in Mexico City last March, the most disagreeable experience he encountered during his series of high-altitude flights was that of having his carburetor freeze when he was 12,411 feet above sea level. This height was 4,550 feet above the aerodome from which he started and he made the distance in forty-six minutes. On the ground the temperature was sixty-eight degrees Fahrenheit. Mr. Garros said that he found it very cold in the upper air lanes and that, even had his carburetor not frozen, it would have been impossible for him to remain aloft much longer, because of the intense cold and the sudden change.

> "Because of the rarefied condition of the air at high altitudes, the engines with which aeroplanes are propelled lose a great deal of their power," continued Mr. Garros. "Let me tell you something that happened to John Moisant, at Memphis, on December 6th, 1910. The temperature on the ground at the time he went up was twenty-four degrees above zero, Fahrenheit. After he had reached an altitude of six thousand feet with a fifty-horse-power motor, he lost about thirty per cent of its power. Climbing steadily to a height of about nine thousand feet—he was trying to break the world's altitude record at the time—he found that at this height of nine thousand feet his fifty-horse-power motor was delivering only about twenty-five-horse-power and that the temperature had very seriously affected the working power of his engine."

Buildings and rivers and parking lots today have no more effect on a modern jetliner flying at 35,000 feet than a fly clinging to the back of a galloping elephant. But in the days when frail aircraft of cloth and wood, with underpowered engines and rudimentary controls, rode the waves of air at lower altitudes, they faced an invisible and potentially deadly obstacle course.

> "Difficult to fly over cities?" repeated Mr. Garros. "Not at great altitudes. There is a difference between flying over cities and over country, but if one is prepared for it and is equipped with a high-powered machine he will not experience any special difficulty. In flying over the city, the buildings send up myriad cross currents, eddies and whirlpools. Occasionally the aviator encounters what, for want of a better name, must be called hills and valleys in the air, and these, curiously enough, always correspond to the hills and valleys on the earth; but after he has made a number of flights he is on the lookout for these

and there is little to be feared from them. The so-called holes in the air are simply talk, as far as my experiences are concerned. Occasionally one will run across a space of rarefied air that offers practically no support for a flying machine, but a powerful engine speedily cuts through these."

While *Leslie's* readers ate up Harriet's first-person accounts like candy from her hand, the "Dresden China Aviatrix," as some in the press had taken to calling her, was also mindful of the price her newfound passion demanded from its faithful.

That the air craft of to-day is in an imperfect state cannot be doubted, but that the greater number of fatalities are due to the imperfections of the machines is doubtful. In nearly every investigated case the fatality has been shown to be due to reckless flying, over-confidence or pure neglect in inspecting the machine before it left the ground. The fatalities of the air come so quickly and unexpectedly and the end is so sudden that the cause of the catastrophe is obviously left to surmise, so we have as many causes as there may be conjectures. None of them may be right. The importance of daily inspection cannot be too greatly impressed upon the aviator who is about to take a flight.

My conclusion is that flying is stripped of its danger or greatest peril whenever the aviator realizes that he is engaged in serious business and that he must carefully consider his surroundings and the condition of the machine which must serve him. It is all very well to do "stunts" and to challenge perils calculated to thrill a vast crowd watching with eager and upturned faces for something to happen. But the real achievement is to master the air as a proof of human progress. It is no idle dream to believe that this mastery can be had. The time is coming when we shall find the means of transportation by bird-like

> flights as safe and satisfactory as transportation by steamship or locomotive and with still greater speed. This is not to be accomplished by racing or doing circus tricks in the air at aviation meets.

Harriet didn't know it then, but her opinion was ultimately backed up by facts. A survey conducted in 1913 attributed 40 percent of aviation accidents to mid-air breakage of the plane, 12 percent to pilot loss of control, 20 percent to wind gusts, 12 percent to mechanical failure, and 10 percent to motor failure. The very best pilots were often put into situations that exceeded their abilities, and more times than not when those moments arose it was fortune, good or bad, that determined who lived and who died. Harriet knew those odds. While arguing that flying was getting safer every year, she never shielded her readers from the realities she faced every time she climbed into a plane. She was so assiduously careful that her articles about the risks of flying and how they could be minimized directly led to the ritual of pilot checklists that are de rigueur today. "Only a cautious person, man or woman, should fly," she told *Good Housekeeping*. "I never mount my machine until every wire and screw has been tested. I have never had an accident in the air." Neither "pluck nor luck" made a good pilot, she insisted in an interview with the *New York Evening World*; rather it was "plain common sense and reasonable care" that kept an aviator safe.

By mid-summer 1911, thirty-six Americans—all men—were licensed pilots, with Harriet and Matilde striving to join their ranks. Most, if not all, of those pioneers experienced some sort of accident in their flying careers, with very few surviving to old age.

15

I JUST WANTED TO BE FIRST

ON A CALM SUMMER day at the end of July 1911, with cicadas buzzing in the tall grass and seagulls meandering lazily among the columns of warm air above, two men arrived at the Moisant School of Aviation. One was G. F. Campbell-Wood, secretary of the Aero Club of America, whose signature graced the club's very first license, awarded to Glenn Curtiss. The other was Baron Ladislas D'Orcy, an aviation official and French nobleman who was an "earnest and careful" student of aviation. This was the time of reckoning for Harriet Quimby.

Scattered between frequent weather delays and equipment mishaps, the aspiring pilot amassed a total of thirty-three lessons, between two to five minutes each. André Houpert watched with growing pride as his star pupil advanced in her abilities over the eleven weeks, but it was an achievement by another female pilot that convinced him to let Harriet take the next step.

Not quite a year earlier, at the Curtiss Flying School in Hammondsport, New York, Blanche Stuart Scott became the first and only woman to be taught to fly by the great Glenn Curtiss himself. Glenn's initial reservations about female aviators were overcome by assurances from his staff that the publicity of training a woman would far outpace the risks. Even so, he insisted on installing a throttle block on Blanche's biplane that prevented her from taking off. That didn't sit well with the woman eventually nicknamed the Tomboy of the Air, who was already an accomplished barrier-breaker. She had entered the record books as the first woman to drive a car across the United States when there were only 280 miles of pavement outside cities. Passing through Dayton, Ohio, during that journey, she paid a visit to the Wright brothers' facilities, which piqued her interest in airplanes. Jerome Fanciulli, head of the Curtiss Exhibition Company, convinced her to attend the school and become part of the team. Blanche did not, however, support the general idea of female fliers, immodestly claiming she was unique: "I have an unusual muscle development," she later told reporters. "I can make my muscles obey my thought instantly. Most women cannot."

On September 2, 1910, during one of her training flights, Blanche used those muscles to either deliberately or accidentally kick off the throttle block. She quickly reached an altitude of forty feet, thus becoming the first woman to successfully solo an airplane. For some unknown reason, Blanche, who heralded from Rochester, New York, never applied for a pilot's license—although that didn't stop her from flying in exhibitions.

A year later, on or about July 28, she reportedly made "a spectacular flight" that attracted quite a bit of national attention, including from one Harriet Quimby. The farm girl from Michigan who had come so far was not about to be outdone within sight of her historic goal. At the first opportunity, Harriet climbed aboard a Moisant monoplane, soared into the air, and immediately, in front of dozens of witnesses (including her astonished instructor), carved a series of figure eights before banking north for a cross-country jaunt over Westbury and Meadowbrook. André Houpert strode into the airfield office and made a call to the Aero Club of America. Harriet recalls the morning of her test:

> Quite unexpectedly on the afternoon of July 31st, while attending my class on the aviation grounds, I was told by my instructor that I must

Autographed photo of Harriet in a monoplane.

> be prepared early the next morning to try for my pilot's license. It was the goal coveted by every student in the school and I was therefore not a little elated to hear that at last my turn had come to make the attempt. It was to be at five o'clock in the morning. At eight-thirty in the evening I was off to slumberland. I confess that sleep was disturbed by many visions. Much to my disappointment, by telephone in the morning, which was to have awakened me for the trial flights, came this message from my instructor: "The fog is thick enough here to cut with a knife."

André advised her to sit tight until he sent a car to bring her to the airfield once the skies were clear. The aspiring pilot, as well as the two judges from the Aero Club, were forced to cool their heels. Finally, Harriet couldn't wait any longer:

> In spite of M. Houpert's message our eagerness to begin the work at hand ruled the hour. So we climbed into the surrey, thoughtfully provided the evening before by the club officials, and driving through the thickest kind of unheavenly mist we groped our way in the dim morning light to the aviation field. The fog seemed to grow thicker every step we took and when we reached the hangar we could scarcely distinguish objects fifty feet across the way. As for the field itself, it was not in sight. It was absolutely blanketed in fog. I turned appealing eyes toward my instructor. He shook his head and in his customary laconic style remarked, "We must wait." And we waited and waited and waited, with how much patience I need not recite. There was gloom without and gloom within the hangar. But we were cheered by the hopeful voice of the chief mechanician prophesying that in half an hour the sun would surely assert itself and clear the field. And it did.

Flight school. Matilde Moisant and Harriet stand behind André Houpert.

The regulations governing the license test Harriet was about to undertake were updated by the Fédération Aéronautique Internationale at its October 28, 1910, meeting. It stipulated that only an organization governing aviation in its own country and that was a member of the federation was authorized to issue licenses. In the US that was the Aero Club of America. Applicants were required to be eighteen years old.

The test itself had three parts: two involving distance and maneuvering skills and one involving altitude and landing accuracy. The pilot would take to the air and, without touching the ground, fly a circuit not less than three miles in length. That circuit was marked by two posts that couldn't be more than 1,600 feet apart to demonstrate the aviator's ability to change directions on a tight course and make "an uninterrupted series of figure eights." The next requirement was to ascend to at least 164 feet above the starting point. Upon landing, the pilot had to "stop his motor not later than the time when the machine touches the ground and to stop his aeroplane at a distance of one hundred and sixty-five feet from the point designated before the flight." The Aero Club considered a safe and controlled landing the most important element, and unless the applicant managed one to the judges' satisfaction, it could deny the license. Said one observer, "The test for the pilot's license has, purposefully, been made as difficult as is consistent with fairness to those competing, in order to eliminate, as far as might be, the possibility of any unfit survivors." Harriet recounts her own test:

> When all was in readiness I was helped into my seat and was eager for the start. I knew that the sooner it was begun, the quicker it would be over. It only remained for the chief mechanic to turn the propellor and thus crank the engine. Now came the last word from my patient and thoughtful instructor, M. Houpert. He explained to me that he would stand not far from the first post and if I lost count while making the

five eights in the air he would signal me on the completion of the final one and I would know it was time to land. The signal was to be the waving of his handkerchief. A moment after the propellor began its revolutions of fourteen hundred and fifty a minute, my machine rolled speedily along the ground for fifty feet or so, then responded promptly to the elevating plane and rose quickly into the air.

In less time than it has taken to write it I was sixty or seventy feet up and circling the second post at the far end of the field. Glancing down I caught a glimpse of the waving hand of Baron D'Orcy, who was watching the flight from his post. Reaching the middle of the field on my return trip I could easily distinguish my instructor, whose signal I was to await. Further on I could see the little group of friends and students of the school, seated about or standing, all with upturned eager faces. Their voices could not reach me, but their waving signals evidenced their interest. Round and round I went, the faithful little engine sending out its steady whirr, which always delights the heart of a pilot.

What did I think of? I thought more of my engine than anything else, for if it failed me I would be obliged to pitch my machine and glide down, a feat I had never attempted. If it continued to hit on every cylinder it meant the speedy accomplishment of my purpose. What did I see? I saw Captain Baldwin's hangars at the end of the field, I saw the cluster of our own hangars at the west, the domes of Garden City in the background, a glimpse of the ocean at the south and Long Island Sound on the north. One who has not made an ascension can scarcely comprehend the clearness with which objects beneath the aviator can be discerned. The ruts in the road, a dog running across the road, the tops of the chimneys and almost every blade of grass are plainly pictured below. I am not surprised at the recent statement that the aeroplane can make the submarine easily distinguishable in any

> harbor and that it will, therefore, seriously interfere with the usefulness of the latter as a weapon of war. How did I feel? I felt like a bird cleaving the air with outstretched wings. There was no thought of obstruction or obstacle. There was no fear of falling because the mastery of a well-balanced machine seems complete.

Harriet's first trial began at 6:42 A.M. and was finished in nine minutes. It covered a distance of twelve miles and consisted of left and right turns in figure eights. She lost track of the number of maneuvers completed, but her instructor's wave of his handkerchief informed her she was entering number six.

> Was I happy when I saw the signal of Professor Houpert, indicating that I had safely gone through the first half of the test? Honestly, I was. Not because I was tired, for driving a monoplane takes little physical strength. Not because I was timid, for I had been too intent on my work for that, but because I felt that my task was half accomplished, and in my frame of mind it seemed to me that half done was all done. I have been fortunate in all of my landings at my school lessons and this test, so dreaded by many, gave me little apprehension. Approaching the point designated before my flight as the place where I should descend, I lowered my plane and made a sharp descent from an altitude of seventy-five feet, then straightened my machine and skimmed the surface of the ground, cutting off the engine just before I reached the ground, then rolled across the grass toward the canvas patch. Before I could leave my seat, my instructor, the Aero Club representatives, Captain Baldwin and my classmates and friends were heaping their congratulations upon me. I was not as presentable as I might have wished, for my face was completely covered with castor lubricating oil, which had been used freely on the engine.

With the hot engine sizzling and popping, Harriet sat quietly until it was cool enough to have a go at her second flight. At 7:22 she returned to the air and carved five perfect figure eights around the markers, landing ten minutes later. The third and final challenge that stood between Harriet and a place in history was the altitude test.

> Again my faithful monoplane was put into service. The flight began at seven-forty-five and ended six minutes later, and then I was once more on earth to receive the welcome greeting of friends whose encouraging words had made my success doubly pleasant. I hope no one will accuse me of being conceited or even proud when I say in conclusion that the honor I sought and prize most highly is that of having secured the first pilot's license ever granted to a woman in America.

One little detail Harriet omitted from her article was that she badly flubbed her first landing, missing the designated spot by a considerable distance. "She forgot to shut off her engine," the *New York Times* reported, "and after striking the ground in an advantageous position she was swept forty feet beyond the mark by her engine. Miss Quimby was almost in tears because her failure in this trial necessitated a repetition of the whole feat." The Aero Club judges graciously agreed to return the next day, and that time when her wheels touched down and she shut off the engine she pulled up to a stop seven feet, nine inches from the mark, a new record for monoplanes. Standing next to her plane, with "her face . . . covered with grease and dirt, but her blue eyes flash[ing] happily," she said to G. F. Campbell-Wood, "I guess I get that license." "I guess you do," he replied.

The following letter arrived later that week:

AERO CLUB OF AMERICA
297 Madison Avenue
New York, August 2d, 1911

Miss Harriet Quimby
225 Fifth Ave., New York City

MADAM: We take pleasure in informing you that at a meeting of the Executive Committee held this afternoon, you were granted an Aviation pilot's license of the Aero Club of America. The book is all made up and lacks only the signature of our acting president, which will be obtained to-morrow morning.

We find that the only other Aviation pilot's license granted to a woman under the 1911 rules is that of Mme. Driancourt, of France, who passed the tests on a Caudron biplane.

Should no mail advices to the contrary reach us within the next few days from Europe you can accordingly consider yourself the only woman to have qualified under the 1911 rules on a monoplane.

Regarding the landing made by you at the close of your first distance-test on August 1st, we would say that accurate landing is not a record internationally recognized, so that we do not know how this performance compares with the best made in Europe. We can state, however, that, at this date, it is the most accurate landing ever made in America on a monoplane under official supervision.

The American record for accurate landing is 1 foot 5 ½ inches by Mr. Sopwith on his biplane; we do not officially make any distinction between types of aeroplanes in this record; we cannot see, however, how there can be any objection to your landing being referred to as an "American record for monoplanes" at this date, as this is what it is in fact.

Yours sincerely,
G. F. Campbell-Wood (Signed)
Secretary

Harriet's official pilot's license, #37, resembling a man's pocketbook "neatly bound in leather," was delivered a day later. It read:

Fédération Aéronautique Internationale
Aero Club of America

The above-named club, recognized by the Fédération Aéronautique Internationale as a governing authority of the United States of America, certifies that Harriet Quimby, having fulfilled all the conditions required by the Fédération Aéronautique Internationale, is hereby licensed as an aviator.

On the back—written in French, German, Russian, Italian, and Spanish—was the declaration: "The civil, naval and military authorities, including the police, are respectfully requested to aid and assist the holder of this certificate." Accompanying the pilot's license were three printed reports, "carefully filled out and duly signed, testifying to all the recorded details of the trial flights and landings."

Reporter Elizabeth Anna Semple caught up with Harriet the day of the test.

> "Does this license make you a regular professional?" I inquired when Miss Quimby, her eyes still shining from the joy of the remembrance, had finished telling me about the main facts connected with that memorable day. "In-so-far as it makes it possible for me to compete in all contests," she explained, "and I'm planning to do quite a little in that line."

"It's not a fad," Harriet told another reporter,

> and I didn't want to be the first American woman to fly just to make myself conspicuous. I just wanted to be first, that's all, and I honestly and frankly am delighted. I have written so much about other people, you can't guess how much I enjoy sitting back and reading about myself for once. I think that's excusable in me.

Over the next weeks and months, adoring articles fluttered onto newsstands. "Here Comes the Air Girl" blared one magazine headline:

> Of course Miss Quimby has ridden bucking broncos out West. After that, a monoplane seems only reasonable. Miss Quimby didn't say what she would do if the monoplane bucked. But I don't think it would get away with her. She'd get a nice quiet grip of the bridle, keep its head up and ride it to the hitching post as tame as a lamb. And when she got down it would eat lump sugar out of her hand.

Overland Monthly included a bit of advice from the freshly licensed pilot:

> "Other women could fly, too. Really," [Harriet] went on, "any woman can—if she wishes to do so. But first she must be quite sure that she

actually does wish to fly beyond anything else—and then she must control her nerves—and that's all."

For all the accolades, it was never far from Harriet's mind that her new profession could be a brief one. Just below the *New York Times* account of her historic accomplishment was a brief mention of the death that same day of a young British aviator named Germal Napier, who was killed when a sudden gust of wind threw his biplane into the ground. Such tragedies had become so commonplace and the public so desensitized to them that the article consisted of a mere two sentences.

16

THE CUTEST LITTLE WITCH

HARRIET QUIMBY WASN'T THE only one hoping to qualify for a pilot's license on August 1; Matilde Moisant and another student, Ferdinand de Murias, were both ready in the discerning eyes of Professor Houpert. The Aero Club of America judges, perhaps wanting to seem unbiased toward the novelty of female flyers, insisted Ferdinand go next.

He clambered into the Moisant School of Aviation's other monoplane (one that Harriet had not used), cranked it up, and took off along the testing course. His exam proceeded flawlessly until he came in for a landing. The airplane lifted briefly on approach, perhaps from a puff of wind, and he missed the target. Overcorrecting, the young pilot nosedived into the rear of Harriet's plane, severely damaging both machines and ending Matilde's shot at a license until the aircraft could be repaired.

Fourteen days later, Matilde passed the three phases of the test perfectly and received US pilot's license #44, becoming the second woman in America to do so and the only person who accomplished that by logging barely thirty-two minutes of flight time. The *New York Times* announced, "With wind eddies flattened to almost a dead calm, Miss Matilda [*sic*] Moisant, sister of the late John B. Moisant, who was killed at New Orleans last January, distinguished herself this morning."

"I could have had my license first," Matilde admitted many years later, "but to me, I only took it up for fun. [Harriet] took it up for commercial reasons. She was taking care of her mother and father, and it [being first] meant a good deal to her, because she intended to make aviation her livelihood." That was likely not idle boasting—André considered Tilly his "most apt student." "You know," he once confessed to Alfred Moisant, "your sister is what I call a natural born flyer." As the chief instructor of the flight school happened to be an employee of Matilde's big brother, he easily could have put her up for the exam first. But for Matilde—the modest, petite, novice pilot who was about to alight onto the world stage—friendship mattered more than fame.

As for Alfred, he was spending most of his time on the road with his Moisant International Aviators, who were thrilling thousands of spectators throughout the country. The problem was, most of those spectators were standing outside the fairground gates, watching for free. Even as the team he assembled was being touted as "The World's Greatest Aggregation of Airmen" by a leading aviation magazine, Alfred lost over a ten-month period an estimated $200,000 between the cost of travel, salaries, and constant repairs, and the underwhelming gate receipts. Something had to be done to bring the crowds inside the turnstiles, closer to his star pilots.

The advertisement covered an entire page in *Aero* magazine. It bragged that the Moisant school employed the world's most accomplished instructors and that lessons were taught using only the finest Moisant-built monoplanes. The ad prominently listed teaching staff who doubled as exhibition flyers: Roland Garros, René Simon, René Barrier, Ralph Johnstone, Edmond "Tiny" Audemars, John J. Frisbie, Ferdinand de Murias (who had perfected his landing since his disastrous first test), André Houpert, and Abram Raygorodsky, who'd just joined the team from Russia. And at the bottom of the roll call: "Miss

Harriet Quimby of U.S.A. (a Record Breaker). The ONLY WOMAN LICENSED PILOT IN AMERICA." The ad did not mention the other "woman licensed pilot in America," even though within days of receiving her certification, Matilde too had joined up with the flying circus "just for fun. I went with my brother's fliers and Miss Quimby. She was flying for money."

But the money had to be right. Harriet knew her worth. When the organizers of an air meet in Chicago refused to meet her financial terms, she politely declined their invitation to appear. A few days later she signed a contract with William S. Van Clief, president of Illinois's Richmond County Agricultural Society to participate in an upcoming county fair.

On the evening of September 4, twenty thousand men, women, and children stayed late at the fairgrounds on Staten Island for one reason: to watch the first licensed female pilot in America take a moonlit flight. But as twilight settled in and the crowd grew restless with anticipation, Harriet was nowhere in sight. All eyes searched the multitude of faces for "a willowy, beautiful brunette with green eyes," as one writer observed.

Whether the ferry was delayed or Harriet's parents took a little too long picking just the right ensembles, the Quimby party was running late. As soon as the barrier rope dropped from the back of the ferryboat, their touring car, borrowed from Mrs. C. H. Fosgate of Quincy, Illinois, roared off down Bay Street toward Vanderbilt Avenue. It was being driven by Rene Porsch, who also doubled as Harriet's chief mechanic. Harriet's mother and father and three other guests rode along with her. As soon as they hit a straightaway the driver stomped on the car's accelerator. The speedometer reached thirty miles an hour, well over the legal limit, before a policeman flagged down the car. No amount of pleading could convince the officer to let the group continue until he finished writing out a five-dollar summons, which Rene dutifully paid the next morning.

By the time Harriet and her entourage reached the fairgrounds at Dongan Hills, the moon perched high in the sky, shining brilliantly in its cloudless realm. Hundreds of bored spectators were wandering around the field, so Harriet asked Rene to slowly drive among the masses while she begged them to get back to the stands so that there was enough room for her to safely take off.

In her fashionable satin flying suit, Harriet climbed as gracefully as possible into the metal seat of her monoplane, which she often joked was a process more like "a monkey crawling along the chassis." She flipped the ignition switch and signaled to Rene to yank on the propeller. The 30-horsepower rotary engine sputtered to life, and the aviator taxied a short distance before taking to the dark air at a sharp angle, eliciting gasps from the audience. "There was hardly a breeze when the monoplane glided into the air. Miss Quimby sent her machine straight ahead to the southwest for half a mile and returned in a wide detour."

She eased back on the controller until she reached an acceptable altitude and then banked the plane south toward Midland Beach. The autumn night was brisk but not overly chilly, and as she flew in a large circle back toward Dongan Hills, Harriet peered down at the scattered lights of the Illinois villages below, enjoying the time alone and the sounds drifting upward from the thousands of rapt onlookers. "I was more interested in the beautiful city view. It was a great temptation not to keep right on flying until I got to New York," she recalled later. "The funny thing about it was that I was so hot up there. I think it was the effect of the applause which made my blood rise. I never had much applause before."

As she neared the fairgrounds, she dipped the plane down. A *New York Times* reporter was there: "On the third time around she passed within a few feet of the judges' stand and waved a handerketchief [*sic*] vigorously at friends in the paddock. She seemed to be enjoying her spin, and the motor worked without a hitch." The crowd responded enthusiastically with applause and cheers. Harriet was forced to pass low over the landing area to shoo some errant spectators away. Then, to avoid plowing into some people who made their way back onto the field, she set the monoplane down in a bit of a dodgy landing: she hit a rut and bounced the plane several times before it came to a stop just a few feet away from a fence. Despite the scare, she was ecstatic as she climbed down. Her mother reportedly

> rushed up to her and kissed her repeatedly. "You were up just seven minutes, Harriet," she said, "and I think that I would have come up after you if you had remained in the air any longer." "Oh! Mother," the daughter replied, "you'll get used to it all right. It was grand. I didn't feel like ever coming to earth again."

William S. Van Clief, the fair organizer, presented Harriet with a $1,500 check. The *New Brunswick Times* swooned, she was the "nerviest, and one of the most beautiful, [aviators] in the world." Harriet's career as a professional exhibition flyer began, and with it fame and the adoration of many. Her mailbox at the Hotel Victoria was often overflowing with letters containing poetry and offers of marriage, and the concierge received flowers and gifts for her almost daily, which she dutifully returned. She was less interested in romance than in encouraging other women to take up the hobby she now loved.

> Driving an aeroplane is more a matter of personality than of sex since it requires so little physical exertion. There is no sport that affords the same amount of excitement and enjoyment, and exacts in return so little muscular strength. Flying is a fine, dignified sport for women, healthful and stimulating to the mind, and there is no reason to be afraid so long as one is careful.

When Alfred Moisant saw the excitement and publicity Harriet was attracting, he knew he'd found the company's salvation. Gone was any thought that his little sister would only be "flying for fun." The elder Moisant was never one to turn away from potential profits.

He booked the Moisant International Aviators in a meet to be held September 23–October 1, 1911, at Long Island's Nassau Boulevard Airfield. It would be the first competition to include female pilots. In addition to Matilde and Harriet, fellow American Blanche Stuart Scott and France's Hélène Dutrieu would also attend.

Elfin and slender, with wide-set, expressive eyes and dark bangs that meandered slightly to the left just above her perfect brows, Hélène's diminutive size belied the muscles and will of an exceptional athlete. Born to a Belgian Army officer, she became a professional cyclist at age fourteen. She set the world record for distance cycled in one hour in 1893 and won the women's speed track world championship three years later. Then she parlayed those accomplishments into a successful career on the stage, where she conducted "spectacular feats on a bicycle and motorcycle that were a sensation." One of those stunts involved driving a motorcycle at full speed and launching herself off the seat in a prone position, as if she were flying, earning her the nickname the Human Arrow. Hélène graduated to performing equally dangerous stunts in an automobile, until one flipped over in front of a packed audience and landed on her. She spent six months recuperating in the hospital, during

Matilde and Harriet, dressed up for an evening event.

which time she read about the exploits of the Wright brothers and decided perhaps the relatively safe occupation of flying airplanes made more sense.

It was about this time that the Clément-Bayard Company, a French airplane manufacturer, was developing a small, maneuverable monoplane named the Demoiselle, the "enraged grasshopper" eventually favored by Roland Garros and Tiny Audemars. The engineers needed an equally bijou person to test fly it while they honed the design. Adolphe Clément-Bayard, a former competitive cyclist, remembered Hélène from her days on the velodromes and signed her to a contract in 1908. Her pay: 2,000 francs ($392) a month, including all expenses and use of a courtesy automobile.

For the next few months, the thirty-one-year-old of "guileless eyes and timid voice" made numerous test flights in the temperamental, unstable plane. After several accidents, some of which were undoubtedly caused by her inexperience and lack of training, she called it quits and tore up the contract. But she wasn't giving up on aviation. The *terrible soif de voler*—terrible thirst to fly—took hold. Hélène enrolled in an aviation school.

In November 1910, she became the fourth woman in the world to qualify for a pilot's license. And in a very short amount of time, she set a flurry of firsts: first woman to carry a passenger, first Belgian woman to fly, and the first woman to fly cross-country. She achieved records for duration, distance, and altitude. When she defeated fourteen men in a speed race for the King of Italy Cup in 1911, newspaper writers gave her a new nickname: *la femme épervier,* Female Sparrow Hawk. The only time she received less-than-glowing public commentary was when it was revealed to scandalized readers that she never wore a corset while flying.

Hélène Dutrieu arrived in New York in late September 1911, as the world's most dominant and famous female aviator. It was her first visit to the US. Fifteen-thousand spectators descended on Nassau Boulevard, each paying between fifty cents and two dollars, depending on the quality of the seating. Fifty planes were assembled for thirty-five pilots from the United States, England, France, and Russia, but most of the crowd was eagerly anticipating an epic competition between France's Girl Hawk and America's trio of female flyers.

Harriet was the first of the women to take to the air that Saturday, but not before a male pilot attempted a landing and crashed right in front of her plane. Nonplussed, she taxied past the crumpled wreckage and lifted off. Matilde soon followed and the two flew in tandem, to the delight of the onlookers.

The next day promised the match that the entire audience was waiting for—an altitude contest between the four women pilots for the Rodman Wanamaker Trophy. But it was not to be. Blanche Stuart Scott was disqualified by the meet rules because she had not yet attained an actual license (she never did). Harriet, in deference to her parents' religious convictions, refused to fly on Sunday. The ship carrying Hélène's Farman biplane arrived too late for it to be assembled and tested. All of which left Matilde as the sole female aviator to go for the record.

Matilde remembered that day very differently. In 1960 she recalled the competition:

> "I said to Harriet, 'Now which one do you want? To me it doesn't make a bit of difference, which one do you want?'
>
> "'I would rather go cross country, if it's all the same to you.'
>
> "'It's all the same,' I said. 'I can only go so high, or I could go so far, and that's all. As you're doing it professionally, you take your choice.'
>
> "So she took the cross country. Well, I took the altitude. We went up. Mlle D[utrieu] went up something like two or three hundred feet now, I guess she went up 500 feet—and I went up 5,000 feet [official

> records state 1,200 feet]. That was the world record for women; I established the world's record for a woman. I don't know what the record was before that.
>
> Well, I didn't know that I had broken the record until afterwards. But I could see that [Hélène] had gone down before I did, and I knew I was always above her. So I thought: well no matter if I come down now, I know I have the record over her. But now, I'm going to frankly tell you—I did it just for the sport. I didn't do it for the glory.

It's entirely possible Matilde spotted another aircraft below her and mistook it for Hélène's, or that recollections looking fifty years into the past were simply clouded by time.

Matilde's wheels barely touched ground when a small caravan of police cars pulled into the airfield parking lot and dozens of deputies converged on the hangars. Nassau County Sheriff Charles De Mott blustered forward and, waving a court injunction, ordered the meet cease operations immediately. The Episcopal bishop of Long Island, Frederick Burgess, and New York Governor John Alden Dix were among a cabal of dignitaries who filed suit against the air show organizers, claiming it violated a blue law banning for-profit sporting events on the Sabbath.

While Timothy L. Woodruff, the former lieutenant governor of New York whose sizable investment bankrolled the meet, argued with the assembled officers, the skies opened up and the rain "fell tardily enough to trap more than 2,000 persons who had journeyed to the grounds. It descended in torrents, ruining gowns and hats and making the long stretch of meadowland between grand stands and railroad station a series of rivulets and ankle-deep rills." The drenched crowd slipped and slid their way back to a waiting train. A passing milkman was talked into removing the empty cans from his wagon and, for one dollar a head, he took as many women wearing "new Fall frocks" as could fit back to the station. The enterprising laborer made several trips. Woodruff continued negotiating out of desperation, promising the sheriff—with no doubt fingers firmly crossed behind his back—that not a dime of prize money would exchange hands and that the flyers would compete for honor alone.

By three o'clock, no decision had been made. Aero Club officials were huddled to one side, debating the matter with pilot representatives T. O. M. (Thomas) Sopwith and Claude Grahame-White. As the *New York Times* reported:

> The American fliers waited for ten minutes, and as the officials showed no indication of concluding their talk with Grahame-White and Sopwith, they became angry and agreed that whatever decision the officials finally reached they would act in opposition to it.
>
> The committee's final decision was that there should be no flying, whereupon Beatty, Ellyson, Hammond, and Beck started up in the air. As they circled around the course, regardless of the drizzle, the megaphone men were proclaiming that the meet was off and that there would be no flying.
>
> Many who left the grounds and boarded railroad trains saw the four machines high above the field and returned to see the flights, but gatemen refused to admit them unless they bought fresh tickets. This caused much confusion, and several hundred forced their way in.

The rebellious pilots stayed in the air for thirty minutes before giving up and landing their soaked aircraft. The next day's *Times* headline dripped with irony: "Rain Stops Flights When Churches Fail."

With the unlicensed Blanche Stuart Scott still sidelined, the meet's only *femme contre femme* contest was a cross-country race on

Publicity poster of Harriet with her signature plum-colored flight suit and Blériot monoplane.

Monday in which Harriet's more powerful monoplane quickly outdistanced Hélène's biplane. Ten thousand spectators stood shivering in the fall chill as Harriet claimed the $600 reward. Hélène, who complained loudly and often that week that the prize money for the women's events had been misrepresented to her, decided to stay in the air in order to set the endurance record, which she did, pocketing the Ives de Villiers prize of $500. The Girl Hawk had good reason to be offended: two of the male pilots took home winnings of more than $4,000 for similar feats.

By mid-week, with the major contests for women concluded at Nassau County, Harriet left the meet early for the Trenton State Fair. There she collected another $1,500 for a seven-minute-long exhibition flight, the first night flight for a female aviator. Aviation was proving to be much more lucrative than newspaper work.

Meanwhile, Matilde was to have one more run-in with Sheriff De Mott. She recalled in 1960,

> One Sunday, Mr. Rene Simone, his father was one of the richest bankers in Paris and he wasn't even as big as I was I don't think, maybe taller but didn't weigh as much as I weighed, 112 pounds, he was at our house for dinner. He said, "Mlle Moisant, you say that you flew the Moisant monoplane with a 50 Gnôme motor." I said, "Yes."
>
> He said, in his half French, half English, "Pardon me, but really, I don't believe it. I don't think a woman can. I've never seen a woman fly a plane with a Gnôme motor, and I don't think she can."

Alfred Moisant was also at the dinner table. He looked at his sister and said, "Tild, if Mr. Simone doubts your word, if I get your plane on the field, will you fly it?" "Sure," she replied. "All right, when we get through dinner," Alfred announced, "we'll get in the car and go."

Before the aviation meet ended on October 1, promoter Woodruff succeeded in getting a temporary injunction against any interference by authorities. That injunction expired the next day, and Sheriff De Mott was determined to arrest anyone who dared fly on a Sunday. He dispatched twenty-two deputies to the Nassau Boulevard Airfield, where a crowd of some five hundred people were gathered to watch Earle Ovington attempt to make the second ever air-mail flight, this one to the West Coast. Arguing that, as a licensed mail carrier, he operated under federal law, not local statues, Ovington convinced the Sheriff's men to let him go, but he promptly suffered engine trouble on takeoff and, abandoning the trip, stowed the bags of mail inside a hangar and headed back to Manhattan. When the Moisants and their French guest arrived, there were still a few hundred aviation fans milling about the airfield.

Matilde continues the story:

> So we got in the car and we went where our planes were, and [T. O. M.] Sopwith was there—he's the one that flies these yachts you know—he was there, and quite a few people. My brother had big locks on all the hangar doors. They were all lined up there, and the field was over here. So Fred said, "Now listen, I don't want you to make a fool of yourself, nor of me. If you want to back out now's the time, but don't back out after I get that door open."
>
> I said, "I won't," so he went to open the door. He had his mechanics there. An officer came up and said, "You can't take out your machine."
>
> "Why not?"
>
> "We have an order that nobody is to fly on Sunday."
>
> Fred said, "I can't see why. This is my property."
>
> "Well," he said, "I'm sorry, but I can't open the door."
>
> "All right," said Fred, "if you won't open the door, I'll have my

> mechanics break the locks, that's all. It's my property and I have a right to go in there, and I have a right to do what I want with my property."
>
> "Well, anyhow," he said to my brother, "I'll tell you something. If you promise your sister won't fly, I'll let you take it out."
>
> He said, "I promise nothing. Either you open that peaceably or I will see that it's opened."

The deputy stepped back and the hangar door was unlocked and opened. The Moisants' mechanics wheeled the monoplane out of the driveway and onto the field. Thomas Sopwith was there as well, but his biplane was surrounded by officers who refused to let him board it. While Thomas was putting up an angry clamor, Matilde managed to climb into her plane unnoticed.

She turned to her former instructor. "Now listen, Mr. Houpert, I won't give this usual signal, but you watch my head, and when I go like that, you give word to the men at the tail to let her go."

Matilde explained that she didn't want to land at the Nassau Boulevard Airfield because it wasn't her family's property, so she told André she'd circle twice, dip down as if she was going to come in for a landing, then bank hard and head towards the Moisants' airfield. "God willing, and I'm going to go and land on our own field. Then you get in the car and take Mr. Simone over to the field." Four police officers stood by on their motorcycles. Another approached Matilde as she sat in her plane. "Listen, young lady, don't forget, if you fly that plane I'll arrest you when you come down."

She replied, "Well, I haven't flown it yet, have I?"

When he walked away, Matilde switched on the ignition, André heaved on the propeller, and she bounded out onto the runway before the deputies could react.

> I circled twice, and came down about ten feet off the ground, and then away I went. They told me afterwards that when I dipped the officers said, 'Now get ready to catch her when she gets out of the machine as we're taking her to headquarters.' They didn't know that the fun was going to be at the other field.

The Moisants' visitor, Rene Simone, turned to one of the deputies who was watching helplessly and said in his droll French accent, "Say, officer, if you want to arrest her, you'd better get wings on your motorcycle."

Turning her monoplane toward Mineola, Matilde was unaware she was being followed on the ground by a police car and a parade of other vehicles, including those of family members, their friends, and the aviation fans who'd come to see Earle Ovington's postal flight.

"I was just so happy that I was flying," Matilde said later, "that I never thought about the officers on the field any more, never thought that I was making a scene of any kind."

It was a scene all right, one straight out of a Mack Sennett Keystone Cops comedy. The high-speed chase wound through Meadowbrook and Westbury before the monoplane touched down at the Moisants' airfield. While Matilde taxied to the hangar, the processional of deputies and spectators slid to a stop in a cloud of dust and noisy recriminations. Two officers tried to haul her out of the cockpit; the enraged crowd began beating them with fists and canes. Matilde, caught up in the melee, suffered a few scratches, and her flying suit was torn.

Suddenly an open-air runabout schussed to a halt next to the battle. Rene Porsch, Harriet's driver and mechanic, jumped out and pulled Tilly into his car. Before they could get free, two deputies leapt onto the running board and began pounding Rene's head with their nightsticks.

During that violent scuffle Matilde managed to slip away from the officer's clutches and climb into the Fiat belonging to her brother's friend. The car dashed back down the road, pursued by more deputies, whose police car immediately broke down. She was almost in the clear, but the youngest Moisant began to have a change of heart. She recalled saying to the driver,

> I haven't done anything that I shouldn't do. That's my property. I'm not flying for money, I'm not flying commercially, I'm flying for fun. I'm not going to run away. Stop the car. I never ran away from anything and I'm not going to run away from this.

The friend did as he was told. Veering to the shoulder of the road, the Fiat was quickly surrounded by the motorcycle officers. After a brief and curt discussion, they ordered her into a police car. She refused.

> Just then my brother came up. He got there just in time. They were ready to pull me out of the car, and Fred came up—"Now," he said, "listen here." He pushed his way through—there was quite a little crowd already—and he said, "Now listen, anyone who lays a hand on her, it's as much as his life is worth."

It was not an idle threat: Alfred was big as a bear with a temper to match. A few of the bystanders vowed to stand by him, declaring, "Yes, Mr. Moisant, we have some clubs here, we'll fix them if they touch her."

That's when Alfred positioned his next chess piece. He suggested the deputies follow them all back to the family airfield to talk it over. As soon as the police cars and motorcycles pulled into the driveway, he whirled on them and announced in a loud voice, "Now listen here. If you officers don't get off of my property I'm going to have you arrested for trespassing!" He glared into the officers' shocked faces until they meekly returned to their vehicles.

"That," Matilde said, "was that."

When her sister Louise, who'd always been fearful about the family's flying business, heard about the incident, she was mortified. "Now your picture will be in the paper! You've disgraced the family!"

"Well," her little sister replied, "you know I always was a tomboy."

Louise was only half correct. The next day, every newspaper in New York did, in fact, feature a story about the airborne odyssey. Pictured above most was, in Matilde's own words, "the cutest little witch you ever saw sitting on a broom, waving to the officers." But rather than being disgraced, the youngest Moisant was now a bona fide folk hero.

17

I'M LIKE A CAT—I THINK I'VE GOT TWO LIVES LEFT

HIS OWN GRANDFATHER LIKENED Francisco Madero's chances of victory at the polls to "a microbe's challenge to an elephant"—a description that proved all too prescient. Before the ballots were even cast in Mexico's 1910 presidential election, the wealthy idealist who dreamed of real democracy and an adherence to the country's constitution was thrown into jail. Porfirio Díaz, former general and wearer of befeathered hats and bedazzling medals, was elected to his seventh term as president, the result of shameless electoral fraud.

With yet another victory under his belt, Díaz assumed Madero—a quiet, contemplative, even quirky landowner—would simply return to his estates in the north once he was freed from jail and fade into obscurity, while his liberal, educated, middle-aged followers would sulk back to their law firms and colleges. Instead, on November 20, Madero called for an armed revolution.

The rural masses, whose labors fueled the burgeoning economy but who saw no hope for a better future, responded first. These were the farmers whose lands were being illegally absorbed into the ruling class's haciendas and the Native Central Americans and mixed-race people. They were followed by city residents, whose belief in *Sufragio Efectivo, No Reelección* (A Real Vote and No Boss Rule), a motto they scrawled on fences and buildings, was summarily crushed by the president's naked power grab.

Within days, rag-tag guerrilla groups began harassing local governments and military outposts, and Díaz's "rusty military apparatus" quickly proved unable to contain it. Díaz too, no longer had a taste for conflict. By May 1911, the elderly president agreed to resign and fled to Spain. Mexico's first free election was held that following November, and Francisco Madero won in a landslide. Little did anyone know, the Mexican Revolution was just beginning.

Born with graceful schooner lines, a low beam, and an iron hull, the steamship *Lampasas* offered its affluent clientele a fast, luxurious ride from New York to points south. Comfortably settled into its well-appointed state rooms in early November 1911 were Harriet Quimby and Matilde Moisant, along with two new Moisant pilots, George Dyott and Patrick Donald Hamilton, who were doubling as chaperones, Harriet's mother, Ursula, Matilde's sister Louise, and Matilde's friend Miss M. C. Long. Traveling by train were Alfred Moisant, André Houpert, five mechanics, and two carloads of planes. The destination: Veracruz, Mexico.

Weeks earlier, Alfred signed a contract with a Mexican government official named Vic Roumagnac to provide five aviators and planes to demonstrate the science of flight as well as celebrate President Madero's inauguration. In return, the Moisant International Aviators were promised $100,000 in gold (almost $3 million today), half from the government, half from local merchants. For the cash-strapped company, it was an offer it couldn't afford to pass up, regardless of the political turmoil. Alfred was also hoping to sell some of his planes to the new administration and perhaps open a flight school at the new Balbuena Military Airport. He agreed to ten days of exhibition flights around Mexico City with plans for stops in other cities as well. Alfred knew Mexico and the country's language and culture well from his business days in Central America.

Not long after unpacking their bags, Matilde asked Louise to go to the airfield with her. Her sister, ever the worrier, asked why. "I was at the flower market this morning," Matilde explained, "and I bought a great big bunch of flowers. I would like to go and fly over Chapultepec this evening and see if I can locate Chapultepec Palace from where we are in the field." The palace featured an enormous and ornate patio. "I would like to see if I could fly over that and drop this bunch of flowers" as a goodwill gesture. She wrote a note to President Madero and asked André to attach it and a rock to the flowers "but not too heavy because I want to be able to lift it into the cockpit and drop it."

At the airfield, Matilde walked over to a local man and asked, in fluent Spanish, which direction was the palace. He pointed and replied, "Over there." She asked again so as to be clear, and he repeated the gesture. "All right," she replied, walking over to her plane and climbing aboard.

> And I cranked my machine. You see, in those days, we didn't have any brakes, we didn't have anything on our machines [to hold them in place] you know. The mechanics, or anybody who was there, hung onto the tail, and then somebody cranked the propeller, spun it, and that cranked the motor.
>
> So I said, "Come on, I'm ready to go." Two or three hung on the tail, and one of them spun the propeller. I felt it was going all right, and I stuck up my hand. Once they let go of the tail, you had to go, you know. There was no way of stopping it, unless you cut off your motor and the motor died, and sometimes then you died too. But I was very lucky. I had a lot of falls but I always came out all right. I'm like a cat—I think I've got two lives left yet.
>
> So we started. I started to the right, and sure enough, I located Chapultepec—beautiful palace, you know—I flew around and

> located it and I had just enough sense to know that when I dropped a thing like that, the air or whatever it was would come up, so I thought, "I'd better cross the patio before I drop my flowers." So when I located it, I flew directly over it, and as I passed over it, I dropped my flowers. I looked back and I could see it going down, and I thought, "Oh boy, I'll hit the patio now." It hit right in the middle of the patio.

The next day, President Madero sought out Matilde and said, "Miss Moisant, I got your flowers. Now if that had been a bomb I wouldn't be here today because it dropped right on the patio." Matilde laughed and said it was only "a bomb of friendship." With that flight, Matilde became the first woman to fly in Mexico.

Once the rest of the team arrived, the reception, at least by the Mexican press, was enthusiastic: "Aviation Field Taken by Assault: The Public Invaded the Field Hoping to See Close-Up the Lady Pilots and Their Machines" blared a headline in *El Imparcial*, which covered the flyer's activities every day. The article featured a photograph of a beaming Matilde and her monoplane. The *Mexican Herald* declared both Harriet and Matilde to be "cultured, frank and intelligent."

The crowds, however, proved to be as thin as the Mexico City air. "The meet has been very successful, so far, from an aviator's point of view," wrote *Aero*'s traveling correspondent,

> because of the number of flights made in such a rare atmosphere; but the attendance has not been good. About 1,000 people were out the first few days of the exhibition, but since Monday the average has sunk to less than 500. The confused political situation here may have something to do with this.

Nevertheless, those who did attend were far from disappointed, when "a laughing girl in a bat-winged, long-tailed monoplane drove her way straight into the hearts of the crowd."

> Miss Harriet Quimby was the star on November 18 when she made a 37-minute flight over Lake Xochimilco and the Hill of the Star. André Houpert also flew well on a 15-minute jaunt over the city, during which he circled Chapultepec. George Dyott was up 22 minutes during Miss Quimby's flight and they engaged in a race to the Estrella (Hill of the Star).

A few days later, Harriet's luck almost changed. She was flying at about 150 feet up when her rotary engine suddenly quit. Remaining calm, "she remembered the three rules her instructor had taught her. Dive the craft at a slight angle to gain air speed and control, look for flat ground, and land quickly." Spotting a wide-open field, she allowed the monoplane to glide toward it, avoiding a copse of trees before setting it down gently. She and the aircraft were unscathed, but the close call did inspire her to write an article about the vicissitudes of flight:

> From my own experience, I can say that an aviator passing over a stretch of ground on his first flight may find certain conditions of the atmosphere which upon his return lap, half an hour later, may be entirely different, and which on the third lap may change again. To navigate safely he must depend on common sense. The difficulty in foreseeing these varying conditions and accurately charting them may easily be recognized. A chart might be a pleasing possession for the flyer to hang in his hangar, but it would scarcely help him to avoid air holes, which he passes through almost before he knows he is in one. So-called air holes or strata of air so light that they fail to give

> sufficient support for the wings of a plane are not found in one place. The atmosphere varies according to the amount that the ground radiates and according to the shifting eddies of wind. It is also affected by the conformation of the ground over which the aviator passes. Seldom does the pilot find the same conditions during two trips over the same ground.

For the first time in their short history, the Moisant International Aviators experienced almost perfect flying weather. But other conditions proved challenging. André compared the flying to "just like a rowboat out in a heavy sea."

"Mexico City is a little over 7,300 feet above sea level," Harriet later told her readers.

> The air is very dry and, therefore, very light. Although there were many days when the wind did not even lift the leaves on the trees, it was impossible for the aviators who were taking part in the festivities incident to President Madero's inauguration to fly. The thin air furnished little or no support for the aeroplanes. The propeller of my machine made the same number of revolutions that it had been making when I flew it at sea level, and the Gnôme engine pulled the same number of pounds; yet there seemed to be a lack of power.

During the team's time in Mexico, both Patrick Donald Hamilton and Matilde were nearly killed when their planes somersaulted, likely when they hit an air pocket, and fell upside down to the ground. Both were saved from serious injury by strong steel-cable guy wires. These were bolted to the motor on one end and to a tripod mast above the cockpit on the other and prevented the engines from crushing them.

As the Mexico City air show drew to a close on November 25, Harriet and Matilde thrilled the crowd by flying side by side. That afternoon, Alfred helped the president climb into George Dyott's pretty little Deperdussin monoplane, and Francisco Madero became the first world leader to take to the air in a powered machine. But unrest and growing disenchantment with the newly installed leader were brewing elsewhere in the nation. Opposition was forming in the personages of Emiliano Zapata and Francisco "Pancho" Villa and their thousands of followers.

While the aviation team prepared to move on to six other Mexican cities, Harriet announced to the stunned troupe she was parting ways with them and heading back to the US. She left unsaid her real reason: a seed of an idea formed sometime while she was performing, perhaps when she flew over Lake Xochimilco, that would become her most daring exploit yet. If successful, her plan would sling her to new heights of aviation fame. She feared that some other flyer would attempt it first, so she kept her secret close to her heart and hurried back to New York to solidify her plans. Other pilots soon abandoned the team as well. The Moisant International Aviators were coming apart at the seams.

With a new contract from the Madero government for five Moisant Blériots and a commitment for five Mexican army soldiers to travel to Mineola for instruction, Alfred salvaged at least part of what was a disappointing trip. Whether he collected on the $100,000 in gold is unclear. It is also unclear why he returned home and left his little sister and chief instructor to oversee the completion of the remaining shows in a suddenly violently unstable country.

As what was left of the troupe made its way to Guadalajara, ominous storm clouds of war were gathering all around the country, with fighting breaking out in dozens of places. Matilde survived yet another accident when the propeller of her plane hit the ground first, causing the rear end to rise and start to topple over. "I thought, 'If that comes on top of me it's goodbye,' but I threw myself back in the machine and I had just enough weight to throw the tail back. That's the only thing that saved me."

A successful showing at León bolstered the flyers' spirits, but the rebel forces were closing in. Heavy fighting forced the Moisant team to cancel events in Veracruz, Monterrey, San Luis Potosí, Puebla, and Hermosillo. For the first time since the Moisant International Aviators was formed, the venues were proving more dangerous than the flying. While the pilots were en route to Chihuahua, federal troops forced their train off the main line and onto a sidetrack near Torreon, 340 miles north of their intended destination. Partisan armies were laying siege to the city. The *federales* managed to break through the rebel lines just long enough to allow the train, with 170 passengers including the Moisant team, to start moving, but this didn't last long. The revolutionary fighters cut the train line again.

For two weeks, Matilde, André, and the other flyers and mechanics were trapped in the Pullman car as fighting raged all around them. They could hear bursts of semiautomatic gunfire. News of other trains being robbed and haciendas sacked by the rebels trickled in. Matilde, the only Spanish speaker among the group, slipped out whenever she could to buy food at a nearby village and haul buckets of water back to the train. Finally, the battle tipped in favor of the Mexican army, and the engine started. The train crept along to Chihuahua and eventually Laredo, Texas. "Not one of us disrobed that night for we expected the train to be held up," Matilde remembered. "All through the night we could see through our car windows the bivouac fires of the rebel army and when our train would halt at the station armed soldiers would put their faces up to the windows of the Pullman car." Within months, Francisco Madero was overthrown and assassinated by his own army. A year later, Alfred sold an 80-horsepower two-seat plane to Pancho Villa, after a Moisant company employee taught some of the rebel soldiers how to "drop 40-pound packages of dynamite upon the Federal garrisons."

"Few men could have managed our affairs as well in Mexico," André Houpert admitted when the team finally arrived in New Orleans. "And had it not been for the cool-headedness of our little woman manager we would have gotten into serious complications at the city of Torreon." But Matilde, ever modest, simply shrugged. "We just got out," she said. "They burned the bridges after we left."

What she didn't realize at that moment was her professional flying career was just weeks away from ending. Coming in for a landing during an exhibition at a golf course in Shreveport, Matilde noticed there was a subtle hill on the manicured fairway below her. "I knew I couldn't do it [land] in front of it, but I thought I might do it over...I just came like that, right in it, and it threw my machine right over, and I came right down." Again, her plane flipped over, landing upside down on top of her. Somehow, again, she survived. She crawled out from under the wreckage to the cheers of the crowd. Richmond Pease, who'd been brought in to help manage the remainder of the exhibition swing, described it thus:

> The occupant [Matilde], jolted from her seat by the first shock, managed to keep her balance until near the ground, when she fell, landing on her hands and knees. A second later the great fabric fell on top of her, completely hiding her from the horrified witnesses. The right wing and propeller were broken and also the right landing wheel. Had it not been for the iron wing supports that stuck in the ground and held up the heavy parts, the girl must have been crushed to death. As it was she wriggled from under the wreck unhurt save for a scratched and blackened eye where her goggles had pressed against it.
>
> She sprang lightly to her feet laughing, and evading the help of those who rushed to her aid, hurried to where Louise sat to prove

> her safety. A few minutes after the accident she merrily approached Houpert saying, "I'll make another flight this afternoon, professor, if you'll lend me your plane." At a sign of dissent from me he shook his head in refusal. "And just think," she sighed, as she regretfully watched the removal of the wrecked monoplane, "I wore a green suit this afternoon in honor of St. Patrick's Day." The scene ended in a rush of souvenir snatchers seeking splinters from the shattered propeller.

Later, in Dallas, Matilde told a reporter she knew her fans would want to see her fly but they "wouldn't care to see me killed." The cat who "had two lives left" seemingly used up both with a pair of narrow escapes in the space of a three-month period. Louise could no longer bear to watch Matilde fly and refused to accompany her to any more aviation events. Sensitive to her sister's concerns, Matilde nevertheless admitted privately, "I have the air intoxications, and only a flier knows what that means."

Although practical in almost every other way, Matilde held a superstition about the number thirteen. She was born on Friday the 13th, took her pilot's license on the 13th, and always insisted that lucky number be painted on the wings of her monoplane. With that clearly in mind, she declared April 13, 1912, would be the last day she took to the air professionally. An exhibition in Wichita Falls, Texas, which Alfred had booked months earlier, would be Matilde Moisant's swan song.

The day dawned to rain and wind, refusing to respect Matilde's numerological ambitions. The momentous occasion would have to wait. Twenty-four hours later, April 14, at six o'clock in the evening, Matilde, in her woolen flight suit and leather helmet, appeared in front of the eager spectators, "as womanly a woman as ever lived," one reporter described her, "attractive, beautiful, demure yet vivacious and highly entertaining." Her dimples flashing, her eyes sparkling, she climbed into the seat and took off smoothly, circling the field for about ten minutes before the

Gnôme engine began to sputter. She landed quickly. André assured her the repair time would be brief, but her former instructor expressed concern about the rising wind. He told her she shouldn't go back up until the next day. Uncharacteristically, given that she was raised in a strongly patriarchal family, Matilde overruled him, saying since it was to be her last flight, it should be "one of my most successful ones."

Once the engine was again running smoothly, she returned to the air, entertaining the audience with skillful aeronautics. As the muggy Texas evening faded into twilight, Matilde dipped the monoplane to make her approach for landing, but a crowd of onlookers, most of whom had never set eyes on an airplane before much less witnessed one landing, wandered onto the stretch of field reserved for the air strip. "They were right in line with the way the wind was," she recalled.

> When they saw me coming down they thought that the minute my wheels touched I was going to stay there. Well, the plane didn't do that. So I saw the line [of people] right in front of me and I thought, "If I don't do something, I'm going to mow right in there." So I just nosed my plane down so that the tail didn't go over, put on a spark [increased power], and I let the wheels touch, and I brought it right back up, but it wouldn't go—only took me over the crowd.

Desperately trying to not kill anyone, Matilde pulled back on the control stick and managed to get the monoplane about thirty feet back into the air, but with the decreased airspeed, it immediately stalled and slammed into the ground just past the spectators. A shard of propeller pierced the gas tank, which exploded, instantly engulfing the wooden fuselage and covering the canvas in flames. "[The tanks] burst their moorings and away we went. The tank went down this way and the gas and oil exploded and got over me."

Matilde Moisant in 1911, in the wool flight suit that likely saved her life. Pinned to her uniform is a swastika medallion, which was popular as a good luck charm with early aviators.

André, who'd been watching nearby and realized what was unfolding, bolted toward the downed airplane. He and another man reached into the flames and pulled Matilde out. Her hair and gloves were singed, but the heavy tweed of her flying suit prevented any more serious burns. While the two men gently carried her a few dozen feet away, she muttered, "That was my last flight." Once clear of the danger, all three stared in disbelief as a Texas cowboy named R. E. Marlow rode up to the burning wreckage, lassoed the Gnôme engine, and yanked it out of the inferno. Within minutes, the airplane was reduced to smoke and ash and "the crowd was swarming around its skeleton."

"I could never watch my brother flying without experiencing great fear within me," she said later. "But after I leave the ground I enjoy every minute without a thought of anything that might happen." Then, more pensively, the second American woman to get a pilot's license admitted ruefully, "The earth is bound to get us after a while, so I shall give up flying before I follow my brother."

18

CAN A MAN KEEP A SECRET?

THE TWENTIETH CENTURY LIMITED was running three hours behind schedule as it sped toward Chicago's LaSalle Street Station. The engineer labored feverishly to make up some time for his well-heeled passengers traveling on the twenty-hour trip from New York. Advertised as "the most famous train in the world," it was also one of the most sumptuous, offering passengers heavily padded couches, barber service, shoeshines, full baths, air conditioning, and restaurant-quality fine dining. In New York's Grand Central Terminal, customers strolled on a "specially designed crimson carpet" to board their reserved cars.

It was not quite noon on January 11, 1912, when the speeding train rammed a pair of empty cars belonging to the Chicago and Eastern Illinois Railroad that had been parked on the track. The two coaches were destroyed, and a porter named A. Eaton, who was on board one of them, sustained internal injuries and a bad cut. The 115 passengers on the Twentieth Century were launched out of their seats and found themselves sprawled amid their luggage and reading matter. Among them was Harriet Quimby, who was on her way to the annual meeting of the Leslie-Judge Company.

"We were progressing smoothly enough," she told one of the reporters who rushed to the scene,

> and just getting ready to step off into Chicago, when—bang!—there came the most fearful jar. I flew out of my seat like a shot and fell across the aisle into another seat and when I looked around I saw people picking themselves up all down the car. Some of them were in the most ridiculous positions, but none of them seemed to be hurt.

Yet all must have considered themselves very fortunate: seven years earlier the Twentieth Century Limited suffered a far more horrific accident that killed twenty-one people.

When asked if she was frightened, Harriet shook her head no, but said,

> I'd rather take a chance in my airship—if the accident wasn't too severe—than get mixed up in a really and truly train wreck. You see, in an airship, if only the engine went wrong or something of that kind, I'd have a chance of gliding safely down. In a train wreck of real size there is one glorious smash, and then—good night! You don't know what's happened to you.

Before the reporter let her continue to the LaSalle Hotel, where she was guest of honor at a luncheon, he invited Harriet to share her vision for the future of aviation:

> Um…that's a hard question. It will undoubtedly be a factor in mail delivery—they've tried that out already, with more or less success. I suppose some day we'll do all our traveling in airships. But, say, isn't it foolish of aviators now, at this stage of the game, to talk about flying over the Atlantic and all that sort of rubbish? Honestly, I think it will be a mighty long time before anybody will cross the Atlantic that way. Those fellows want to do big, sensational things, but why don't

> they first fly over Lake Michigan or some other body of water somewhat smaller than the ocean? Bless us, they haven't crossed many rivers yet!

Harriet didn't disclose that she was at that very moment well into planning to do a "big, sensational thing" and fly across a large body of water—just not the Atlantic. Her eyes were on the English Channel, the vision quest that drew her away from the Moisant troupe's tour of Mexico. Concerned that a European female aviator would beat her to it, she was desperate to keep her scheme under wraps. "Without mentioning the matter to a soul," she said later, "for fear that some one across the sea might anticipate my idea."

Harriet didn't waste a single moment upon her return to New York in hiring a business manager. Albert Leo Stevens, who went by Leo, was a friend of the Wright brothers and an accomplished promoter. An unassuming but attractive thirty-nine-year-old with tousled dark hair and darker eyes, a chiseled chin, and prominent nose, Leo was considered one of the world's leading experts on balloons and dirigibles. He was the proud holder of the Aero Club of America's second license for balloon pilots. There were rumors over the years, never confirmed by either party, that Harriet and Leo's relationship blossomed into more than just one of business.

Leo was born with an aversion to gravity. At age eleven, in his hometown of Cleveland, Ohio, he volunteered to work for a balloonist who was selling tethered rides at a local park. "I shoveled the iron, carried the acid, helped to haul the water, and chopped the ice," he said, "ruining my knickerbockers with the acid." (Hydrogen gas was produced by the combination of sulfuric acid and iron filings). When the concessioner refused to let him take a ride, he slipped inside the balloon unnoticed, cut away the ropes, and hung on tightly as it shot into the sky. After eventually crash-landing into a tree, miles away, he walked home uninjured. His livid parents were forced to pay for damages to the balloon. Undeterred, the life course for Leo was firmly plotted: he ran away from home the next year and started a career making balloons with his older brother, Frank, and performing high-wire acts and parachute jumps.

During an 1897 test flight—as one of the brothers' early creations meandered over Rahway, New Jersey, on its way to New York City for an exhibition—a storm blew in, pushing the brothers out to sea. They tried to change direction, but the winds were too strong. Within a short time, Leo and Frank found themselves far from land. There were only two choices: cut themselves free from the balloon or risk disappearing somewhere over the vast ocean. The basket they were in was made of willow with a canvas covering. With one hand each on the railing, they began sawing desperately on the ropes. When the last threads parted, the basket plunged four hundred feet to the Atlantic. Somehow, they both survived the fall.

The brothers, exhausted and soaked from the squall, clung to their makeshift boat for six hours, until a passing schooner, the *Mary Jane*, hove into view just before sunset. The captain and his crew pulled the boys onboard and turned up the Shrewsbury River to Monmouth Beach, where the Stevens brothers were treated to warm clothes and food at a local house. With weary grins they told their hostess it was their most exciting day, but one they had thought would be their last.

By the turn of the century, Leo Stevens had invented the first manually operated safety pack parachute as well as the first dirigible airship in America. He was also a colorful and daring showman. His most popular stunt was called the Human Bomb, which he first featured at the 1901 Pan-American Exposition in Buffalo. Thousands watched as a large balloon rose into the air trailing a round ball, which the young promoter referred to as the bomb. At a designated height, the "bomb" exploded

Leo Stevens, visionary balloonist and inventor of the safety parachute who became Harriet's business manager.

and Leo flew out of it, plunging toward earth before deploying a parachute. He floated softly to a landing amid uproarious cheers. At other events, he jumped from an airplane or balloon wearing three parachutes: red, white, and blue. As he fell, he popped one open, then cut it loose, opened the next, and repeated until his feet returned to earth.

A few months before joining up with Harriet, Leo demonstrated the newest version of his emergency parachute, built in his factory on Ninth Avenue in New York. An assistant wearing the device leapt out of a Wright biplane. "The parachute itself is wrapped in a square of cloth," *Aeronautics* magazine explained. "As the jump is made the parachute opens up, the cloth cover remaining with the belts. A pin with spring affords release" of the cotton and linen chute, sixteen feet in diameter.

Leo believed that the death rate among aviators could be lessened if all flyers were outfitted with his invention. He devoted the rest of his life to working toward that goal. The fact that he was willing to take time away from that mission, his successful businesses, and personal appearances to take a job as Harriet's business manager speaks to his belief in her ambitions. Or, possibly, his addiction to her charms.

Harriet's second course of action upon returning to the US was to set about acquiring an airplane that could safely carry her across the English Channel. Since she learned how to fly on a Blériot-style monoplane, that was the type of aircraft in which she had the most confidence. Tellingly, rather than buy a Moisant copy, she decided on an actual Blériot. There is no record of Alfred Moisant's reaction when he found out, but Harriet's choice must have stung, given it was he who helped her launch her aviation career.

Harriet secured a letter of introduction to Louis Blériot—from whom is unclear—and included with it an order for a newly designed 70-horsepower model with seating for two. She intended to meet him at his factory in France and take possession of the flying machine there.

Blériot's representative in the US, Bernard Alfieri, met Harriet in New York City in late February or early March 1912, and she reportedly gave him a bit of a fright by speeding him around Central Park in her open-air runabout. When he finally gathered his wits about him, Bernard agreed that the first successful female English Channel crossing would be invaluable publicity for the Blériot company.

On March 7, Harriet and Leo boarded the ocean liner *Amerika*, the same luxurious Hamburg American Line cruise ship on which she started her around-the-world journey for *Leslie's Illustrated Weekly*. Fifty Aero Club members saw their celebrity pilot off at the dock, believing the reason for her trip was to compete in Europe with the best aviators in the world. Only a handful of her closest friends and her *Leslie's* editor, John A. Sleicher (who gave her time off from her reporting duties in return for a series of articles about her adventure), knew her real plans.

Perhaps inspired by G. K. Chesterton's 1908 spy novel, *The Man Who Was Thursday*, Harriet adopted an alias the moment the ship's crew dropped its mooring lines. As "Miss Craig" she enjoyed the trappings of the luxury liner: tea at four o'clock on the deck, with stewards serving cakes and small sandwiches, and evenings at the Ritz-Carlton Restaurant, reserved for first-class passengers only, where she and Leo dined on turbot à la Catalane, sweetbreads à la Adlon, sorbet in oranges, and pudding Rothschild. The daughter of poverty never lost her appreciation for the finer things in life: "Some people eat to live," she once remarked, "but the majority live to eat."

It shouldn't be much of a surprise that the Michigander suffered from chronic seasickness, often lamenting how much she disliked being on the water: "I never was the best kind of sailor." She was so fond of the *Amerika* in part because she rarely felt nauseated on that ship. Certainly its enormous size—669 feet long with a 74-foot beam—reduced the pitch and roll, but the ship's chief steward, G. Scholz, told her that her comfort was also likely due to a new invention: refrigeration. As Harriet related to her readers:

> Only a few years ago it was a common sight to see passengers lying deathly pale in steamer chairs refusing everything in the food line offered by solicitous stewards. Many did not appear in the open air at all, being unable to leave their cabins. Now, on any of the larger steamers, the passengers snap their fingers at the waves. They are as much at home as they are in a hotel on land. Some pale faces are noticed among passengers comfortably tucked up by the stewards on the promenade deck, and especially in sheltered nooks and corners; but it is a rare occasion when one of them is humiliated by having an attack of seasickness while on deck. This general enjoyment of good health no doubt has much to do with the especial attention given to the kitchen departments.
>
> "Thirty years ago," Mr. Scholz said, "the company endeavored to give passengers the very best, but the fresh meats, eggs, fish and poultry were not as well preserved as a fastidious diner would wish. At that time these were all packed on ice, and if the ice gave out the food suffered. Now no such difficulty is possible. Under the modern system of refrigeration, everything is in as perfect condition as in the best hotels."

It took the *Amerika* a week to reach Cherbourg, France. During that time, Harriet pecked away on her typewriter in her stateroom, catching up on her *Leslie's* commitments that would be translated into Morse code and sent back to New York via the ship's wireless radio transmitter: "Latest Plays and Popular Players," "Kubelík Earns $1 Million Dollars with a Violin," and, with information gathered from the Moisant exhibition swing, "Notable Observations of Holy Week in Mexico." "Poor, troubled Mexico!" the article begins. "Upset by revolution, facing dangers from within and without, with Madero's new government tottering on its foundation, it is not strange that it turns to religion for a rest."

Her first order of business upon arrival was to meet with Alexander Kenealy, editor of the London *Daily Mirror*, whom Harriet later described as an "inspired editor" and "bar-room gladiator of note." Kenealy, a brute-faced bull of a man who had accompanied Admiral Robert Peary on the first Arctic expedition, knew a good story when he saw one. "He was delighted with the idea and immediately offered me a handsome inducement if I would make the trip as the *Mirror's* representative." Leo and Alexander negotiated exclusive European rights to the story of her flight. The pair also met with an unnamed British businessman and secured a $5,000 loan to purchase the Blériot.

> The next thing necessary was to get a monoplane. I went to Paris, saw Mr. Bleriot and placed an order with him for a seventy-horse-power passenger machine, regarding which I had had some correspondence with the firm. At the same time I readily arranged with Mr. Bleriot for the loan of a fifty-horse-power monoplane of the type I had been accustomed to use in the United States [the more powerful model could not be built in time for the Channel attempt].
>
> Mr. Bleriot has a hangar at Hardelot, where he has a seaside home. It seemed prudent to try out the new machine first in some quiet way. So it was shipped to Hardelot. I followed soon after. The control of the new machine was a trifle different from that which I had been using in the United States, hence my desire to have a trial flight.
>
> It was not so easy finding Hardelot. It is a summer resort of recent creation and its exclusive character, as well as its remoteness from the crowded cities, made it a good place to test my machine without attracting attention.

Leo stayed behind while Harriet made her way from Paris to Boulogne, the closest rail stop to Hardelot. When she stepped off the train, she was dismayed to discover there were no cabs or vehicles for hire in all of Boulogne, only a "ramshackle tramcar" packed full of Easter holiday travelers. She managed to squeeze aboard and stood sandwiched in between raucous family members headed to the beach, "while everybody tumbled over my luggage lying on the floor." She continues,

> After one change of cars and an hour and a half of much discomfort on a bleak and chilly April day, I got into Hardelot just as it was getting dark. I had heard of its fine hotel, but to my surprise, on reaching the end of the tramcar line, I saw the hotel in the distance was in absolute darkness. I learned that it was open only in summer.
>
> Here was a bad dilemma. With a knowledge only of fragmentary French and among total strangers, I was in something of a fix. I found a little cafe that took lodgers, but it was full. At another little place I had better luck and was stowed away in the single room remaining unoccupied. It had no fire or carpet—nothing but the bed and a chair. But the people were kind. They gave me a simple dinner, with plenty of hot tea, and, weary as I was, the bed, with its cardboard covers and diminutive pillow, was a haven of refuge most acceptable. I had scarcely sat down to eat before a little girl hesitatingly stepped up to me and, showing a postal card, asked if I would give her my autograph. I inquired why she wanted it. The French maid who waited on my table spoke a little English, and she said that they understood that I was in Hardelot to fly across the channel! And this after all our studied efforts to secure secrecy! I found that some one in the Bleriot hangar had been talking—quite innocently—too freely in Hardelot. I gave the girl and a number of others who came up my autograph, but enjoined secrecy. Question: Can a man keep a secret?

Eager to test out her new Blériot, Harriet rose early the next morning. Outside the window of the small café she watched as gale-force winds blew brown sheets of sand off the beach.

> Usually it dies out in the evening, but it kept constantly increasing, until it whistled around the corners of the house at a velocity of forty miles. The next morning, at five, once more I prepared to go out into the chilly air to make a trial. Still the wind blew a gale, and it continued to blow throughout the day. There was nothing left but to sit in my cheerless room and wait.

Hardelot today is a beautiful vacation town with an eclectic and vibrant downtown and wide, sandy beaches, popular with French and English visitors. It was much smaller and more modest in 1912, but no less welcoming. A British family that lived nearby heard about Harriet's plight, "the lonesomeness of an American girl, a stranger in a strange land," and invited her to join them for lunch. She gratefully accepted. A hired car pulled up to her boarding house at noon. Harriet spent the better part of a pleasant afternoon with Mr. and Mrs. J. Robinson Whiteley and their daughter. As they parted, no one guessed fate would conspire to reunite the new friends sooner rather than later.

During that week, Harriet often found herself staring out at the gray fog and churning waters, thinking about Dover and Calais, "like two grim bulldogs glaring at each other, these cities, twenty-two miles apart, bristle with fortifications of the most formidable type. The surging channel typifies the antagonism between two great European nations, now happily less than it has been."

As the days crept by it became clear that she would not be able to test out the new plane before departing for the English coast.

> The persistent gale at Hardelot would not permit me to carry out my plan to try out the machine. Time was flying—even if I was not. I had promised the *Mirror* editor to be at Dover promptly. So I arranged to have the Blériot monoplane shipped across to Dover at once and wired the *Mirror* to have its photographers and reporters meet me at the Hotel Lord Warden, at Dover. The famous Dover Castle stands on the cliffs, overlooking the channel. It points the way clearly to Calais. Those who have made the channel crossing by steamer at this point, with more or less discomfort during its period of a little more than an hour, will appreciate the delight with which I contemplated making an absolutely smooth journey across its spiteful waters in a swift and graceful monoplane. There was real satisfaction in contemplating a crossing in the air and mocking at the waves which had so often made me uncomfortable.
>
> It was vitally important that nothing should be known of my contemplated journey, so the machine was shipped very secretly to the aerodome on Dover heights, about three miles back from the channel, a fine, smooth ground from which to make a good start.

But despite all their precautions, rumors began circulating among the villagers that "several English and French woman pilots were to attempt the crossing in the next few days."

At the end of March, while the Quimby team huddled at Dover, waiting for the monoplane's arrival, Harriet made the acquaintance of Gustav Hamel. He was a twenty-two-year-old Brit whose boyish looks belied his considerable flying experience. Already the proud possessor of numerous aviation records, crashes, and two channel crossings, Gustav's reputation was that of a future superstar in the sport. Louis Blériot himself said he'd "never seen a pilot with such natural ability."

The charming aviator magnanimously offered his advice to Harriet, and the two likely talked late into the night.

Three days later, the *Daily Mail* carried the headline "Lady Crosses Channel by Air."

That lady was not Harriet Quimby.

19

I WAS NOT A BIT NERVOUS

> Miss Eleanor Trehawke Davis [*sic*], the first woman to cross the English Channel in an airship, arrived in Paris at 5:30 this evening, having left Hendon, near London, in a Blériot monoplane at 9:38 A.M.

WHEN HARRIET AND HER team heard a brief notice about the accomplishment on April 2, 1912, they were devastated. Gone was the *Daily Mirror's* "handsome inducement." Gone, they feared, was Harriet's place in the history books. Shuttered in her room at the Hotel Lord Warden, she was inconsolable.

"I saw Miss Davies shortly after she landed," the *Mirror* reporter wrote, "Her cheeks were glowing like roses with exposure to the wind, but she was looking very pleased and was carrying a large bunch of beautiful flowers which a gallant Frenchman had presented to her." With movie-star looks and a craving for adventure, Eleanor Trehawke-Davies was a wealthy Londoner who developed an early obsession with aviation. By the time of her channel crossing, she was already a survivor of a two-day-long journey from Hendon and Brighton and back, and eventually became the first woman to "loop-the-loop" seven times in one flight.

But Trehawke-Davies was never a pilot. She was what was known as an "air companion"—a passenger ever and only. The aviator who actually did the flying across the channel that day was none other than the young man who only days before had talked to Harriet about crossing the channel, Gustav Hamel. "I was an extremely useless passenger," Trehawke-Davies told the *New York Times*, "for I did not do my work. I promised to keep the pressure pump going but failed miserably. Mr. Hamel had to do all the work, which makes his trip all the more wonderful."

A knock on her hotel room door the next morning brought Harriet the truth. Grief quickly gave way to anger, which eventually morphed into cold, steely, determination. Summoning Gustav, she swallowed her disappointment, hired him as a consultant, and even praised him in subsequent interviews. But under the surface, resentment seethed. Months later she bitterly recounted confiding her plans to a fellow pilot "I trusted very much (I will not mention his name) [who] took a woman as passenger across the Channel, robbing me of the distinction of being the first woman across."

Why the betrayal? Was Gustav's motivation one of patriotism, so that a fellow Britisher could be the first woman across? Loyalty to an old friend? Trehawke-Davies had accompanied him on previous flights and would again. Or perhaps he, having experienced a handful of close calls already in his young life, was so concerned for Harriet's safety that it was misguided chivalry intended to discourage the dangerous attempt. He never explained his actions except, perhaps, to Harriet, his offended employer, who refused to disclose his reasons publicly. Even more mystifying was his bizarre suggestion, days later, that he dress up in Harriet's signature plum-colored flying suit, take the Blériot across the channel himself, and then trade places with her once he landed on a predetermined deserted French beach. "I laughed," she recalled, "and told him I was going to make that flight myself."

While the team waited for its aircraft to arrive, Harriet pondered the enormity of what she was about to do. Even though other male aviators

Still frames from a newsreel of Harriet with her friends preparing to take off from the cliffs of Dover.

succeeded in following Louis Blériot's pioneering voyage three years earlier, the channel crossing was still an exceedingly risky endeavor.

> On Saturday, April 13th, I took an automobile and drove three miles out from the city to inspect the grounds from which Mr. Bleriot started to make the first successful aeroplane flight across the channel, in July 1909. A fine granite monument marks the spot. Mr. Bleriot flew from Calais to Dover. It seemed to me that the Dover cliffs were higher, and I preferred to make the flight in reversal of Bleriot's program. So historic was Bleriot's achievement regarded that his landing place, not far from Dover Castle, was also marked by a permanent monument. This is in the form of a stone representation of his full-sized monoplane, suitably inscribed, lying flat upon the grassy hillside where Bleriot landed. This was only three years ago.

Harriet's close friend Carrie Vanderbilt, who traveled to Dover from New York along with Linda Arvidson to witness the channel attempt, took photographs of the women standing at the Blériot monument.

> On Sunday, the day after our arrival at Dover, our party drove out to see the aerodrome on the heights. It seemed absolutely necessary to try out the new machine before making the channel trip. Everybody insisted that I must do this, and I wanted to do it myself; but it was not to be. Sunday, April 14th, was a perfect day for flying across the channel. There was no wind. The sun was bright and warm. The air was so clear that by straining our eyes a little we could see the French coast dimly outlined across the channel. Everybody said, "Start now. It is your chance. We may have high winds to-morrow and they may last two weeks. That has been the experience of everyone who has come here to make the channel flight."

But Harriet steadfastly refused to break a promise she made to her devout parents. Flying on a Sunday was simply out of the question. Her team reluctantly agreed to try again early on Monday morning, weather permitting, and the American, registered as "Miss Craig," kept to her room as much as possible to avoid recognition.

> Monday, at four A.M., we were called and had a cup of tea. An automobile hurried us off to the aerodrome while it was still dark. The wind was strong. Worse than that, it came in dangerous gusts which no aeroplane could withstand. All day Monday, in a chilly wind, we hovered about the aerodrome or sat restlessly in our automobiles, hoping that the wind would go down. To add to our discomfort, clouds cut off the sun's warmth and splashes of cold rain fell. Our only respite was a hurried trip to the hotel for a hot luncheon.

The Quimby team was beginning to attract attention. Residents of Dover and other nearby towns grew curious, chewing on rumors of an imminent channel crossing attempt by an unknown woman. The Sunday on which Harriet refused to fly presented perfect weather for a shake-out flight in the new monoplane, so Gustav taxied it out and bounced it down the grassy field and into the air as a crowd gathered at the aerodrome fences to watch. Reporters, too, were keeping gimlet eyes on the activities, but once the Gaumont Cinematograph Company of London's camera started filming Gustav's flight, the crowds dispersed, figuring the assembled strangers were just making a movie. In fact the camera crew, hired by *Daily Mirror* editor Alexander Kenealy, was in position to capture Harriet's shot at history.

"After all our patient waiting and hoping against hope that the wind would go down toward evening," Harriet later told her *Leslie's* readers,

Louis Blériot on his historic flight.

> there was no abatement in its strength. We went back to our hotel at seven P.M., tired, chilled and disgusted. The wide-awake *Mirror* reporters who had taken a tug out into the choppy sea in midchannel and another group who were waiting back at Calais to witness my landing were even more disappointed than we. My greatest disappointment was that I had had no chance to try out the new machine.

Tuesday morning April 16, 1912, at three-thirty, there was a knock on Harriet's door. Make ready, she was told; the weather appeared to be improving. Harriet, Carrie, and Linda had a quick sip of hot tea while her crew scurried off to prepare the Blériot. Thirty minutes later, the women arrived at the cliffs just as the plane was being wheeled out of the hangar. A sense of urgency hung in the air, mingling with the drapes of fog stubbornly refusing to surrender. Harriet noted there was scarcely a breath of wind stirring, which foretold of a smooth flight but which also meant there was no empyrean hand to sweep away the low-hanging clouds.

Standing next to her frail wood and fabric aircraft, Harriet focused her gaze into the mist, urging her eyes to pierce the thick, gray veil that obscured her path to the far coast. Occasionally, the clouds would shift, and Dover Castle materialized into view, which afforded some small amount of hope.

> I saw at once that I had only to rise in my machine, fix my eyes upon the castle, fly over it and speed directly across to the French coast. It seemed so easy that it looked like a cross-country flight. I am glad I thought so and felt so, otherwise I might have had more hesitation about flying in the fog with an untried compass, in a new and untried machine, knowing that the treacherous North Sea stood ready to receive me if I drifted only five miles too far out of my course.

She later learned that was the unfortunate destiny of another young aviator, D. Leslie Allen, who took off later that day in a monoplane with the goal of crossing St. George's Channel from Holyhead, Wales to Dublin, Ireland. He was never seen again.

Finally, after what seemed like a thousand lifetimes of waiting, Harriet felt a shifting of the air, a breeze that nuzzled her face and lifted the windsock ever so slightly. The sky, in patches, was mutating from blackish gray to blue. Gustav reacted first, declaring he would give the engine a quick try-out and report back on the flying conditions. After a brief run out over the channel he returned, "making one of the beautiful and easy landings for which he is famous." Climbing down from the open-air seat, he told Harriet there was still fog over the water, but the conditions might not get any better. Time to go.

Days earlier, he had warned Harriet that the air up high would be frigid, perhaps colder than she'd ever flown in before. Under her wool-backed satin flying suit she wore two pairs of silk long underwear. She added a long woolen coat as well as a rubberized raincoat, and a long sealskin stole. Completing the ensemble were two pairs of long gloves. Reaching around her waist, Gustav insisted on tying a large leather hot-water bag to her midsection "like an enormous locket." Harriet's female friends fussed about, helping her on with her coats and a scarf. Linda Arvidson held a mirror as the aviator touched up her make-up before hugging them all and climbing aboard. In film footage of the moment, Harriet's smile is effervescent and relaxed. Leo Stevens kneels next to the airplane like a gallant knight as his friend and star client uses his thigh as a step to climb aboard.

> It was my turn at last. Everybody was expectant. I was eager to get into my seat and be off. My heart was not in my mouth. I felt impatient to realize the project on which I was determined, despite the protest of

> my best friends. For the first time I was to fly a Blériot monoplane. For the first time I was to fly by compass. For the first time I was to make a journey across the water. For the first time I was to fly on the other side of the Atlantic. My anxiety was to get off quickly.

When the 50-horsepower engine growled to life, six assistants clung to the underside of the bucking monoplane to keep it rooted to the earth. Gustav climbed onto the chassis behind Harriet to give her a last-minute word of warning. He leaned in close to her ear so she could hear him above the din of the motor and the blast of the propeller, "Be sure to keep your course, for if you get five miles out of the way, you will be over the North Sea, and you know what that means." He reported the clouds were low and spent several minutes "explaining precisely the use of the compass and the direction she must follow. He set the compass for south-east, and placed a red mark upon it." His last words to her were "Don't go too high." When the Englishman clambered down from the cockpit, Harriet waved her hand in the air. "All right! Let's be off!" She shouted over the engine noise, "I don't care what happens. I'm going now!" Her first-person account of the flight appeared in both *Leslie's Illustrated Weekly* and *Fly* magazine:

> The sky seemed clear, but patches of cloud and masses of fog here and there obscured the blue. The French coast was wholly invisible, by reason of moving masses of mist. The wind had not come up yet. The smooth grounds of the aerodrome gave me a chance for a perfect start.
>
> It was five-thirty A.M. when my machine got off the ground. The preliminaries were brief. Hearty handshakes were quickly given, the motor began to make its twelve hundred revolutions a minute, and I put up my hand to give the signal of release. Then I was off.

The mechanics anchoring the plane let go and dove out of the way. It instantly leapt forward and was airborne after taxiing barely seventy feet.

> The noise of the motor drowned the shouts and cheers of friends below. In a moment I was in the air, climbing steadily in a long circle. I was up fifteen hundred feet within thirty seconds. From this high point of vantage my eyes lit at once on Dover Castle. It was half hidden in a fog bank. I felt that trouble was coming, but I made directly for the flagstaff of the castle, as I had promised the waiting *Mirror* photographers and the moving-picture men I should do.
>
> In an instant I was beyond the cliffs and over the channel. Far beneath me I saw the *Mirror*'s tug, with its stream of black smoke. It was trying to keep ahead of me, but I passed it in a jiffy. Then the thickening fog obscured my view. Calais was out of sight. I could not see ahead of me at all nor could I see the water below. There was only one thing for me to do and that was to keep my eyes fixed on the compass.

Harriet's hands were safe from the cold, thanks to her Scottish woolen gloves, but her goggles were so clouded from the fog and rain and castor oil the engine threw off that she had to push them up onto her forehead to see. The Blériot sped along at a mile a minute.

Easing back on the control stick, she climbed the monoplane until it reached an altitude of six thousand feet, hoping to punch through the mist that enveloped her. The cold at that height was bone chilling. Another quick glance at the compass assured her she was still going in the right direction, but the thick fog would not relent, so she decided to take the aircraft lower in hopes of finding clear air. That's when fate reared up and took a nearly fatal swipe.

Harriet had repeatedly met this challenge, but never before under such dangerous circumstances. "Frequently when I have been flying it has seemed to be as if a huge cloud-hand were mischievously rocking my slender little monoplane," she once told a reporter. "It seemed, with a playful finger, to be lifting the tail of my machine. That giant hand grows more and real the longer I fly."

Piloting a small fabric and wood aircraft over open water is far from a smooth experience even under the best conditions. Air pockets caused by slight variations in temperature can tug on a wing or rudder. Soaring from clear air into a cloud changes the plane's aeronautic characteristics. Water molecules add density to the atmosphere and weight to the canvas wings. All of this requires constant adjustment to the flight control surfaces. It can feel at times like cantering a horse on an icy pond. As Harriet angled downward to descend, the Blériot hit a patch of turbulence. The tail snapped upward at a steep angle, and the Gnôme engine flooded. She later mused in a reflective moment:

> When flying is in its infancy, as now, the navigator of the air is beset by dangers and difficulties not unlike those presented to the navigator of the water who sails on an uncharted sea. Yet even he can be warned by the ripples he sees ahead or by the foaming and roaring of the surf of the dangers that may be lying in wait for him. But the flyer has no such warnings; moreover, he must be prepared for instant action in any and all emergencies, and this preparation is the one absolute essential for the person who resolves to conquer the air. The skillful aviator is the one who has not alone the daring to do risky things, but who has, as well, the intuition, the knowledge and the ability to meet and conquer the waves and whirlpools and even the so-called air-rocks that may confront him without losing his head.

With her motor sputtering and misfiring, the pilot calmly assessed her options. "I was not a bit nervous," she later declared. Leaning out over the edge of her seat, she began scanning for a patch of water on which she could pancake the plane, preferably without flipping it over. This is what Hubert Latham had done a few years earlier on both of his failed attempts to cross the channel.

> But, greatly to my relief, the gasoline quickly burned out and my engine resumed an even purr. A glance at the watch on my wrist reminded me that I should be near the French coast.
>
> The distance straight across from Dover to Calais is only twenty-two miles, and I knew that land must be in sight if I could only get below the fog and see it. So I dropped from an altitude of about two thousand feet until I was half that height. The sunlight struck upon my face and my eyes lit upon the white and sandy shores of France. I felt happy, but I could not find Calais. Being unfamiliar with the coastline, I could not locate myself. I determined to reconnoiter and come down to a height of about five hundred feet and traverse the shore.
>
> Meanwhile, the wind had risen and the currents were coming in billowy gusts. I flew a short distance inland to locate myself or find a good place on which to alight. It was all tilled land below me, and rather than tear up the farmers' fields I decided to drop down on the hard and sandy beach. I did so at once, making an easy landing.

It would be a mistake to interpret that last sentence as a blasé conclusion to an everyday occurrence. Rather, that was simply a classic example of Harriet's understated style when she wrote about her beloved avocation. At some point in her journey to aviation fame, she made the conscious decision to go against the popular trend of melodramatics. Instead she portrayed flight as something that should be accessible to all, especially women, and not as much a heroic undertaking as one of caution, learning, and common sense. Harriet was the anti-elitist of the air—wanting anyone and everyone who had the wherewithal to hop into a plane, to join her in that joy.

Her eastern course to France was a little more meandering than originally planned by a distance of some forty miles. It took her not over Calais, but south of Boulogne to a spot near the fishing village of Équihen-Plage.

Nevertheless, after one hour and nine minutes in the air, the little girl from a Michigan dirt farm became the first woman to fly solo across the English Channel.

20

WOMEN ARE MORE FEARLESS THAN MEN

ON A WIDE STRETCH of sandy beach, bordered by a rim of slender native grasses that waved languidly in the breeze like wispy green bangs above a broad forehead, Harriet Quimby's Blériot settled to a stop. She killed the engine and climbed down, grateful to finally be in somewhat warmer surroundings. Wiping the moisture and oil from her face she looked around, marveling that she was alone on the vast shore. "But," she then noticed,

> it was only for a few moments. A crowd of fishermen—men, women and children each carrying a pail of sand worms—came rushing from all direction towards me. They were chattering in French, of which I comprehended sufficient to discover that they knew I had crossed the channel. These humble fisherfolk knew what had happened. They were congratulating themselves that the first woman to cross in an aeroplane had landed on their fishing beach.

After the adrenaline rush faded and relief set in, Harriet realized she was quite hungry. A glance at her watch showed it was seven o'clock, and the hasty spot of tea she sipped back in the hotel almost four hours earlier was about as nutritionally fortifying as the fog that her wings had parted. It then dawned on her that her friends and the assembled reporters and photographers were probably still waiting for her on a beach at Calais. Somehow, she had to get word to them that she was alive.

> I knew that friends at Dover and Calais were anxious to hear the result of the trip. Just before I had started, some one had thrust a *London Mirror* between my woolen coat and my raincoat, as a further protection from the cold. I tore off the margin of this paper, sat down on the sand and wrote a telegram, while curious fishermen pressed about me. From one of them I learned that Hardelot was the nearest place and was about two miles distant. I asked a fisherboy to take the message for me. I had no money with which to pay him, as I had expected to land at Calais among waiting friends. But the fisherboy took the message and the operator sent it. Who paid for it I do not know.

A photograph of the moment shows Harriet seated on the sand next to some fishing boats, her calf-high boots crossed at the knee, as she composes the note. A half-dozen young boys sit next to her, straining their necks to see what she was doing.

As word spread and the crowd of excited locals grew, Harriet momentarily worried about the safety of her plane, but later admitted she misjudged the fishermen, who were

> helpful and thoughtful in every way. Taking note of the rapidly rising tide, they made me understand that the aeroplane should be moved higher up on the beach. An aeroplane is a difficult thing to handle. I did not want my machine harmed, so I picked out an elderly, sensible-looking fisherman, who seemed greatly interested in the mechanism, and put him in charge of the moving. It was pleasant to notice with what care these fishermen, even the children, handled the aeroplane under my direction, while pushing it up the beach to a place of safety.

While the villagers struggled valiantly to haul the airplane to higher ground, Harriet was shown to a table next to one of the buildings and invited to sit. A woman brought her bread, cheese, and a cup of hot tea.

> The tea was served in a cup fully six times as large as an ordinary teacup and was so old and quaint that I could not conceal my admiration of it. The good-hearted woman insisted upon giving it to me, and no cup that I have ever won or ever shall win as an aero trophy will be prized more than this.

About this time, "all of Hardelot was racing to the beach." Hundreds of ecstatic Frenchmen gathered all around her. Then Harriet spotted a familiar face. It was her English friend Miss Whiteley, whose parents had hosted the lonely American for lunch only days before. Whiteley and her companion were so overjoyed to see her that they

> lifted me impulsively on their shoulders and bore me over the sands. I felt more uncomfortable than I had at any time during the trip. Perhaps I ought not to admit it, but I note the fact because the *Mirror* photographers and moving-picture men, who, on hearing of my landing, had rushed over from Calais in their automobiles, caught this particular scene with their cameras, and that means that they will give it to the public.

Immortalized by the Gaumont Cinematograph Company of London's camera, that singular instant mirrors the fantasies of every athlete who ever competed. Harriet Quimby, the victorious conqueror of the English Channel, was carried away from the watery field of battle on the shoulders of two women, as dozens of admirers cheer and wave their hats while they walk along beside her.

> The good-natured fishermen were wild with delight. They were ready to do anything for me. They were only too willing to tote my machine over two miles along the beach and to put it back into the Bleriot hangar, where a week before I had seen it reposing peacefully and invitingly by the sands of Hardelot.

But before the monoplane was taken away, the *Daily Mirror's* photographers convinced Harriet to climb back into the Blériot for posterity; one more lasting image of her historic achievement. A reporter produced a bottle of champagne and popped the cork, handing her a small glassful, which she lifted toward her new devotees in a toast and downed in two swallows as they jumped and cheered. She threw her head back and laughed, the sheer unadulterated joy of that moment visible on her face. "But the real refreshment, I confess it, was a cup of hot and fragrant tea and some delicious little cakes that Mrs. Whiteley served in the warm and spacious dining-room of her hospitable mansion."

After enjoying the company of her new acquaintances for a few hours, Harriet shrugged on her long sealskin coat (which a considerate reporter had thought to bring) to cover her oil-soaked flying suit, climbed into a hired automobile, and drove thirty miles back to Calais. A train then sped her on to Paris, where she arrived at 7 P.M., "a very tired but a very happy woman." She closed her eyes that night knowing that she did what she set out to do, against the odds, and that her world was about to change.

It did change, but not in the ways she imagined.

The next morning, she picked up the newspapers left at her hotel room door and scanned the front pages, anticipating the headlines announcing her historic flight.

There was not a word.

On the evening of April 14, 1912, the cruise ship on which Harriet and Leo sailed from New York to Europe, the SS *Amerika,* was on its return

Still frames from a newsreel of Harriet's English Channel crossing, as friends and villagers carry her triumphantly off the French beach where she landed.

voyage to the US when a crewmember spotted icebergs. The captain sent out a wireless message warning all ships in that part of the Atlantic to beware. One did not heed the call.

Three hours later, the largest ship in the world's starboard hull plates buckled on impact with an iceberg, and five of its sixteen watertight compartments flooded. The RMS *Titanic*, carrying many of the wealthiest people alive, slipped beneath the surface of the ocean at 2:20 A.M., taking with it more than 1,500 passengers and crew. Days after the sinking, passengers on passing boats could still witness the macabre results:

> What appeared to be a large number of little white dots floating in the water, some in clusters, others alone. The dots were in fact hundreds of lifeless, marble-like, pale bodies still floating, rigidly upright in their white, cork life jackets, bobbing up and down on the surface of the sea. It was not only possible to clearly see what the corpses were wearing but also their faces and make out whether the bodies were male or female. It was a heart-rending experience. One such body clearly seen was that of a young woman dressed in a night gown, still clutching an infant tightly against her breast. Another woman appeared fully dressed with her arms clinging tightly around what appeared to be the rigid and matted body of a shaggy dog, looking much like a St. Bernard. Dozens more bodies passed by for what were several minutes but must have seemed like hours. The ship passed groups of bodies, one with a cluster of three men still grasping solidly to a deck chair, and scores of other aimlessly drifting in the open sea. Many, many more little white dots bobbed up and down.

Such horrifying descriptions of the deadliest peacetime marine disaster dominated the pages of newspapers around the world for weeks, even months.

The day after her crossing, Harriet burrowed deep into the pages of the *New York Times* to find any mention of her flight. She eventually tracked down a narrow column on page fifteen.

To her credit, she never publicly complained about the cruel twist of fate that robbed her of international acclaim for "the most remarkable feminine exploit of modern times." Obviously, she was sensitive to the enormous loss of life. But when she returned to New York, no parades awaited her, no rapturous throngs lined the avenues, no speeches were made in her honor by puffed-up politicians. It was as if the achievement of a lifetime never happened. Not even until May 16, a full month later, did her first-person account appear in *Leslie's Illustrated Weekly*, "An American Girl's Daring Exploit":

> The Editor of *Leslie's* asked me to write "the thrilling story" of the crossing of the English Channel, on April 16, in a monoplane, for the first time, by a woman pilot. I am afraid I shall not be able to make it "a thrilling story," although there were some very doubtful moments for me while passing through the heavy banks of fog that rose from the chilly waters of the notoriously treacherous channel.

The fateful coincidence between her historic flight and the Titanic's sinking was not her only undoing; political passions, too, conspired against Harriet taking her rightful place in cultural status and history. A woman aspiring to do something formerly exclusive to men was becoming increasingly controversial. The America Harriet returned to was seething in resentment toward a suffrage march that had been held just days earlier, wherein fifteen thousand people swarmed down Fifth Avenue in support of voting rights for women. The journalist was ever cautious about expressing her personal views publicly, and so her achievement was tacitly ignored by those in the feminist movement because she refused to be their poster girl. To them, "the only thing worse than an anti-suffragist was an independent woman who wasn't interested in their cause." Journalist Elizabeth Anna Semple reported:

> Miss Quimby assured me that she doesn't care for bridge, nor is she a suffragist—notwithstanding various alluring propositions from sympathizers of "Votes for Women" to call her machine after one of the leaders—the "Pankhurst," for example, or even the "Catt." "The latter might have been the more appropriate," the monoplane's driver said with that little humorous look in her big eyes that, somehow, seems her most pronounced characteristic after you've talked with her a little while. "Really, you'd be surprised to know how purely feminine a monoplane can be when it wants to, but personally I preferred to call my machine 'Genevieve'—because 'Genevieve' always seems to me to fit someone who is remarkably versatile—and my monoplane possesses that quality to a degree!"

Neither were the male-dominated editorial boards quick to herald her accomplishment. Some went so far as to pooh-pooh it with a "been there, done that" haughtiness. On April 18, 1912, the *New York Times* opinion-page banner declared "Exultation Is Not in Order":

> Even at a time when so much of public attention is concentrated on the loss of the *Titanic,* the fact that a woman, alone and depending wholly on her own strength, skill, and courage, has driven an aeroplane across the English Channel does not pass unnoticed. Miss Quimby's flight is recognized as a considerable achievement. Not so many months ago this same flight would have been, and indeed was, recorded as one of the most daring and in every way remarkable deeds ever performed by man. Since then, however, the passage has

> repeatedly been made by men, and now for them there is little or no glory in it. The serial passage of the strait, for the male aviator, is now regarded as hardly anything more than proof of ordinary professional competency.
>
> Hence should the feminists be somewhat cautious about exulting over Miss Quimby's exploit. They should not call it a great achievement, lest by so doing they invite the dreadful humiliating qualification, "great for a woman." A thing done first is one thing; done for the seventh or eighth time is quite different. Of course it still proves ability and capacity, but it doesn't prove equality.

The *Times* editors conveniently and disingenuously ignored the fact that male pilots were still losing their lives attempting to cross the channel and would for some years to come. Gustav Hamel himself disappeared between France and England almost exactly two years after coaching Harriet, at the age of twenty-four. He was transporting a new high-powered Morane-Saulnier monoplane when it went down on July 6, 1914. The crew of a fishing vessel spotted a body matching his description in the waters of Boulogne, but high seas prevented them from retrieving it. The channel crossing was still one of the most dangerous twenty-two miles on earth for fliers, male or female.

The *Times* critique stung. Harriet knew it was less about what she accomplished than her sex, but she had to face the fact that no matter how much she tried over the years to keep gender politics out of her public life, they were unavoidable. Women who dare step into the established realms of men inevitably become targets of rancor. "I wish my views on feminism could be understood," she complained in a direct response to the opinion piece. "[Flying] is not a fad, and I did not want to be the first American woman to fly just to make myself conspicuous. I am just living my life, going after goals, and continuing to evolve."

Gustav Hamel. Harriet hired him as a consultant on her English Channel crossing. The twenty-four-year-old's plane disappeared over that same body of water two years later.

The inherent double standard being leveled against Harriet, symptomatic of much larger issues, was not lost on some of her contemporaries: "Woman's advent into the aviation field was not welcomed by the man flier," early aviation correspondent Elizabeth Hiatt Gregory wrote in 1912.

> He resented it as an intrusion on what he regarded as an occupation that belonged exclusively to man. Some were outspoken in their protests and frankly said it was not a woman's business, while others put it on a sentimental basis. It was dangerous, they thought, and women should not be allowed to risk their lives in aeroplanes. There were those who were so vigorous in their opposition that they carried it so far as to refuse to sell a machine to a woman or instruct one in aviation.

As the world's attention gradually shifted away from the *Titanic* disaster, Harriet did finally gain some measure of fame and appreciation for her feat. Americans, ever searching for homegrown heroes to admire, eventually returned their gaze to the beautiful aviator in their midst. Harriet's celebrity status soared. Articles began appearing in popular magazines like *Good Housekeeping*, some written by Harriet herself, in which a theme emerged: rather than making speeches or leading marches, she was subtly planting the flag of sexual parity by allowing her accomplishments to speak for themselves:

> Any woman with sufficient self-confidence and a cool head could fly across the English Channel as easily as I did. The men flyers have given out the impression that aeroplaning is very perilous work, something that an ordinary mortal should not dream of attempting; but when I saw how easily the men flyers manipulated their machines

> I said I could fly. While I have not exactly followed in their footsteps I have at least accomplished something along the line of flying. I believe women are more fearless than men, or at least I have more requests for rides from them.

Matilde Moisant, tracked down in California by the *Alameda Daily Argus,* said, "Nothing has pleased me more than to hear of Miss Quimby's achievement," but then tweaked her former flying partner by adding, "although I had my eye on doing the same thing."

In an odd twist that did nothing to further confidence in the female flyer, Professor Rudolph Hensingmuller of Vienna published a dubious study claiming to explain why women would be better pilots than men:

> Because she has retained the primitive faculty of seeing with full retina; enforced modesty and flirting have caused this; because she has scattered attention instead of concentration; this is invaluable to an aviator who must notice many things at once; because she has the faculty of intuition—that quality of the mind which can take in a number of causes simultaneously and induce a conclusion—an essential in aviation; because her specific gravity is less than man's; because she needs less oxygen and therefore can better meet the suffocating rush of air; altitude affects her less than it does man; because her sneezes, in man an actual spasm, have been controlled by ages of polite repression; because she feels more quickly warning atmospheric changes; because she loves to speed.

His argument was immediately—and rightfully—ridiculed, and Harriet refused even to comment on it.

Once back in the United States she had more important work to do—a backlog of writing commitments and, as the official aviation editor of *Leslie's*, oversight duties on the magazine's first issue devoted entirely to flight, which hit stands on May 9, 1912. On the cover was a photo of Harriet suiting up in preparation for her channel crossing.

Leo Stevens was busy, too, hustling up exhibition flights for which Harriet was paid $1,000 or more, as well as product endorsements. Her experience in San Francisco as an actress and model came in handy. In a first for advertising, which previously featured only male spokespeople, the smiling young pilot is pictured on a poster holding up a glass of Vin Fiz grape soda, whose color perfectly matched that of her flying costume. The beverage company also pioneered aerial advertising and painted its name prominently on the underside of the Vin Fiz Flyer that toured America. Unfortunately, the drink's pure cane sugar was prone to spoiling if not refrigerated, leading one newspaper to describe Vin Fiz as a cross between river water and horse slop.

As she traveled the country for exhibitions and endorsements, Harriet grew increasingly frustrated over broken promises, unpaid fees, and legal troubles. Aviation increasingly involved a shifty conglomerate of hucksters and con men, and its entertainment side was becoming almost unbearable for her. It didn't help that, in her view, her native land was ceding its dominance of the air to Europe. "America is the birthplace of aviation," she argued, and "for this reason America, more than any other nation, should forge ahead and stand in the front ranks with a well equipped aerial army and a system for using the aeroplane as a commercial vehicle, instead of lagging behind and of being the last of the large nations interested in flying science."

Her outlook hadn't always been so glum, nor her thoughts always so serious. In a photograph of Harriet sitting in her monoplane, taken just prior to her channel attempt, she is seen with a broad smile, holding up a small object. It was the brass figure of a Hindu deity, Ganesha, which, weeks earlier, she had selected from a pile of similar objects in the offices of the *Daily Mirror* in London. For unknown reasons, the paper often received talismans and good luck charms in the mail, and once a year the editors asked readers what should be done with them. The ones readers deemed unlucky were usually burned or otherwise destroyed. Harriet picked out the tiny statuette and announced it was her new lucky token. Before the propeller was pulled and the engine of the Blériot coughed to life, she affixed the little metal figure to a guy wire at the front of the plane. It made the journey across the channel with its new owner.

Weeks later, Harriet jokingly began to blame the elephant-headed "little devil"—the Ganesha figure that had flown with her across the channel—for her troubles and decided an exorcism of sorts was in order. She penned a lighthearted article for *World* magazine:

> It is a curious thing, but all women flyers are superstitious, and again it isn't so curious either. All people who follow a calling in which chance enters largely are superstitious. My own superstition is Ganesha, a little ancient brass idol. He brought me such bad luck.
>
> He had belonged to a French aviator who met with reverses and gave the brass god to a country gentleman, who in turn sent him [to the *Daily Mirror*] to be burned. I was arranging for my flight across the English Channel in a Bleriot monoplane and wanted the flight kept secret until it was accomplished.
>
> Here is where Ganesha got in his first licks. I confided the hope that I might be the first woman to fly across the Channel to an aviator whom I trusted very much.

That was an obvious reference to Gustav Hamel, whose trip with Eleanor Trehawke-Davies robbed her of the distinction of being the first woman across. But Harriet's troubles didn't end there.

> Then the man who had promised me $5,000 for the flight went back on his word. Disgusted, I left for America, returning home a few months ago. Ganesha came along, too, because I did not suspect anything. No sooner had I landed than I was embroiled in financial disputes, none of them serious, but all annoying and a bit unpleasant. In the past two months I had to see my lawyer about thirty times. Before that I do not remember ever talking over matters with him ten times in a year.
>
> I began to suspect Ganesha. I believe he meant to do the things I accused him of; that is, it seemed that way to me. So I spanked him and set him out as a paper weight, a most humiliating position for one so ancient.

Within a few days after she had banished Ganesha to her desktop, those closest to Harriet began noticing a new charm around her neck: a bolo tie with a silver necklace and the clay head of an ancient Aztec deity, Huehueteotl, the god of fire and creator of all life. She had picked it up during her time in Mexico. The little Aztec god accompanied her on every flight for the rest of her life.

21

WE ACCEPT WHAT WILL BE, WILL BE

WHEN IT OPENED IN 1906, the US Custom House in New York was described in the press as "a fearsome symbol of federal authority" where patience was required to "unravel those coils which bind the goods that enter this port in a maze of red tape." After considerable negotiations, Harriet Quimby finally walked out of the massive new Beaux-Arts building on a late spring day with the correct documentation for her new acquisition.

> My machine, a Bleriot, made in France, arrived at New York on the 21st of May. While going through the details necessary to get the machine through the custom house, I found that, although, as the president of the Aero Club of America states, America is the birthplace of the aeroplane and several of the most famous flyers in the world are native Americans, the United States government has not yet given the subject of the mastery of the air serious consideration. The best proof of this is that the aeroplane has not yet been given the importance of a separate clause in the foreign entry rules for clearage through the custom house. My beautiful and powerful machine of the very latest model was subjected to the indignity of being entered as "a polo pony!"
>
> On a legal appearing paper a customs official wrote a number indicating the legal clause under which the machine was to be

entered. From this department I was sent to the law department to have some technical point approved. The lawyer said something about a pony.

"No, it is not a pony," I said, "it is an aeroplane."

"Well, this number is that of the polo pony clause," returned the lawyer.

I went back to the first department, where the official who had entered the figures opened a book and soon proved that he was not in the wrong. Under the present law the aeroplane simply is not. For some reason the flying machine does not come under the head of motor car or wagon or sleigh. Just why it is "a polo pony" nobody seemed to know, but polo pony it is, or "phantom horse," as William Sweeney, the obliging chief customs official in the foreign department, facetiously termed it.

The new, gleaming white "polo pony," with wings that could be folded or removed altogether, was designed for ease of transport. Harriet arranged for the monoplane to be trucked out to the Moisants' airfield in Mineola and began familiarizing herself with a machine much more powerful than any she had flown. From her time on horses, in automobiles, and in airplanes, Harriet loved to go fast above all else, and her new monoplane was speedy. Louis Blériot created the Blériot Type XI-2 "Artillerie"—a 70-horsepower model featuring two seats, one behind the other—with military applications in mind. But flight controls and aviation technology were not yet keeping pace with advances in horse-power. The Type XI-2 was notoriously difficult to fly due to a center of gravity that had a pronounced forward bias. Nevertheless, Harriet immediately set about learning its quirks before daring to use it for exhibitions.

William Willard and Harriet in the new two-seat Blériot just before takeoff.

In early June, 1912, she took Shakir S. Jerwan, one of her early classmates and the newly installed director of the Moisant Aviation School, for a practice flight in the two-seater over Long Island. He later told her of his concerns about what he observed that morning; the plane could be nose heavy. She assured him if there wasn't a passenger on board she would always put at least 170 pounds of sandbags in the rear seat to equalize the balance. She later decided she disliked the way the sand shifted during maneuvers and vowed to fly the Type XI-2 only with a passenger in the back.

During Harriet's second flight in the Blériot, her scarf escaped her neck and fluttered back, tangling on the rudder. Her passenger, Walter Bonner, impulsively reached back to rescue it with no apparent adverse effect on the stability of the aircraft. Cruising homeward on the return leg of that outing to Mineola, Harriet spotted a plane flown by Cecil Paoli—at eighteen the youngest licensed pilot in America—and, using hand signals to instigate a race, the two lined up in parallel before speeding back to the airfield. Harriet pulled away to cross the imaginary finish line a full length ahead of Cecil, despite her passenger's added weight.

In the third flight in her new machine, the Blériot showed a tendency to misbehave. With sandbags acting as ballast in the rear seat, Harriet was taking the plane higher when the nose shot suddenly upward and the wings dipped sharply to the side. The engine stalled and the plane canted, plummeting powerlessly toward the earth. She remained calm and, rather than fight the spin, she let go of the controls, neutralizing them so the aircraft could find its own flight trim. She may have been thinking of advice she once received from John Moisant:

> If you wish to be a pilot, you must not be of an excitable, nervous disposition. You mustn't be dull nor slow; you must be, above all, a good

> guesser, feeling ahead of time what's going to happen. You cannot tell ahead of time when the bottom is going to drop out of the air and you go plunging down for several feet.

Once her plane settled into a glide, Harriet guided it down to an uneventful landing. When, upon later inspection, she and her mechanic could find nothing out of the ordinary, he chalked the failure up to a quirk of airplanes to sometimes lose their balance in the air, perhaps when hit by a gust of wind. With her cautious nature only exceeded by confidence in her abilities, Harriet declared she was ready to introduce her new airplane to the world at an upcoming air show in Boston.

Four months earlier, *Aero* magazine featured this announcement:

> William A. P. Willard, a member of the executive committee of the 1910 and 1911 aviation meets at Atlantic and father of [pilot] Charles F. Willard, has organized a group of local businessmen for the purpose of holding an aviation meet on the Harvard Aviation field, the scene of Boston's previous meets, from June 29 to July 7 inclusive.

William "Bill" Willard was a forty-eight-year-old electrical engineer by trade who developed a deep fascination with aviation in mid-life. Widowed after thirty years of marriage, he found inspiration in the new science with the help of his oldest son, Charles, a Harvard University graduate and former race-car driver who was one of the first licensed pilots in America. Charles claimed his license at Glenn Curtiss's school and won $250 in the spot-landing contest at the first air meet in the US at Dominguez Field in Los Angeles. His father, a modestly successful businessman but certainly no Andrew Carnegie, discovered a latent skill in finding financial backers among his wide-ranging group of friends and business acquaintances. Bill was also a quick study. The first two air meets he managed were plagued with logistical problems the Boston native was determined to correct.

After raising $8,000 in seed money, he set about finding a suitable venue for the event. He eventually decided on a seven-hundred-acre vacant field at Squantum, near Harvard, jutting out into Boston Harbor between Quincy and Dorchester bays. Surveyors began work at the new site, laying out plans for a half-mile-long, 150-foot-wide runway, a row of hangars that could accommodate twenty airplanes, and an enormous grandstand with seating for ten thousand spectators. The advertised price of admission was twenty-five cents, one dollar for a grandstand seat. Parking in the new three-thousand-space lot would cost one dollar per car. Bill had already received commitments from fifteen pilots, including Lincoln Beachey, Charles C. Witmer, Charles K. Hamilton, and Glenn Martin. But what he really wanted was an appearance by America's brightest new star.

Leo Stevens was well aware of Harriet's value. An ad in *Aeronautics* touting various aviation opportunities listed him as the general manager of the "First Aviatrice in the World to Fly Across the English Channel." He drove a hard bargain with Bill Willard, reportedly guaranteeing Harriet more than $100,000 for her participation, although that seems an unlikely sum given the organizer's slim profit margins. As an additional publicity stunt, Leo convinced the postmaster general to allow Harriet to fly a load of mail from the Harvard meet to New York City on July 7 to mark the end of the air show; this would be yet another first for women flyers.

Before departing for Boston, Harriet confided to some friends that her goal was now to earn enough to retire from such events in order to write novels for a living before the age of thirty-five. "I will [quit] after I make enough money to pay for my aeroplane," she wrote. "I feel awfully poor with the debt hanging over my head." She had accomplished her life's mission of creating a secure financial future for her parents, and the already thirty-seven-year-old was growing weary of the strain of travel and performing. Hardelot, the French resort town near which she landed after her channel crossing, announced it would present its most famous visitor with a bungalow and a large piece of ground in which she could settle down and work on her books.

Warm, sunny skies and thousands of spectators heralded the opening day of the Squantum Aviation Meet on June 29, 1912. Unfortunately, for Bill Willard and his fellow investors, many of the fans chose to stay outside the fence and watch for free; this was a common frustration for air-show organizers. Bill was in the middle of a quarrel with the Aero Club of America, the official sanctioning body, because the promoters were unable to guarantee prize money. The club suspended a number of pilots for participating in the meet. Still, he was heartened to see the grandstand eventually filling up and the good weather holding. It was the first time that most in the crowd laid eyes on a flying machine. A columnist for *Outlook* magazine captured the novel atmosphere:

> An aeroplane close at hand makes more noise than anything of its size in creation. Take a motor bicycle, a rolling mill, and a buzz saw, and blend them, and you get something like it. It makes an aeroplane, like a peacock, an undesirable neighbor, in spite of its other charms. But, unlike the peacock, the aeroplane does not stay in one place with its noise. Its mechanicians whirl the arms of the propellers and start them revolving, fast, faster, faster. The birdman steps into his seat and gives the signal—the wheels begin to run on the grass, the mechanicians are left kicked in a heap by the recoil, and suddenly, from the grass, the wheels lift a bit and, taking hold on the air, at once run lightly up into it, and, Lo! The plane is half a mile off before one can say Jack Robinson.

The first day of the meet saw pilots performing spot-landing competitions, aerobatics, flybys, and flour bombing demonstrations. Those with airplanes large enough, including Harriet and her new two-seater, took paying customers for short joy flights. When not in the air, she posed for photographs with fans and talked to the dozens of reporters who were following her every move. As she leaned against her machine, one asked her about the dangers of engine failure while flying over a body of water such as the harbor. She said,

> A water landing is alright in a Blériot, unless you come down head first. In that case, the heavy motor at the extreme forward end of the machine would drag the monoplane deep into the water and sink it. But if we came down "pancake" the broad wings would float us for two hours or more.

"But," she added with a brilliant smile, "I am a cat—and I don't like cold water." She then announced to the surprise of the assembled journalists that she was going to attempt to break Claude Grahame-White's speed record later that week.

Turning to a new acquaintance, fellow journalist Gertrude Stevenson of the *Boston Herald*, Harriet said, "I'll be back in 20 minutes to get you, you'll have to hurry and get into your togs." Her intention was to first make a test flight over Dorchester Bay to the Boston Light and back, which was the route she would take in the record attempt, and then chauffeur Gertrude up for a pleasure ride.

"From the moment that I was introduced to Miss Quimby any lack of confidence I might have had [in the safety of flying] was immediately dispelled," Gertrude later wrote.

> Never have I seen a more fearless, confidence-inspiring person in my life. Her expressive, intelligent gray eyes just commanded confidence. If she had the slightest fear she gave absolutely no sign of it. There wasn't a trace of doubt or uncertainty in her manner.

"You know," Harriet said to her, "this thing will make dandy cable news. I suppose that you are the first woman passenger to fly with a woman pilot. That's good enough news to be cabled all over Europe."

Gertrude joked that that she would get a good story out of the trip, and Harriet countered with a wink that she would as well. Turning serious, the *Herald* reporter asked, "How did you ever dare to get into the game?" Harriet replied,

> It really doesn't take half as much courage as you'd think. And I know that instead of being at all afraid you'll just love the flying and will probably be anxious to go up with me again. I had run a motor car for several years in all kinds of traffic and one day at an aviation meet it suddenly dawned on me that driving a car and an aeroplane was one and the same thing—the only difference being the vehicle. I determined to drive an aeroplane as soon as I could learn.

Then, almost as a premonition, she added,

> You'll have to keep still in the machine. I don't suppose you'll want to move around very much. But then it doesn't make any particular difference except that it might affect the balance of the monoplane.

The *Boston Herald* reporter's account continued from there:

> Miss Quimby jumped lightly into her seat in the monoplane and with familiar and skilled fingers began to work on the various pieces of mechanism of the steering wheel. Some man in the crowd remarked that "she had a devil of a nerve," and more than one declared that they wouldn't be hired to go up in the machine. The women about frankly confessed that they would give anything to go. They crowded about me, declaring that they wished they might have my chance and asking me if I realized how lucky I was at being chosen for a trip. I admitted that safe in the office I had been much more keen on the trip than I was now with the whirr of the motor being tried on in my ears.
>
> Miss Quimby turned to me quick as a flash.
>
> "You're not afraid, are you?" she asked, and looked at me searchingly, "because I have never taken anyone up who was afraid."
>
> I laughed and declared it was natural that I should have some qualms.
>
> "You'll just love it when you get up there." She assured me again. "Tie your veil around your bonnet good and tight because there's an awful rush of wind, a sixty-miles-an-hour wind up there, and if your bonnet isn't tied on tight you'll lose it."

Gertrude stepped back and watched as Harriet finished her meticulous preparations, marveling that

> she was laughing all the time—for the photographers—to her friends, giving good-natured directions, and apparently as much at home in the hollow of that monoplane as any girl would have been in her own room. For me it was love at first sight. She fascinated me by her skill and cleverness and unconscious bravery. In spite of the fact that she was the center of attraction, admiration and breathless wonder, she was as unconscious of it all and as unaffected as any one could possibly be.

The chief mechanic, a man only referred to in press accounts as Mr. Hardy, made one last inspection of the warping mechanism and wire connections under the plane's carriage and emerged, announcing everything looked fine. Helpers wheeled the Blériot out of the hangar area and onto the runway as five thousand spectators looked on, buzzing in anticipation.

It was either Harriet or Leo who invited the beleaguered meet promoter, Bill Willard, to come along as passenger. They were well aware of the financial anxiety he was under, with gate receipts coming in far under expectations. Bill turned to his youngest son, Harry, who was equally eager to fly in the new Blériot, and proposed they flip a coin for the honor. The father won the toss.

He was a large man, tipping the scales at two hundred pounds or more. Friends described him as somewhat spontaneous in his enthusiasms. As the assembled crowd teased the widower about venturing skyward for the first time with such a beautiful guide, Leo stepped close and warned him to "sit tight" once they were in the air lest he throw off the plane's balance.

"Willard's getting his flight at last," someone said.

Harriet signaled for the four men holding her machine to the ground to let go, and "as easily and gracefully as a great powerful bird the monoplane rose up in the air." Her watch showed 5:30 P.M.

Not yet twelve pages of the calendar had been turned since Harriet Quimby achieved her pilot's license, but even her fiercest competitors admitted she was a natural in the air, as competent and intuitive a pilot as anyone who ever escaped the grasp of gravity. Despite a handful of close calls, she was one of the few aviators who had not suffered a serious accident. Harriet attributed this to an obsession with checking every bolt and wire of her airplane prior to takeoff and a supreme confidence in her training.

The Blériot Type XI-2 cut through a mild breeze on its way east toward the Boston Light on Little Brewster Island, with the late-day sun glinting off its white wings. Harriet made a gentle turn around the nation's first lighthouse and eased the throttle forward, picking up speed for the downwind portion of the twenty-minute trip.

"It was one of the most beautiful performances I ever saw Miss Quimby or any other aviator make," Leo remembered.

> At all times... she had the Blériot under splendid control. As the speck grew larger and larger until the dragonfly outline of the Blériot again shaped itself against the blue sky we could see that Miss Quimby was coming down, flying at a speed of about eighty-five miles per hour.

The monoplane reached the edge of the airfield at three thousand feet. Harriet put it into a wide circle to bleed off altitude before entering her approach path at about one thousand feet over the tidal flats.

At that moment, Ursula and William Quimby were on their way to Grand Central Station in New York City to catch a train to Boston, in anticipation of watching their daughter set the new world-record for speed the following day.

At that moment, Matilde Moisant, newly retired from flying, was probably sitting down to dinner at the family hacienda, Santa Emilia, in El Salvador.

At that moment, reporter Gertrude Stevenson, wrestling on her flying togs inside a dressing room, heard "cries of horror."

Five thousand pairs of eyes watched as the monoplane bucked suddenly, its nose veering hard toward the earth, its tail shooting straight up as if a giant finger flicked it violently. Recalled Leo, "The next instant we saw a body hurl itself upwards out of the machine, apparently leaping fifty feet in the air, describe an arc, then come plunging downward well ahead of the monoplane." Unsure of what they were witnessing, the crowd grew hushed for a split second. Then came the screams of realization as William A. P. Willard began to fall.

Harriet wrestled with the now-unstable Blériot. With the plane suddenly freed of its two-hundred-pound ballast, she was in a losing battle against physics and gravity. For the briefest of instants, the pilot righted the machine and it appeared she would regain control. But there came a violent shudder, and the monoplane dipped again, its tail flung into a perpendicular position, before turning completely upside down.

Bill Willard had not yet hit the water when Harriet, too, was catapulted from the plane, arched clear, and began to fall, her purple flight suit silhouetted against the setting sun. Both bodies reached terminal velocity within seconds, before slamming into the concrete-hard tidal flats two-hundred feet from shore and sinking deeply into the mud. The monoplane followed closely behind. Having rid itself of the two passengers, it regained its flight trim and descended "in gentle spirals until the wheels touched the water and flipped it over on its back relatively undamaged."

Watching in horror from the shore, Leo cried out and collapsed. Harriet's close friend Carrie Vanderbilt fell prostrate to the ground.

"My God, they're killed!" yelled a man. Harry Willard rushed to the shore and desperately slogged forward in the shallow waters before being restrained by a member of the signal corps. "Let me go!" he cried. "I want to save my father!"

Sixteen-year-old Myron Savage and his friend were watching the air show from his father's rowboat in Dorchester Bay when they saw the two fliers fall not one hundred feet away. He quickly rowed over to the rescuers wading out to where Harriet lay embedded in the mud. "They placed her body in my boat," he recalled sixty-seven years later. "I took it to a nearby wharf where the men took her ashore. Needless to say it was a

Harriet's lifeless body being carried to shore.

dreadful experience for me, and in all the years since I have never forgotten it." Photographs show Harriet was completely limp in the arms of a rescuer, her satin jumper torn and muddy.

As a crowd of spectators surged forward, ghoulishly intent on reaching the downed flyers and the airplane, corpsmen and state police brought in to help with security began bludgeoning some of them to push them back. Amid the chaotic scene, volunteers carried Harriet and Bill to dry ground and resuscitation efforts began. It took only moments for the doctor and two nurses to realize they were gone. Autopsies showed they both had multiple potentially fatal injuries, including broken limbs, skulls, and backs. There was water in Bill's lungs, indicating he may have drowned. The coroner stated Harriet likely died on impact with the shallow water. The watch that graced her wrist on the channel crossing was frozen at the moment of her death: ten minutes past six.

Blanche Stuart Scott, who was in the air at the time, witnessed the entire event. The stampeding crowd preventing her from immediately landing. "A dozen people would have been cut down by my propeller," she recalled. "They were running in every direction, all over the field." When she finally found a clear section of ground, she put her biplane down, rolled to a stop, and fainted.

"If aviators choose to stay in the game," Blanche later mused, "the reality is we may die. We all know this and that's why all flyers are fatalists. We accept what will be, will be."

EPILOGUE:
Something tells me that I shall do something some day

ON THE EVENING OF July 4, 1912, services for Harriet Quimby were held at the funeral parlor of Frank E. Campbell in downtown Manhattan. In attendance were William and Ursula Quimby, high society's biggest names, dozens of reporters from around the world, representatives from the Italian Club and the New York chapter of the Aero Club of America, her friends and coworkers from *Leslie's Illustrated Weekly*, and close friends Carrie Vanderbilt, Linda Arvidson, and Leo Stevens. Her mother stood at the entrance and handed out a single rose to every visitor to place on her daughter's casket. Harriet was attired in a simple white dress, which she purchased days before for an aviation luncheon in her honor. Earlier, while her body rested in the morgue, souvenir seekers made away with her satin flying costume and antique jewelry. "And I wanted the Smithsonian to have them!" Ursula sobbed to a reporter. The Aztec necklace, too, disappeared, either left behind in the muck of Dorchester Bay or spirited away in the hands of a thief.

The Reverend James B. Wasson took to the podium and read from the Book of Revelation. "Her name is added to the long list of those who have freely given their lives in order that the world might be larger and better," he intoned,

> in order that life might be greater and grander. But, in our sorrow tonight, there rests still a joyous note of triumph. For we realize that through this death there has come progress and that, therefore, Miss Quimby's life was a victory over those very elements which at the end brought on her tragic end. For through such as she was, do we reach near and nearer to the far-off goal of our hope.

He then concluded the service by reciting Harriet's favorite psalm:

> The Lord is my shepherd; I shall not want. He maketh me to lie down in green pastures: he leadeth me beside the still waters. He restoreth my soul: he leadeth me in the paths of righteousness for his name's sake. Yea, though I walk through the valley of death, I will fear no evil.

In the days that followed it seemed to many still in grief that within minutes of the accident there was an unseemly flurry of opinions put forth about why it happened. Some blamed Harriet. Pilot Lincoln Beachey suggested she lost consciousness while in flight.

> I had a hunch that something was going to happen on that flight. I am almost positive that Miss Quimby fainted while she was in the air. She was coming down at a high rate of speed and her semi-conscious control caused the machine to lurch. When she recovered it was too late.

Mr. Hardy, Harriet's mechanic, fiercely rejected any suggestions of equipment failure and instead believed she came down at "too steep a glide. The machine lost its balance." A cruel rumor spread that Bill Willard, distraught over his wife's death and the financial strains of the air show, leapt to his death, thus destabilizing the aircraft.

America's first airmail pilot, Earle Ovington, was one of the first people to arrive at the fallen Blériot after the accident. What he saw there led him to conclude the accident was caused by a flaw in the aircraft's design. He sent a letter to *Scientific American* stating,

> When we reached the wreck, I scrambled on top of it, and the first thing I saw was the rudder wire caught over the lower end of the warping lever. If you examine my sketch, you will see that by the wire catching as indicated the rudder would be thrown to the left and the monoplane turned toward the left as it plunged downward.

Engineers later speculated what Earle noticed could have been a result of the accident itself, rather than a cause.

It took some time, but Leo Stevens eventually pulled himself together enough to write a defense of Harriet in the journal *Aeronautics*:

> The tragic deaths of Miss Harriet Quimby and William A. P. Willard, who fell in midair from Miss Quimby's Bleriot monoplane at Boston, July 1st, have aroused universal speculation on the cause of that most unfortunate mishap.
>
> Out of all the maze of conflicting opinions two or three seem to have gained preeminence over all the others: that something "went wrong" with some factor in the monoplane control or machinery; that a sudden wind-puff whipped it out of Miss Quimby's control, or that Miss Quimby became a victim of sudden mental panic, or even fainted.
>
> Knowing as I do the machine's condition before the flight, I discard the first theory. Knowing Miss Quimby as I did, I emphatically reject the third theory. The second theory I consider so purely speculative that I cannot seriously entertain it.

Leo then went on to place the blame squarely on the shoulders of Harriet's passenger.

> My last warning to Willard, before he entered the machine and even after he had climbed aboard was not to leave his seat under any circumstances. This warning I was very particular to give because I knew him to be a man of sudden impulses. I was fearful lest under sudden impulse and effervescing enthusiasm he should suddenly lean from his seat to communicate with Miss Quimby. This I knew would be an exceedingly dangerous thing to do. But I received his assurance that he would "sit tight."
>
> Now then, this is what I believe really happened. I believe that as the flight drew to its conclusion, Willard, enthusiastic over Miss Quimby's splendid performance, for a moment forgot the danger of moving, and suddenly stretched forward over the deck to shout a word of congratulations.
>
> Miss Quimby, unable to see what was going on behind her, had no warning of Willard's movement until his shifted weight caused the machine to dip and the tail to flip upward. That same flip of the tail, I believe, threw Willard into the air. That theory is based upon my knowledge of the machine and my close personal acquaintance with Miss Quimby and Willard and their personal characteristics.
>
> That Miss Quimby even for an instant lost her head is disproven by her instantaneous attempt to right the machine. Not only as her manager but as a close personal friend, I know her to be a woman of great coolness and judgment and an operator of extraordinary ability. With Willard's weight gone—a weight absolutely necessary to the control of the monoplane—she was pitted against a circumstance over which no aviator, no human ingenuity, or knowledge, or skill or practice could have control.

For Leo Stevens, whose life's mission was to create safety equipment for aviators, it must have been heart wrenching to realize a simple device—seat belts—could have saved Harriet and Bill. These were not yet in widespread usage, as some pilots considered such "straps" would prevent them from leaping free of their aircraft in the event of a crash. But Harriet herself seemed in favor of them. A month before her accident she authored an article in *Leslie's* about aviation improvements; it featured a photograph of a pilot wearing a harness-type restraint. To this day, the question of whether Harriet and Bill were strapped into the plane remains unanswered, but the evidence argues against it.

Almost immediately, the Squantum Aviation Meet tragedy was seized upon by critics of female flyers as proof the sky was no place for them. "The sport is not one for which women are physically qualified," wrote the editor of the *New York Sun*.

> As a rule, they lack strength, presence of mind, and the courage to excel as aviators. It is essentially a man's sport and pastime. In the world's now long list of aviation fatalities, none has caused more profound grief than the tragic demise of Harriet Quimby.

"Women are temperamentally unfit for flight because they are prone to panic," Claude Grahame-White opined. "When calamity overtakes women pupils as eventually I fear it will, I shall feel in a way responsible for their sudden decease."

With the most prominent voice of women's involvement in aviation now silenced, the condescension went largely unchallenged until, decades later, one of the most famous pilots in history said of Harriet,

Flying over the salt marshes moments before the accident.
William Willard is visible in the rear seat.

> Without any of the modern instruments, in a plane which was hardly more than a winged skeleton with a motor, and one, furthermore, with which she was totally unfamiliar, to cross the Channel in 1912 required more bravery and skill than to cross the Atlantic today. Always we must remember that, in thinking of America's first great woman flier's accomplishment.

Those words were spoken by none other than Amelia Earhart.

John A. Sleicher, the editor at *Leslie's Illustrated Weekly* who first spotted Harriet's journalistic talent and who later encouraged her aviation career, penned a heartfelt tribute two weeks after her funeral. "A brilliant light in the literary firmament has been extinguished," it began. "She firmly believed in aeronautics as crucial for the progress of the century, and gave her young life as sacrifice to a sense of duty." Only weeks earlier, Harriet named John executor of her estate.

Sometime later, while cleaning Harriet's desk at *Leslie's*, a newspaper staffer discovered one of her unfinished articles. At the top was written a single word: lost!

> Nobody likes to be lost. There is a wretchedness about it most pathetic. Our hearts go out to the lost child, we join in the search for the missing, whether we be strangers or neighbors. The instinct to go to the rescue is always the same.
>
> It is a new experience to be lost in the sky, but it is as real and trying as to be lost in the midst of earth's wilderness or on the infinite expanse of the waters of the sea. I speak with knowledge. Twice I have been lost in the sky while driving a monoplane.
>
> The sense of loneliness and helplessness one feels while driving a thousand feet above the earth in a swiftly moving monoplane, with nothing but the everlasting sky above and the horizon around

> and with no signs of recognition from the distant earth below, is overwhelming and indescribable. One can do nothing but look and hope. One must drive on.

One must drive on. From a failed Midwest farm, to an unknown future in California, to a tradition-busting career in journalism, to the heights of human achievement. One must drive on.

"Stricken before her mission was fulfilled," wrote the poet, Lilita Lever Younge in 1913, saying Harriet lost her life "in the realm of air she loved with all her dauntless heart, fearless, with steady hand upon the helm, in life's last drama played the hero's part."

The world continued to circle around the sun. Aviation continued to evolve and become more of a fixture in twentieth-century society as technology and the understanding of aeronautics improved. Woodrow Wilson became the twenty-eighth president of the United States, the first president to fly in an airplane while in office. Bulgarian pilots Radul Minkov and Prodan Toprakchiev successfully introduced airplanes into warfare by bombing a railway station in Turkey. And Matilde Moisant, after being rejected as a fighter pilot in WWI because of her gender, served out the war as a volunteer Red Cross nurse. As the news media focused on fighting in Europe and steady advances in aviation, the name Harriet Quimby was forgotten by all but those who knew the woman who broke so many barriers. Seven years after her death, Clara Bell Brown published this appreciation in *Leslie's*:

> It is with a peculiar pleasure that I record some of the unknown incidents of the life of Harriet Quimby, who, had her career not terminated so early, would have been a woman "ace."
>
> I first met her in San Francisco.... My manager said: "I will send you a reporter." The next day, at the hour appointed, a sweet-faced

young girl stepped in.... She was shabbily dressed in black, and the thin silk bows on her hat were dusty. But her qualities as an interviewer soon drew a veil over her shabbiness; and when she left, she had won me. There was a shrewd but joyous satire—a native wit—qualified by a courtesy and dignity that must have been born in her, for, as I grew to know her well—and love her well—I never saw her without both attributes....

She lived in one large attic room, in a business building with no elevator. She had divided the barnlike apartment into a sleeping-room for her parents, a little corner for the inevitable oil cooker; and the main part was her own domain.... Nothing could hide or adorn the poverty of that attic. But nothing could hide or adorn the proud silence with which she dwelt there.... And amid all the squalor of the home surroundings, Harriet came and went with the serene air of one favored by the gods.

"Something tells me that I shall do something some day," she said. And so it was to be....

Then began the part of her career, that reads like an old tale of adventure. She began to fly. And—the shop girl, extra girl, space writer, and artist's model flew in France, made much money; received lands and gold; won the prize for flying across the English Channel, and was the most famous woman flyer in the world. At this time Miss Quimby was on the staff of LESLIE'S.

One day I was pondering upon her wonderful career. I picked up the evening paper, and on the first page—a place she had ardently desired—was the face of the girl I had known and loved, in her flying costume and beneath, the story of her fall to death.

Harriet Quimby was young, brave, patient and courageous. She was of the stuff that gives heroines to the world.

That summer night before she took the train to Boston, Harriet sat at her desk in the Hotel Victoria to tie up some loose ends, perhaps pay a few bills, finish an article, maybe even respond to fan mail. It's not hard to imagine she thought of her elderly parents as they slept in the next room, of the family's long, difficult, unlikely journey together from poverty to providence, invisibility to international acclaim. She scribbled a handwritten note Ursula found a few days later. "If bad luck should befall me," it read in part, "I want you to know that I will meet my fate rejoicing."

ACKNOWLEDGMENTS

I FIRST STUMBLED ON the story of Harriet Quimby almost three decades ago while reading an obscure aviation magazine. It was stunning to me that someone who accomplished so much was virtually lost to history because of a cruel and horrific twist of fate. I tracked down a few good articles from the 1980s, such as Terry Gwynn-Jones's excellent "For a Brief Moment the World Seemed Wild about Harriet" in *Smithsonian* and Weston George's "Beauty and the Bleriot" in *Aviation Quarterly* but, for the most part, Harriet's name was almost absent from the national press in the years after WWI. She was mentioned in a few books about aviation history, but no major account of her fascinating life had yet been published. A screenplay I wrote about her was optioned by a Hollywood producer but, as often happens, it never made it to production. So the boxes of research went into storage until the day I was ready to tackle a thorough biography of this amazing woman and her times.

It was a phone conversation in the winter of 2020 with my literary agent, Claudia Cross, that convinced me the time was right. We were bouncing around a few ideas for what would be my next novel when I mentioned Harriet. Without hesitation, Claudia declared that should be our project. A few weeks later, Lynn Grady of Princeton Architectural Press responded to our proposal with an enthusiasm and passion that have never wavered. Thank you, Lynn, for believing, and for your wonderful guidance. Thank you, Claudia, for putting us together.

In addition, I'd like to express my appreciation and admiration to Doris Rich for her excellent book about the Moisant family, *The Magnificent Moisants*; Eileen Lebow for her fascinating tales of the earliest female pilots, *Before Amelia*; Gavin Mortimer for the riveting account of the seventeen days in 1910 that changed aviation, *Chasing Icarus*; Terry Gwynn Jones for numerous books about the first pilots and planes; and authors Leslie Kerr, Ed. Y. Hall, Sterling Brown, Henry Holden, and Giacinta Bradley Koontz for their hard work and devotion to the woman we all admire so much. I am especially indebted to Giacinta for her compilation of photos and documents contained in *The Harriet Quimby Scrapbook*. Sadly, she passed away in March 2020, still working to see Harriet get her due.

Mike Wallace's excellent *Greater Gotham* supplied fascinating descriptions of the New York City Harriet chose as her ultimate home. It is dense with detail and incredibly entertaining.

Thank you to Susan Brinchman, author of *Gustave Whitehead: First in Flight*, for her great research and help.

Professor Emeritus Francis X. Blouin Jr. of the University of Michigan gave invaluable guidance and insight into life in Michigan for the early pioneers and fact checked that section of this book.

Anna Koether, you're an angel for putting in so many hours proofreading an early version of the manuscript.

Clare Jacobson and Kristen Hewitt, your deft copyediting, gentle corrections, and insightful suggestions were invaluable. Credit also goes to the very talented art director Paul Wagner and marketing director Kim Dayman, who made this book look so good and brought it to as many readers as possible.

Joan Mathys, I can't thank you enough for your detective work in tracking down some of the rarer images of Harriet and the other fearless heroes of her time.

Kate Igoe, of the Smithsonian National Air and Space Museum, was kind and incredibly helpful in finding the collection's archival photographs.

Maile Ramzi and Richard Houpert told me so many wonderful stories about their grandfather, André Houpert, and generously added to the collection of historic photographs in this book.

Siobhan Dee of the National Film and Sound Archive of Australia patiently guided me through the acquisition and rights process for the movie stills of Harriet's channel flight.

I'd also like to thank the digital archival teams of the Smithsonian National Air and Space Museum, the Library of Congress, *New York Times, Boston Globe,* Newspapers.com, and Accessible Archives, without whom this book would not be possible.

Finally, my deepest gratitude goes to Katie, Callie, and Jack for their support and patience. Living with an obsessed writer can seem like being in a haunted house; you know someone's there, but the appearances are rare. Love you guys, much and more.

NOTES

Prologue: If you are afraid, you shall never succeed

11. *Not even a heartbreaking:* Terry Gwynn-Jones, "For a Brief Moment the World Seemed Wild about Harriet," *Smithsonian* (January 1984).

11. *A spindly frame made out of ash:* Charles B. Ragnaud, "Bleriot Monoplane," *Practical Aeronautics* (1912), 727–57.

13. *"Take a motor bicycle":* "First Impressions of the Aero Meet," *Outlook* (October 21, 1911).

13. *Not yet a decade had passed:* Orville Wright, "Telegram from Orville Wright in Kitty Hawk, North Carolina, to His Father Announcing Four Successful Flights" (1903), World Digital Library, Wdl.org.

13. *Rickety wood-and-linen airplanes:* Joshua Stoff, *Picture History of Early Aviation* (New York: Dover Publications, 1996), 118–23.

13. *The year before:* Gwynn-Jones, "For a Brief Moment."

13. *Attendance at air shows:* Weston George, "Beauty and the Bleriot: The Story of Harriet Quimby, Pioneer Aviatrix," *Aviation Quarterly* (1980), 61.

13. *Fliers could earn:* Gavin Mortimer, *Chasing Icarus: The Seventeen Days in 1910 That Forever Changed American Aviation* (New York: Walker Publishing, 2009), 193.

13. *"There's another good man":* Doris L. Rich, *The Magnificent Moisants: Champions of Early Flight* (Washington, DC: Smithsonian Institution Press, 1998), 98.

14. *The first air show:* "Explorers, Daredevils, and Record Setters—An Overview," Centennial of Flight, https://www.centennialofflight.net/essay/Explorers_Record_Setters_and_Daredevils/EX_OV.htm.

14. *One of those was named:* David Langley, "The Life and Times of Glenn Hammond Curtiss," The Aviation History Online Museum, last modified November 18, 2009, http://aviation-history.com/early/curtiss.htm.

16. *"a brilliant smile":* Gwynn-Jones. "For a Brief Moment."

16. *Among many:* Ed. Y. Hall, *Harriet Quimby: America's First Lady of the Air* (Spartanburg, SC: Honoribus Press, 1993), 35.

16. *No one who enjoyed:* Hall, *Harriet Quimby: America's First Lady of the Air*, 20.

16. *"The wings of a flying machine":* Harriet Quimby, "A Japanese Aeronaut to Startle the World," *Leslie's Illustrated Weekly* (August 5, 1909).

17. *"If you are afraid":* Leslie Kerr, *Harriet Quimby: Flying Fair Lady* (Atglen, PA: Schiffer Publishing, 2016), 42, 43.

Chapter 1: A tomboy full of verve and spunk

21. *A member of a large Irish:* Giacinta Bradley Koontz, *The Harriet Quimby*

Scrapbook (Prescott, AZ: Running Iron Publications, 2003), 7.
21. *The unlikely pair:* Wedding certificate of William and Ursula Quimby, dated October 9, 1859, Branch County Records.
21. *William enlisted:* Samuel S. Whitt, "Miss Harriet Quimby," *National Aeronautics* (1973).
21. *On his enlistment letter:* US Army Clerk. "Volunteer Enlistment" *Military record,* 1864.
21. *William's unit found:* Frederick Phisterer, *New York in the War of the Rebellion 1861–1865* (Albany: J. B. Lyon, 1912), 290.
22. *A few more bloody:* William Quimby's Pension File, 1895, US Government Archives.
22. *188th received the honor:* Joe Servis, "The Surrender Meeting," National Park Service, updated August 6, 2020, https://www.nps.gov/apco/learn/historyculture/the-surrender-meeting.htm.
22. *William managed to survive:* Leslie Kerr, *Harriet Quimby: Flying Fair Lady* (Atglen, PA: Schiffer Publishing, 2016), 9.
22. *Of the 370,000:* Phisterer, *New York in the War,* 22.
22. *Some 800,000 soldiers:* Frank D. Lewis and Claudia D. Goldin, "The Economic Cost of the American Civil War: Estimates and Implications," *Journal of Economic History* (1975): 304.
23. *"Conquering, holding":* Walt Whitman, *Leaves of Grass* (Brooklyn: James and Andrew Rome, 1865), 183, https://whitmanarchive.org/published/LG/figures/ppp.00707.191.jpg.
23. *William and Ursula:* William Quimby's Pension File.
23. *The only condition:* "Homestead Act, 1862," Our Documents, https://www.ourdocuments.gov/document_data/document_info_text/document_031_description.html.
23. *Tall Michigan white pines:* Francis X. Blouin Jr., email to author, November 14, 2020.
24. *"We were hungry":* Roger Rosentreter, *Michigan: A History of Explorers* (Ann Arbor: University of Michigan Regional, 2013), 81.
24. *The most agonizingly vexing pest:* Blouin email to author.
24. *He spent his days:* Daniel Stewart, "The Diary of Daniel Stewart," https://web.archive.org/web/20160609080701/http://www.macombhistory.us/adl/3501_Diaryfrm_bgn%201872-75.pdf.
25. *Between three and nine:* Kerr, *Harriet Quimby,* 9.
25. *A massive fire in 1871:* Bradley Koontz, *Harriet Quimby Scrapbook,* 4.
26. *In scribbled handwriting:* Census of Arcadia, Michigan, 1880, US Census Archives.
26. *"tomboy full of verve":* Hall, *Harriet Quimby,* 19.
26. *Judd Calkins, who grew up:* Ibid., 193.
27. *In 1880:* Bradley Koontz, *Harriet Quimby Scrapbook,* 6.
28. *William finally began:* Whitt, "Miss Harriet Quimby."
28. *Independent Order of Odd Fellows:* Bradley Koontz, *Harriet Quimby Scrapbook,* 7.
28. *By 1884, the Quimbys had had enough:* Kerr, *Harriet Quimby,* 10.
28. *A stagecoach took:* Ibid.
29. *"A California woman":* Elizabeth Anna Semple. "Harriet Quimby, America's First Woman Aviator," *Overland Monthly* (1911).
29. *She eventually claimed:* Whitt, "Miss Harriet Quimby."
29. *The days in Arroyo Grande:* NOAA. *National Centers for Environmental Information.*
29. *Chicago Yeast Powder:* "Be It Remembered," Vanderburgh County Records and Archives, https://vanderburghcountyclerkrecordsandarchives.wordpress.com/2016/09/06/groceries-notions-flour-and-feed-in-1890/.
29. *Terrifyingly high, 171-foot-long:* "Swinging Bridge," California Highway 1 Discovery Route, https://highway1discoveryroute.com/activities/swinging-bridge/.

30. *The West finally bid:* "America at the Turn of the Century: A Look at the Historical Context" (Early Films of New York, 1898–1906).
30. *"from sea to shining sea:"* Katharine Lee Bates, *America the Beautiful and Other Poems* (New York: Thomas Y. Crowell, 1911), 4.
30. *It began in the wheat fields:* David O. Whitten, "The Depression of 1893," EH.net, posted January 2021, https://eh.net/?s=The+Depression+of+1893.
30. *Philadelphia and Reading Railroad:* James L. Holton, *The Reading Railroad: History of a Coal Age Empire* (Laury's Station, PA: Garrigues House, 1989).
31. *A quarter of Pennsylvanians:* Gerald Parshall, "The Great Panic of '93," *U.S. News & World Report* (1992).
31. *William's pension application:* Bradley Koontz, *Harriet Quimby Scrapbook*, 11.

Chapter 2:
Weaving spiders come not here

32. *From about the time:* "Early San Francisco History," HiddenSF, http://www.hiddensf.com/400-san-francisco-attractions/brief-early-san-francisco-history.html.
33. *One such particularly horrific:* Edgar Myron Kahn, "Andrew Smith Hallidie" (June 1940), The Museum of the City of San Francisco, https://www.sfmuseum.org/bio/hallidie.html.
33. *Like 1899's mercurial:* "America at the Turn of the Century: A Look at the Historical Context" (Early Films of New York, 1898–1906).
33. *not much better than a hovel:* Leslie Kerr, *Harriet Quimby: Flying Fair Lady* (Atglen, PA: Schiffer Publishing, 2016), 12.
34. *From the moment:* "Early San Francisco History."
34. *and certainly one could be forgiven:* Annabel Fenwick Elliott, "Rare Nineteenth-Century Photos Offer a Glimpse into Everyday Life in America's First Chinatown," *Daily Mail*, 2017.
34. *A map from 1885:* Willard B. Farwell, "Farwell's Map of Chinatown in San Francisco," https://commons.wikimedia.org/wiki/File:Willard_B._Farwell,_Official_Map_of_Chinatown_1885,_Cornell_CUL_PJM_1093_01.jpg.
34. *She slapped a fresh coat:* Hugh Powell, "Harriet Quimby: America's First Woman Pilot," *AAHS Journal* (1982).
34. *William's curriculum vitae:* Ed. Y. Hall, *Harriet Quimby: America's First Lady of the Air* (Spartanburg, SC: Honoribus Press, 1993), 18.
34. *Articles from as recently:* Powell, "Harriet Quimby."
35. *Thanks to her good old:* Samuel S. Whitt. "Miss Harriet Quimby," *National Aeronautics* (1973).
35. *Harriet pitched in:* Giacinta Bradley Koontz, *The Harriet Quimby Scrapbook* (Prescott, AZ: Running Iron Publications, 2003), 16.
35. *It's also likely:* Terry Gwynn-Jones, *Aviation's Magnificent Gamblers* (Sydney: Landsdowne Press, 1981), 10.
35. *"Weaving spiders come":* Peter Martin Phillips, "A Relative Advantage: Sociology of the San Francisco Bohemian Club" (University of California, Davis, 1994).
35. *Although originally established:* Albert Parry, *Garretts & Pretenders: A History of Bohemianism in America* (Cosimo, 2005), 13.
36. *Numbered among the early:* Kerr, *Harriet Quimby*, 13.
36. *Rumors of "bawdy gatherings":* Bradley Koontz, *Harriet Quimby Scrapbook*, 17.
36. *she sat for a nude portrait:* Kerr, *Harriet Quimby*, 26
36. *later accounts claimed:* Elizabeth Anna Semple, "Harriet Quimby, America's First Woman Aviator," *Overland Monthly* (1911).
37. *a network of hundreds:* Thomas Postlewait, *The Cambridge History*

of American Theatre, vol. 2, *1970–1945* (Cambridge, UK: Cambridge University Press, 1999).

37. *"O, speak again, bright angel . . ."*: William Shakespeare, "The Tragedy of Romeo and Juliet (1594)," OpenSource Shakespeare, last updated 2021, https://www.opensourceshakespeare.org/views/plays/playmenu.php?WorkID=romeojuliet.

37. *The young actress playing:* Bradley Koontz, *Harriet Quimby Scrapbook*, 76.

38. *Harriet was working:* Kerr, *Harriet Quimby*, 13.

38. *They would remain:* Bradley Koontz, *Harriet Quimby Scrapbook*.

39. *Still pathetically short:* Mrs. D. W. Griffith [Linda Arvidson], *When the Movies Were Young* (New York: E. P. Dutton & Company, 1925), 10.

39. *Phelan was also:* Robert W. Cherny, "City Commercial, City Beautiful, City Practical: The San Francisco Visions of William C. Ralston, James D. Phelan, and Michael M. O'Shaughnessy," *California History* 73: 4 (1994).

39. *But on that day:* Griffith, *When the Movies.*

39. *From the* San Francisco Chronicle*:* Bradley Koontz, *Harriet Quimby Scrapbook*, 23.

40. *"the recital didn't"*: Griffith, *When the Movies*, 11.

40. *Harriet made a few:* Jean Patriquin, letter to Mrs. Gregory, 1934, UCLA Special Collections Library.

Chapter 3:
Why, I just began to write

41. *a low voice and a brilliant smile"*: Bonnie R. Ginger, ". . . So Easy Now to Learn . . . ," [possibly] *World* (1911).

41. *He was to become:* Robert V. Hudson, *The Writing Game: A Biography of Will Irwin* (Ames, IA: Iowa State University Press, 1989).

42. *"Slowly but surely"*: Harriet Quimby, "The Artists' Colony at Monterey," *San Francisco Sunday Call*, October 1, 1901.

44. *"Why, I just began to write"*: Ibid.

44. *"Two o'clock in the morning"*: Harriet Quimby, "A Day with the Fishermen," Bradley Koontz, *The Harriet Quimby Scrapbook.*

47. *1901 was a cacophonous: Appletons' Annual Cyclopaedia and Register of Important Events* (D. Appleton & Company, 1902).

47. *Gustave was twenty-seven:* Megan Adam, "Gustave Whitehead—Pioneer Aviator," Gustave Whitehead's Flying Machines, http://www.gustave-whitehead.com.

48. *On August 14, 1901:* Susan Brinchman, *Gustave Whitehead: First in Flight* (La Mesa, CA: Apex Educational Media, 2015).

48. *At the start of the experiment:* "Flying," *Bridgeport Herald*, August 18, 1901.

48. *"so lightly"*: "Flying."

49. *the* New York Evening World*:* "Bridgeport Man Says His Airship Will Surely Fly" (October 1, 1901), "News Reports of Whitehead Flights, 1901/1902," http://www.gustave-whitehead.com.

49. *he promised the editor:* Gustave Whitehead, "1902—Letters to American Inventor from G. Whitehead," *Gustave Whitehead's Flying Machines*, last modified 2006, https://web.archive.org/web/20130803021728/http://gustavewhitehead.org/news_journalism/1902_-_letters_to_american_.html.

49. *Fame and fortune:* John Brown, "Gustave Whitehead: A Short History," Gustave Whitehead: Pioneer Aviator, http://www.gustave-whitehead.com.

49. *In 1911, Gustave invented:* William J. O'Dwyer and Stella Randolph, *History by Contract* (Fritz Majer & Sohn, 1978). See also "Did Whitehead Fly?" *Air Enthusiast* 35 (1988).

50. *Was the Bridgeport flight:* "Harvard Teacher Hits Wright Claim," *Reading Eagle* (1937).
50. *And a group of aviation experts:* "Whitehead Reproductions," *Flight Journal* (June 2006).
50. *"Down on the fringe":* Harriet Quimby, "The Sacred Furnaces of Mon War," *Overland Monthly* 39 (1902).
53. *Before long, she:* Terry Gwynn-Jones, "For a Brief Moment the World Seemed Wild about Harriet," *Smithsonian* (January 1984).

Chapter 4:
Come full of faith in yourself

57. *Fruit stands, piled high:* Guy Jones, "1903—Scenes in New York City" (via Framepool, March 4, 2017).
58. *The boarding house:* Bonnie R. Ginger, "Here Comes the Air Girl," *World* (1911).
58. *"If you are a journalist":* Harriet Quimby, "The Home and the Household: A California Journalist Making Her Way in New York," *Leslie's Illustrated Weekly* (September 7, 1905).
59. *But Harriet's luck:* "John A. Sleicher, Publisher, Dies," *New York Times,* May 6, 1921.
59. *What began as:* Joshua Brown, *The Great Strikes of 1877* (Champaign: University of Illinois Press, 2008), 19–22.
60. *It's worth noting:* Phillip W. Steele and Steve Cottrell, *Civil War in the Ozarks* (Gretna, LA: Pelican Publishing, 1993), 74–83.
60. *Weeklies like* Leslie's: Frank Luther Mott, *A History of American Magazines 1885–1905* (Cambridge, MA: Harvard University Press, 1957).
60. *boxwood blocks:* Brown, *Great Strikes,* 19–22.
60. *Joseph Pulitzer commanded:* William Andrew Swanberg, *Pulitzer* (New York: Scribner, 1967), 67.
61. *Skyscrapers were surpassing:* John J. Newman and John M. Schmalbach, *United States History* (New York: Amsco School Publications, 2018), 363.
61. *S. S. McClure, a mustachioed:* Mike Wallace, *Greater Gotham: The History of New York City from 1898 to 1919* (New York: Oxford University Press, 2017), 77.
62. *"grip of gambling on women":* Quimby, "Home and Household."
62. *"Dens of infamy masked":* Harriet Quimby, "How White Slaves Are Shackled," *Leslie's Illustrated Weekly* (June 15, 1911).
63. *short-stay hotels:* The Committee of Fifteen, *The Raines Law Hotel and The Social Evil* (New York: G. P. Putnam's Sons, 1905).
63. *"high-powered group of bankers":* Wallace, *Greater Gotham,* 109.
63. *She reignited concerns:* Ed. Y. Hall, *Harriet Quimby: America's First Lady of the Air* (Spartanburg, SC: Honoribus Press, 1993).
63. Leslie's *was among those:* Mott, *History of American Magazines.*
64. *twenty thousand aspiring writers:* Ibid.
64. *"It began in an interview":* Quimby, "Home and Household."
65. *A Cantonese immigrant:* Alvin F. Harlow, *Old Bowery Days: The Chronicles of a Famous Street* (New York: D. Appleton & Company, 1931).
65. *"I found the Chinese settlement":* Quimby, "Home and Household."
65. *"The educated and the illiterate":* Harriet Quimby, "Curious Chinese Customs," *Leslie's Illustrated Weekly* (January 22, 1903).
66. *with its polyglot population":* Quimby, "Home and Household."
66. *to retire to write fiction:* Weston George, "Beauty and the Bleriot: The Story of Harriet Quimby, Pioneer Aviatrix," *Aviation Quarterly* (1980).
67. *"If one strays in":* Harriet Quimby, "The Spicy Hungarian Quarter of New York," *Leslie's Illustrated Weekly* (August 17, 1905).
67. *"Success cannot be spelled":* Quimby, "Home and Household."

Chapter 5:
Hang on for dear life

69. *On July 23, 1903:* Robert Lacey, *Ford: The Men and the Machine* (New York: Little, Brown and Company, 1986).

70. *"The chauffeur, his lean, sun-tanned face":* Harriet Quimby, "Trick Automobiling and How It Is Done," *Leslie's Illustrated Weekly* (August 13, 1903).

71. *"One of the marvels of this century":* Harriet Quimby, "Automobiling: The Society Women's Latest Fad," *Leslie's Illustrated Weekly* (January 26, 1905).

71. *the annual Gordon Bennett Cup:* "Dawn of Automobile Racing," Grand Prix History, https://www.grandprix.com/people/james-gordon-bennett-jr.html.

72. *three-hundred-thousand-a-week readership:* Sterling Brown, *First Lady of the Air: The Harriet Quimby Story* (Greensboro, NC: Tudor Publishers, 1997), 15.

72. *"So you are going to ride":* Harriet Quimby, "A Woman's Exciting Ride in a Racing Motor-car," *Leslie's Illustrated Weekly* (October 4, 1906).

74. *Somewhere along:* Hugh Powell, "Harriet Quimby: America's First Woman Pilot," *AAHS Journal* (1982).

Chapter 6:
It's the smile that's the hard part of dancing

75. *"As a curtain-raiser":* Harriet Quimby, "Where the Play's the Thing," *Leslie's Illustrated Weekly* (October 28, 1909).

75. *"Miss Harriet Quimby":* Giacinta Bradley Koontz, *The Harriet Quimby Scrapbook* (Prescott, AZ: Running Iron Publications, 2003), 62.

75. *scores of shows that appeared:* "Broadway Shows by Year—Opened in 1906," Broadway World, https://www.broadwayworld.com/browseshows.cfm?showtype=BR&open_yr=1906.

76. *Harriet could now afford:* Samuel S. Whitt, "Miss Harriet Quimby," *National Aeronautics* (1973).

76. *It boasted the distinction:* "Hotel Victoria," *Pittsburgh Press* (1907).

76. *"The first thing that impresses":* Harriet Quimby, "Rose Stahl Tells the Secret of Stage Success," *Leslie's Illustrated Weekly* (November 1, 1906).

79. *"Not long ago a young woman":* Harriet Quimby, "Chances of the Homely Girl on the Stage," *Leslie's Illustrated Weekly* (March 1, 1906).

80. *"I was awakened from a sound slumber"* "Eyewitnesses to the Earthquake and Fire," The Museum of the City of San Francisco, http://www.sfmuseum.org/1906/ew.html.

81. *"As they watched":* Gordon Thomas, Max Morgan-Witts, *The San Francisco Earthquake: A Minute by Minute Account of the 1906 Disaster* (New York: Open Roads Media, 1971), Chapter 6.

82. *which consumed some 28,000 buildings:* "The Great 1906 San Francisco Earthquake," USGS Earthquake Hazards Program, https://earthquake.usgs.gov/earthquakes/events/1906calif/18april/.

82. *Among the multitudes:* Mrs. D. W. Griffith [Linda Arvidson], *When the Movies Were Young* (New York: E. P. Dutton & Company, 1925), 18.

82. *to Harriet's delight:* Bradley Koontz, *Harriet Quimby Scrapbook*, 75.

83. *"Margaret Anglin's return":* Harriet Quimby, "Intimate Glimpses of Some Worthwhile Plays on the New York Stage," *Leslie's Illustrated Weekly* (October 7, 1909).

83. *"Harriet Quimby was now":* Griffith, *When the Movies*, 111.

84. *"What Miss Quimby—and others—had achieved":* Richard Shickel, *D. W. Griffith: An American Life* (Brisbane: Limelight, 1988), 72.

84. *"I work in them":* Griffith, *When the Movies*, 29.

85. *the Lumière brothers:* "Edison and the Lumiere-brothers," *Encyclopedia Britannica,* https://www.britannica.com/art/history-of-the-motion-picture/Edison-and-the-Lumiere-brothers#ref507907.
85. *D. W. and Linda worked with miniscule budgets:* Griffith, *When the Movies,* 134.
86. *Over a period of twelve months:* Bradley Koontz, *Harriet Quimby Scrapbook,* 76.
89. *"We do know":* Shickel, *D. W. Griffith,* 164.
89. *The director already had a reputation:* Seymour Stern, "D.W. Griffith: An Appreciation," *New York Times,* August 1, 1948.
89. *In recalling D. W. Griffith:* Thomas Leitch and Leland Poague, *A Companion to Alfred Hitchcock* (Hoboken, NJ: John Wiley and Sons, 2011), 50.

Chapter 7:
We must see the sphinx by moonlight

90. *He possessed a swoop:* Ray Robinson, *Matty: An American Hero* (New York: Oxford University Press, 1994), 9.
90. *"They are as fast as lightning":* Brendan Macgranachan, "The Cuba Trip of 1911," Seamheads, September 4, 2009, https://seamheads.com/blog/2009/09/04/the-cuba-trip-of-1911/.
90. *The Giants, however:* Jorge S. Figueredo. *Cuban Baseball: A Statistical History, 1878–1969* (Jefferson, N.C.: McFarland & Company, Inc. 2003), 96.
91. *One of those was Harriet Quimby:* Harriet Quimby, "Curious Sights and Picturesque Scenes in Cuba," *Leslie's Illustrated Weekly* (August 16, 1906).
91. *Harriet was also able:* Hugh Powell, "Harriet Quimby: America's First Woman Pilot," *AAHS Journal* (1982).
92. *"stuffy cabin":* Harriet Quimby, "Wonderous Transformation of Ocean Travel," *Leslie's Illustrated Weekly* (May 23, 1907).
92. *"lavishly decorated" Amerika:* "America II (Id. No. 3006): 1917–1919," posted March 25, 2020, Naval History and Heritage Command, https://www.history.navy.mil/content/history/nhhc/research/histories/ship-histories/danfs/a/america-ii.html. Note: The ship named "Amerika" was renamed "America II" when the US Navy commandeered it.
92. *"an array of dainty sandwiches":* Quimby, "Wonderous Transformation."
92. *"It was tea-time":* Harriet Quimby, "Afternoon Tea in Quaint Old Cairo," *Leslie's Illustrated Weekly* (August 13, 1908).
93. *"Mystery, together with a veil":* Harriet Quimby, "The Mysterious Women of Egypt," *Leslie's Illustrated Weekly* (August 29, 1907).
94. *"prigs ignorant":* Harriet Quimby, "Why American Travelers Are Criticized," *Leslie's Illustrated Weekly* (June 20, 1907).
95. *"young and good-looking":* Harriet Quimby, "Striking Fads and Fancies of London Town," *Leslie's Illustrated Weekly* (July 18, 1907).
95. *In Nice Harriet noted:* Harriet Quimby, "Curious Contrasts in Nice, the Gayest of Health Resorts," *Leslie's Illustrated Weekly* (September 19, 1907).
95. *The native divers:* Harriet Quimby, "Delights of a Four Weeks' Cruise in the American Tropics," *Leslie's Illustrated Weekly* (July 15, 1909).
95. *When she stood:* Harriet Quimby, "The Panama Canal an Attraction for Tourists," *Leslie's Illustrated Weekly* (April 22, 1909).
95. *Given her affection for automobiles:* Harriet Quimby, "Pleasures and Penalties of Motoring Abroad," *Leslie's Illustrated Weekly* (August 27, 1908).
96. *The National Geographic Society:* Robert M. Poole, *Explorers House: National Geographic and the World It Made* (London: Penguin Press, 2006).
96. *Her photographs introduced:* Giacinta Bradley Koontz, *The Harriet Quimby Scrapbook* (Prescott, AZ: Running Iron Publications, 2003), 51.

Chapter 8:
A pretty woman is pretty whatever her dresses may be

98. *By 1908, women's clothing:* "Women's Clothing, 1900's," The University of Vermont, https://glcp.uvm.edu/landscape_new/dating/clothing_and_hair/1900s_clothing_women.php.

99. *"When Eve plucked a fig leaf":* Harriet Quimby, "The Tragedy of Dress," *Leslie's Illustrated Weekly* (October 1, 1908).

99. *Harriet managed to maintain:* Elizabeth Anna Semple, "Harriet Quimby, America's First Woman Aviator," *Overland Monthly* (1911).

100. *She'd taken to wearing:* Leslie Kerr, *Harriet Quimby: Flying Fair Lady* (Atglen, PA: Schiffer Publishing, 2016), 25.

100. *In 1907:* "Hailing the History of New York's Yellow Cabs," posted July 8, 2007, NPR, https://www.npr.org/templates/story/story.php?storyId=11804573.

100. *The latest spectacular:* Mike Wallace, *Greater Gotham: The History of New York City from 1898 to 1919* (New York: Oxford University Press, 2017), 399.

101. *She likely attended:* Kathrine Sorley Walker, "Anna Pavlova," *Encyclopedia Britannica*, February 8, 2021, https://www.britannica.com/biography/Anna-Pavlova.

101. *"the delightful revival":* Harriet Quimby, "Gossip of the Theatrical World," *Leslie's Illustrated Weekly* (June 20, 1912).

101. *Afterward, Harriet and her entourage:* Wallace, *Greater Gotham*, 426.

102. *For a more intimate experience:* "What's on the menu? 1908," http://menus.nypl.org/menus/decade/1900s.

102. *or on the excellent prime rib:* Georgia Kral and Nicole Levy, "Oldest Restaurants in NYC: Delmonico's, P.J. Clarke's, Katz's and More," posted July 6, 2018, amNY.com, https://www.amny.com/eat-and-drink/old-restaurants-nyc-1-19634651/.

102. *a 1908 law banned women:* Erin Blakemore, "When New York Banned Smoking to Save Women's Souls," last modified April 7, 2021, History.com, https://www.history.com/news/when-new-york-banned-smoking-to-save-womens-souls.

102. *maybe even told a joke or two:* Harriet Quimby, "From the Theatrical Critic's Sketch Book," *Leslie's Illustrated Weekly* (April 7, 1910).

102. *Bands everywhere:* Wallace, *Greater Gotham*, 413.

103. *"Nor was all the intercourse mock":* Ibid.

103. *she took a dim view of women:* Harriet Quimby, "The Girls That Do NOT Go Wrong!," *Leslie's Illustrated Weekly* (September 7, 1911).

Chapter 9:
An epoch-making event

107. *a large white rectangle of cloth:* Gavin Mortimer, *Chasing Icarus: The Seventeen Days in 1910 That Forever Changed American Aviation* (New York: Walker Publishing Company, 2009), 124.

108. *"The wires have been kept hot":* "Seven Airmen Brave Rain at Belmont Park," *New York Times*, October 23, 1910.

108. *The best parking places at the track:* Royal Feltner, "Early American Automobiles: 1910 Models," https://www.earlyamericanautomobiles.com/1910.htm.

108. *Five thousand parking spots:* Mortimer, *Chasing Icarus*, 118.

108. *"What astonished you most":* "Meet at Belmont Park," *Outlook* (1910).

109. *"At night, returning":* Ibid.

109. *receipts showed only a fraction:* "Seven Airmen Brave Rain."

109. *Thousands more:* "First Impressions of the Aero Meet," *Outlook* (October 21, 1911).

109. *spectators "were enthusiastic":* "Meet at Belmont Park."

110. *"the world's greatest":* "Belmont Park Opens To-Day with Big Race," *New York Times*, 1905.

110. *"like you deal cards":* Ring W. Lardner, *The Big Town: How I and the Mrs. Go to New York to See Life and Get Katie a Husband* (Indianapolis: Bobbs-Merrill Company, 1921).
110. *"fifty feet long":* Mortimer, *Chasing Icarus*, 117.
110. *"breeziest race track":* "Seven Airmen Brave Rain."
111. *where a week prior:* "The Birdmen at Belmont Park," *American Heritage* (1956).
111. *an upstart American:* Doris L. Rich, *The Magnificent Moisants: Champions of Early Flight* (Washington, DC: Smithsonian Institution Press, 1998), 68.
112. *"I took up flying as a hobby":* Mortimer, *Chasing Icarus*, 55.
112. *Twenty-four months had passed:* Harriet Quimby, "A Japanese Aeronaut to Startle the World," *Leslie's Illustrated Weekly* (August 5, 1909).
114. *John Moisant, soon after:* Rich, *Magnificent Moisants*, 54.
115. *When one reporter asked:* Mortimer, *Chasing Icarus*, 62.
115. *"not one man":* Rich, *Magnificent Moisants.*
115. *The jewel of the air show:* Henry Serrano Villard, *Blue Ribbon of the Air* (Washington, DC: Smithsonian Institution Press, 1987).
116. *"I climbed as high":* Henry Serrano Villard, *Contact! The Story of the Early Aviators* (Garden City, NY: Dover Publications, 2002), 83.
117. *Authoritarian and vain:* Ibid., 13.
118. *Inside one of the thirty hangars:* Mortimer, *Chasing Icarus*, 137.
118. *The Brit, he wrote, "delights":* Colgate Baker, "Belmont Park Meet," *New York City Review* (1910).
118. *John eased his monoplane up:* Rich, *Magnificent Moisants*, 55.
119. *"It was sheer carelessness":* Mortimer, *Chasing Icarus*, 56.
119. *lugging along with him:* Rich, *Magnificent Moisants.*
120. *Three days later:* "Seven Airmen Brave Rain."
120. *"At the dawn of the opening day":* Mortimer, *Chasing Icarus*, 118.
120. *"The grand stand and concourse":* Ibid.
121. *J. Armstrong scratched:* Ibid.
121. *The final event of the day:* Rich, *Magnificent Moisants*, 57.
122. *"They waited until it was out of sight":* "Seven Airmen Brave Rain."
122. *his heading east by one-eighth south:* Arthur H. Gleason (likely Harriet Quimby), "How to Learn to Fly: What the Sky Chauffeurs Say, A Remarkable Interview with the Noted Birdmen," *Leslie's Illustrated Weekly* (December 29, 1910).
123. *John approached the field:* Rich, *Magnificent Moisants*, 62.
123. *Not everyone was impressed:* "Seven Airmen Brave Rain."
124. *one such article:* Gleason (Quimby), "How to Learn to Fly."
126. *Claude Grahame-White took the:* Mortimer, *Chasing Icarus.*

Chapter 10:
King of the air

127. *"In the morning the storm":* "John B. Moisant," *New York Times*, August 18, 1910.
128. *His older brother Alfred:* Doris L. Rich, *The Magnificent Moisants: Champions of Early Flight* (Washington, DC: Smithsonian Institution Press, 1998), 5.
129. *In 1907, the two eldest Moisant brothers:* Gavin Mortimer, "The Daring Mr. Moisant," *Air & Space* (2010).
129. *It didn't help relations:* Rich, *The Magnificent Moisants.*
130. *There came a point:* "John B. Moisant."
130. *John and his remaining fighters:* Rich, *Magnificent Moisants*, 22.
130. *In July, he stormed aboard:* Ibid.
131. *"People talk of shooting at flying machines":* Mortimer, "Daring Mr. Moisant."

132. *In spite of the fact that:* Albert Burnelli. "Pioneer Air Pilots: John B. Moisant," *Popular Aviation* (1928).
133. *He and his band of merry tinkerers:* Henry Serrano Villard, *Contact! The Story of the Early Aviators* (Garden City, NY: Dover Publications, 2002), 114.
133. *Humbled but not defeated:* Rich, *Magnificent Moisants*, 39.
135. *"During the trip he slept":* Burnelli, "Pioneer Air Pilots."

Chapter 11:
Indeed, at that time it was a miracle

137. *"Fleecy clouds moved lazily":* "Thousands Watched Racers in Flight," *New York Times*, October 31, 1910.
137. *Seventy-five thousand people paid:* Doris L. Rich, *The Magnificent Moisants: Champions of Early Flight* (Washington, DC: Smithsonian Institution Press, 1998), 57.
137. *eighteen dollars would buy one a heavy black coat:* Gavin Mortimer, *Chasing Icarus: The Seventeen Days in 1910 That Forever Changed American Aviation* (New York: Walker Publishing Company, 2009), 212.
138. *The event they all came to see:* Rich, *The Magnificent Moisants.*
138. *Most of the pilots shared:* Gavin Mortimer, "The Daring Mr. Moisant," *Air & Space* (2010).
139. *"Just be careful John":* Mortimer, *Chasing Icarus*, 233.
139. *Claude and Jacques:* Rich, *Magnificent Moisants*, 67.
140. *"Grahame-White was the first":* "Thousands Watched Racers in Flight," *New York Times*, October 31, 1910.
140. *At the clubhouse, Alfred:* "Moisant Wins Liberty Flight," *New York Tribune*, 1910.
140. *"I want to buy your craft":* Mortimer, *Chasing Icarus*, 238.
141. *"[Grahame-White] thinks he's safer":* "Thousands Watched Racers."
141. *He took a few moments:* Rich, *Magnificent Moisants*, 66.
142. *With Claude Grahame-White:* "Thousands Watched Racers."
142. *Then, as the Moisants' new monoplane:* Mortimer, "Daring Mr. Moisant."
142. *"Oh, but it's a shame!":* "Thousands Watched Racers."
142. *"Roll her out, boys!":* Rich, *Magnificent Moisants*, 239.
143. *"regarded by aviators":* Ibid.
143. *"Miss Liberty was at home":* "Moisant Wins Liberty Flight."
143. *"Moisant made a very sharp turn":* "Thousands Watched Racers."
144. *A photograph of that instant:* Joshua Stoff, *Picture History of Early Aviation* (New York: Dover Publications, 1996), 99.
144. *"He's got two minutes to beat Grahame-White":* Mortimer, *Chasing Icarus*, 239.
145. *"He's won! He's won!":* Rich, *Magnificent Moisants*, 68.
145. *The scoreboard showed:* Mortimer, "Daring Mr. Moisant."
145. *"Aeronautics was neither":* Henry Serrano Villard, *Contact! The Story of the Early Aviators* (Garden City, NY: Dover Publications, 2002), 7.
146. *The meet manager:* "Thousands Watched Racers."
146. *"He doesn't fly to land":* Rich, *Magnificent Moisants*, 69.
146. *"Almost as soon":* Thomas Naughton, "The Birdmen at Belmont Park," *American Heritage* (1956).
148. *cheers and shouts of "Moisant! Moisant!:* "Thousands Watched Racers."
148. *Looking on was a woman:* Terry Gwynn-Jones, *Aviation's Magnificent Gamblers* (Sydney: Landsdowne Press, 1981), 11.

Chapter 12:
There's another good man gone

153. *"Americans are called an inquisitive race":* Harriet Quimby, "How a Woman

Learns to Fly," *Leslie's Illustrated Weekly* (May 25, 1911).
153. *When a tire blew:* Terry Gwynn-Jones, "For a Brief Moment the World Seemed Wild about Harriet," *Smithsonian* (January 1984).
154. *"Long Island Folk Discover":* "Woman in Trousers Daring Aviator," *New York Times*, May 11, 1911.
155. *Alfred, fully convinced:* Doris L. Rich, *The Magnificent Moisants: Champions of Early Flight* (Washington, DC: Smithsonian Institution Press, 1998), 74.
157. *The former law student:* Ibid.
157. *"Nothing so excruciatingly funny":* Graham Wallace, *Claude White-Grahame: A Biography* (New York: Putnam, 1960).
158. *Joining the three Frenchmen:* Rich, *Magnificent Moisants*, 75.
159. *It was Roland:* Ibid., 78.
160. *"There is a deeply rooted belief":* Harriet Quimby, "The Dangers of Flying and How to Avoid Them," *Leslie's Illustrated Weekly* (August 31, 1911).
161. *On the morning of New Year's Eve:* Rich, *Magnificent Moisants*, 95.
162. *"I think there is no danger":* "Moisant Left $125,000," *New York Times*, January 2, 1911.
162. *After making two circuits:* "How Moisant Fell," *New York Times*, January 1, 1911.
162. *Other witnesses described:* Rich, *Magnificent Moisants*, 96.
165. *The coroner declared:* Ibid., 97.
165. *"Everybody who knew him loved him":* "How Moisant Fell."
165. *Moments after hearing of the accident:* Rich, *Magnificent Moisants*, 97.

Chapter 13:
To become a companion of the birds

167. *"Four o'clock in the morning":* Harriet Quimby, "How a Woman Learns to Fly," *Leslie's Illustrated Weekly* (May 25, 1911).
167. *A June 1911 advertisement:* Steve Remington, "Early Bird Aviator" (Collect Air, n.d.), https://collectair.org/steveremingtonart.html.
168. *"The student of aviation":* Quimby, "How a Woman."
168. *In the days after "Johnny" was laid to rest:* Doris L. Rich, *The Magnificent Moisants: Champions of Early Flight* (Washington, DC: Smithsonian Institution Press, 1998), 103.
169. *"the only natural prairie":* Remington, "Early Bird Aviator."
170. *He fed a tip that appeared:* "To Start Aviation Schools," *New York Times*, June 25, 1911.
170. *In fact, the class Harriet joined:* Rich, *Magnificent Moisants*, 130.
170. *"it didn't interfere":* Weston George, "Beauty and the Bleriot: The Story of Harriet Quimby, Pioneer Aviatrix," *Aviation Quarterly* (1980).
170. *By 1910, 27 percent of New York State's:* Mike Wallace, *Greater Gotham: The History of New York City from 1898 to 1919* (New York: Oxford University Press, 2017), 757.
170. *characterized by Daisy Miller:* Ruth Bordin, *Alice Freeman Palmer: The Evolution of a New Woman* (Ann Arbor: University of Michigan Press, 1993), 19.
171. *Leaders of the Catholic Church:* Kathleen Sprows Cummings, *New Women of the Old Faith* (Chapel Hill: University of North Carolina Press, 2009), 19.
171. *Many of the anti-suffrage:* Lynda G. Dodd, "The Rhetoric of Gender Upheaval During the Campaign for the Nineteenth Amendment," *Boston University Law Review* (May 2013): 709–727.
171. *In the US, Elizabeth:* "Women's Suffrage," posted Oct 29, 2009, History.com, https://www.history.com/topics/womens-history/the-fight-for-womens-suffrage.
172. *Both the Wright brothers:* Rich, *Magnificent Moisants*, 132.
172. *"If a woman wants to fly":* Quimby, "Woman Learns to Fly."

173. *The youngest Moisant:* Matilde Moisant. "The Reminiscences of Matilde Moisant" (New York: Oral History Department, Columbia University, 1960).
174. *"The first lesson of the beginner":* Quimby, "Woman Learns to Fly."
176. *"Like most monoplanes":* Charles Hayward, *Practical Aviation* (Chicago: American Technical Society, 1912), 730.
177. *"TRUEING UP FUSELAGE":* Anonymous. "Bleriot" (unknown. Chapter fragment).
178. *As early as 1912, engineers:* Hayward, *Practical Aviation,* 88.
178. *The Blériot XI measured twenty-seven feet:* "The Bleriot Aeroplane," *Scientific American* (1909).
179. *"J'ai été à la peine":* B. A. Elliot, *Herald of an Age* (London: Stroud, 2000), 113.
180. *As Louis Blériot was trying:* Terry Gwynn-Jones, *The Air Racers: Aviation's Golden Era 1909–1936* (London: Pelham Books, 1983), 11.
181. *"As soon as I am over the cliff":* "Bleriot Tells of His Flight," as told to *The Daily Mail,* quoted in *New York Times,* July 26, 1909.
182. *"How could I help believing in him":* "Madam Bleriot," *Daily Mirror* (Over-Seas edition), 1909.
182. *One advertised:* Henry Serrano Villard, *Contact! The Story of the Early Aviators* (Garden City, NY: Dover Publications, 2002), 9.
183. *Matilde evidently skipped:* Moisant. "Reminiscences."
183. *"If Professor Houpert's":* Quimby, "Woman Learns to Fly."
184. *an indictment of America's:* Harriet Quimby, "Saving 1,000 Babies' Lives," *Leslie's Illustrated Weekly* (August 3, 1911).
184. *protect endangered bird:* Harriet Quimby, "How Can We Save Our Birds?," *Leslie's Illustrated Weekly* (June 8, 1911).
185. *"There is no exaggeration":* Quimby, "Woman Learns to Fly."
186. *"Why shouldn't a woman fly if she wants to":* Rich, *Magnificent Moisants,* 136.

Chapter 14:
Only a cautious person should fly

187. *"It was a happy day for me:* Harriet Quimby, "How a Woman Learns to Fly," *Leslie's Illustrated Weekly* (May 25, 1911).
188. *André Houpert was the first:* "André Houpert, Aviator, 77, Dies," *New York Times,* April 7, 1963.
188. *"an aircraft was probably":* Terry Gwynn-Jones, "For a Brief Moment the World Seemed Wild about Harriet," *Smithsonian* (January 1984).
189. *One day in mid-summer:* Doris L. Rich, *The Magnificent Moisants: Champions of Early Flight* (Washington, DC: Smithsonian Institution Press, 1998), 133.
190. *There is reason to believe:* Richard Houpert and Maile Ramzi, telephone conversations with and emails to the author, February 2021.
190. *During a practice takeoff:* Leslie Kerr, *Harriet Quimby: Flying Fair Lady* (Atglen, PA: Schiffer Publishing, 2016), 45.
192. *"Everyone," she wrote, "asks":* Quimby, "Woman Learns to Fly."
194. *"That the air craft of to-day":* Harriet Quimby, "The Dangers of Flying and How to Avoid Them," *Leslie's Illustrated Weekly* (August 31, 1911).
195. *A survey conducted in 1913:* Henry Serrano Villard, *Contact! The Story of the Early Aviators* (Garden City, NY: Dover Publications, 2002), 240.
195. *the ritual of pilot checklists:* Ed. Y. Hall, *Harriet Quimby: America's First Lady of the Air* (Spartanburg, SC: Honoribus Press, 1993), 90.
195. *"Only a cautious person":* Eileen F. Lebow, *Before Amelia: Women Pilots in the Early Days of Aviation* (Washington, DC: Brassey's, Inc., 2002), 152.

Chapter 15:
I just wanted to be first

196. *two men arrived at the Moisant School:* Harriet Quimby, "How I Won My Aviator's License," *Leslie's Illustrated Weekly* (August 24, 1911).

196. *Not quite a year earlier:* "Blanche Stuart Scott," National Women's Hall of Fame, https://www.womenofthehall.org/inductee/blanche-stuart-scott/.

197. *Passing through Dayton:* Doris L. Rich, *The Magnificent Moisants: Champions of Early Flight* (Washington, DC: Smithsonian Institution Press, 1998), 165.

197. *"I can make my muscles":* Ibid.

197. *On September 2, 1910:* Claudia M. Oakes, *United States Women in Aviation through World War I* (Washington, DC: Smithsonian Institution Press, 1978), 18.

197. *She reportedly made "a spectacular flight":* Eileen F. Lebow, *Before Amelia: Women Pilots in the Early Days of Aviation* (Washington, DC: Brassey's, Inc., 2002), 151.

197. *"Quite unexpectedly":* Elizabeth Anna Semple, "Harriet Quimby, America's First Woman Aviator," *Overland Monthly* (1911).

201. *"When all was in readiness":* Quimby, "How I Won."

204. *"She forgot to shut off her engine":* "Miss Quimby Wins Air Pilot License," *New York Times,* August 2, 1911.

204. *"her face . . . covered with grease":* Hugh Powell, "Harriet Quimby: America's First Woman Pilot," *AAHS Journal* (1982).

204. *The following letter:* Quimby, "How I Won."

207. *"Does this license make you":* Semple, "Harriet Quimby."

207. *"It's not a fad":* Sterling Brown, *First Lady of the Air: The Harriet Quimby Story* (Greensboro, NC: Tudor Publishers, 1997), 31.

207. *"Of course Miss Quimby":* Bonnie R. Ginger, "... So Easy Now to Learn ...," [possibly] *World* (1911).

207. Overland Monthly*:* Semple, "Harriet Quimby."

208. *Just below the* New York Times*:* "Miss Quimby Wins."

Chapter 16:
The cutest little witch

209. *Harriet Quimby wasn't the only one:* Henry M. Holden, *Her Mentor Was an Albatross: The Autobiography of Pioneer Pilot Harriet Quimby* (Mt. Freedom, NJ: Black Hawk Publishing, 1993), 57.

209. *"With wind eddies flattened":* "Miss Moisant Wins License," *New York Times,* August 14, 1911.

210. *"I could have had my license first":* Doris L. Rich, *The Magnificent Moisants: Champions of Early Flight* (Washington, DC: Smithsonian Institution Press, 1998), 135.

210. *That was likely not idle:* Steve Remington, "Early Bird Aviator" (Collect Air, n.d.), https://collectair.org/steveremingtonart.html.

210. *"You know," he once:* Rich, *The Magnificent Moisants,* 134.

210. *The advertisement covered:* Rich, *Magnificent Moisants,* 135.

211. *"just for fun":* Remington, "Early Bird Aviator."

211. *"a willowy, beautiful brunette":* Shirley Wilcox, "Aviatrix Harriet Quimby: She Showed the Way," *American History Illustrated* (1985).

211. *It was being driven by:* Hugh Powell, "Harriet Quimby: America's First Woman Pilot," *AAHS Journal* (1982).

212. *By the time Harriet:* Weston George, "Beauty and the Bleriot: The Story of Harriet Quimby, Pioneer Aviatrix," *Aviation Quarterly* (1980).

212. *"a monkey crawling":* Eileen F. Lebow, *Before Amelia: Women Pilots in the Early Days of Aviation* (Washington, DC: Brassey's, Inc., 2002), 153.

212. *"There was hardly a breeze"*: "Girl Flies by Night at Richmond Fair," *New York Times*, September 5, 1911.
213. *William S. Van Clief*: Lebow, *Before Amelia*, 154.
213. *Her mailbox at the Hotel Victoria*: Leslie Kerr, *Harriet Quimby: Flying Fair Lady* (Atglen, PA: Schiffer Publishing, 2016), 51.
213. *"Driving an aeroplane"*: Harriet Quimby, "American Bird Woman: Aviation as a Feminine Sport," *Good Housekeeping* (1912).
214. *She set the world record: Le Veloce-sportif: organe de la velocipedie française* (Gallica, 1893).
214. *"spectacular feats"*: Lebow, *Before Amelia*, 22.
216. *"guileless eyes"*: Rich, *Magnificent Moisants*, 163.
217. *Matilde remembered that day*: Matilde Moisant, "The Reminiscences of Matilde Moisant" (New York: Oral History Department, Columbia University, 1960).
218. *Matilde's wheels barely*: Rich, *Magnificent Moisants*, 166.
218. *"fell tardily enough"*: "Rain Stops Flights When Churches Fail," *New York Times*, October 2, 1911.
219. *promising the sheriff*: Rich, *Magnificent Moisants*, 167.
219. *"The American fliers"*: "Rain Stops Flights."
219. *With the unlicensed Blanche Stuart Scott*: Rich, *Magnificent Moisants*, 167.
221. *The Girl Hawk*: Lebow, *Before Amelia*, 29.
221. *Harriet left the meet early*: Kerr, *Harriet Quimby*, 53.
221. *"One Sunday, Mr. Rene Simone*: Moisant, "Reminiscences."

Chapter 17:
I'm like a cat—I think I've got two lives left

227. *His own grandfather likened*: Alan Knight, *The Mexican Revolution* (Lincoln: University of Nebraska Press, 1990).
228. *Born with graceful schooner lines*: "Fire in the Lampasas," *New York Times*, November 24, 1894.
228. *Comfortably settled*: "$100,000 for Aviators," *New York Times*, May 28, 1911.
229. *Matilde asked Louise*: Matilde Moisant, "The Reminiscences of Matilde Moisant" (New York: Oral History Department, Columbia University, 1960).
230. *Once the rest of the team arrived*: Eileen F. Lebow, *Before Amelia: Women Pilots in the Early Days of Aviation* (Washington, DC: Brassey's, Inc., 2002), 171.
230. *The* Mexican Herald: Doris L. Rich, *The Magnificent Moisants: Champions of Early Flight* (Washington, DC: Smithsonian Institution Press, 1998), 171.
230. *"The meet has been very successful"*: Ibid.
231. *"Miss Harriet Quimby was the star"*: "Politics Effect Attendance in Mexico" (*Aero*, 1911).
231. *Harriet's luck almost changed*: Henry M. Holden, *Her Mentor Was an Albatross: The Autobiography of Pioneer Pilot Harriet Quimby* (Mt. Freedom, NJ: Black Hawk Publishing, 1993), 73.
231. *"From my own experience"*: Harriet Quimby, "In the World of People Who Fly," *Leslie's Illustrated Weekly* (January 18, 1912).
232. *"Mexico City is a little over 7,300"*: Harriet Quimby, "With the Intrepid Flyers," *Leslie's Illustrated Weekly* (February 1, 1912).
232. *André compared*: Lebow, *Before Amelia*, 172.
233. *While the aviation team*: Weston George, "Beauty and the Bleriot: The Story of Harriet Quimby, Pioneer Aviatrix," *Aviation Quarterly* (1980), 174.
233. *With a new contract*: Rich, *Magnificent Moisants*, 174.
233. *Matilde survived yet another*: Moisant, "Reminiscences."
234. *A year later, Alfred sold*: Steve Remington, "Early Bird Aviator" (Collect Air, n.d.).

235. *"Few men could have managed":* Rich, *Magnificent Moisants*, 176.
235. *Coming in for a landing:* Remington, "Early Bird."
236. *Later, in Dallas:* Lebow, *Before Amelia*, 175.
236. *Louise could no longer bear:* Rich, *Magnificent Moisants*, 181.
236. *Matilde held a superstition:* Henry Serrano Villard, *Contact! The Story of the Early Aviators* (Garden City, NY: Dover Publications, 2002), 144.
236. *The day dawned to rain:* Lebow, *Before Amelia*, 177.
237. *Matilde dipped the monoplane:* Rich, *Magnificent Moisants*, 182.
237. *Desperately trying to not kill:* Leslie Kerr, *Harriet Quimby: Flying Fair Lady* (Atglen, PA: Schiffer Publishing, 2016), 52.
237. *"[The tanks] burst their moorings":* Rich, *Magnificent Moisants*, 182
239. *Within minutes, the airplane:* Holden, *Her Mentor Was an Albatross*, 74.

Chapter 18:
Can a man keep a secret?

240. *The Twentieth Century Limited:* "20th Century Limited—Decades TV Network," December 3, 2015, YouTube video, 1:51, https://www.youtube.com/watch?v=Zy2-QVuA21E.
240. *customers strolled on:* Bob Johnson, Joe Welsh, and Mike Schafer, *The Art of the Streamliner* (New York: Metro Books, 2001), 146.
240. *It was not quite noon:* "20th Century in Crash," *New York Times*, January 12, 1912.
240. *"We were progressing smoothly":* "Miss Quimby Prefers Aviation to Wrecks," *Mexican Herald*, June 12, 1912.
241. *seven years earlier:* Thomas Mantowitz, "Wreck of the 20th Century Limited," posted November 20, 2016, City of Mentor, https://cityofmentor.com/wreck-20th-century-limited/.
242. *Concerned that a European female aviator:* Harriet Quimby, "An American Girl's Daring Exploit," *Leslie's Illustrated Weekly* (May 16, 1912).
242. *Harriet didn't waste:* Claudia M. Oakes, *United States Women in Aviation through World War I* (Washington, DC: Smithsonian Institution Press, 1978), 28.
242. *He was the proud holder:* Leslie Kerr, *Harriet Quimby: Flying Fair Lady* (Atglen, PA: Schiffer Publishing, 2016), 53.
242. *At age eleven:* Giacinta Bradley Koontz, "Of Balloons and Parachutes: The Remarkable A. Leo Stevens (1877?–1944)," posted January 1, 2012, D.O.M. Director of Maintenance: The Business of Aircraft Maintenance, https://dommagazine.com/article/balloons-and-parachutes-remarkable-leo-stevens-1877-1944.
243. *During an 1897 test flight:* "Two Aeronauts Rescued," *New York Times*, March 16, 1897.
243. *He was also a colorful:* "Trophies of Pioneer Otsego Aeronaut to Be Preserved by Institute of Aeronautical Sciences in New York," *Binghamton Press*, 1945.
245. *A few months before joining:* "Stevens Life Pack," *Aeronautics* (1912).
245. *Leo believed:* Tom D. Crouch, *The Giant Leap: A Chronology of Ohio Aerospace Events and Personalities 1815–1969* (Columbus: Ohio History Connection, 1971).
245. *to set about acquiring an airplane:* Eileen F. Lebow, *Before Amelia: Women Pilots in the Early Days of Aviation* (Washington, DC: Brassey's, Inc., 2002), 156.
246. *Blériot's representative in the US:* Giacinta Bradley Koontz, *The Harriet Quimby Scrapbook* (Prescott, AZ: Running Iron Publications, 2003), 116.
246. *Fifty Aero Club members:* Hugh Powell, "Harriet Quimby: America's First Woman Pilot," *AAHS Journal* (1982).
246. *the Michigander suffered from:* Ed. Y. Hall, *Harriet Quimby: America's First Lady of the Air* (Spartanburg, SC: Honoribus Press, 1993), 104.

247. *"Only a few years ago"*: Harriet Quimby, "How the Ocean Traveler Is Fed," *Leslie's Illustrated Weekly* (June 13, 1912).
247. *"Poor, troubled Mexico"*: Harriet Quimby, "Notable Observations of Holy Week in Mexico," *Leslie's Illustrated Weekly* (April 4, 1912).
248. *Her first order of business:* Bradley Koontz, *Harriet Quimby Scrapbook*, 118.
248. *Kenealy, a brute-faced bull:* "Alexander Kenealy," Prabook, https://prabook.com/web/alexander.kenealy/733536.
248. *"He was delighted"*: Quimby, "American Girl's Daring Exploit."
248. *The pair also met:* Hall, *Harriet Quimby*, 102.
248. *"The next thing necessary"*: Quimby, "American Girl's Daring Exploit."
251. *But despite all their precautions:* Terry Gwynn-Jones, *Aviation's Magnificent Gamblers* (Sydney: Landsdowne Press, 1981), 14.
251. *He was a twenty-two-year-old:* "Hamel, Gustav," Oxford Dictionary of National Biography, https://www.oxforddnb.com/view/10.1093/ref:odnb/9780198614128.001.0001/odnb-9780198614128-e-39597.
252. *Three days later:* "Lady Crosses Channel by Air," *Daily Mail*, 1912.

Chapter 19: I was not a bit nervous

253. *"Miss Eleanor Trehawke Davis"*: "Woman in Flight: London to Paris," *New York Times*, April 3, 1912.
253. *"I saw Miss Davies shortly"*: "Lady Crosses Channel by Air," *Daily Mail*, 1912.
253. *She was what was known:* "Woman in Flight."
254. *Months later:* Terry Gwynn-Jones, *Aviation's Magnificent Gamblers* (Sydney: Landsdowne Press, 1981), 15.
254. *Even more mystifying:* Elizabeth Hiatt Gregory, "Woman's Record in Aviation," *Good Housekeeping* (September 1912).
256. *"On Saturday, April 13th"*: Giacinta Bradley Koontz, *The Harriet Quimby Scrapbook* (Prescott, AZ: Running Iron Publications, 2003), 132–136.
256. *"On Sunday, the day after"*: Harriet Quimby, "An American Girl's Daring Exploit," *Leslie's Illustrated Weekly* (May 16, 1912).
257. *"After all our patient waiting"*: Ibid.
260. *Harriet's female friends fussed about: Flying* (35 mm film from the National Film and Sound Archive, Australia).
260. *"It was my turn at last"*: Quimby, "American Girl's Daring Exploit."
261. *Gustav climbed onto the chassis:* Hiatt Gregory, "Woman's Record."
261. *He reported the clouds were low:* "First Woman to Fly the Channel," *Daily Mirror*, 1912.
261. *"All right! Let's be off"*: Quimby, "American Girl's Daring Exploit."
262. *"Frequently when I have been flying"*: "Little Miss Dresden China Doll Broken at Last," *Omaha Sunday Bee Magazine*, 1912.
263. *"When flying is in its infancy"*: Elizabeth Anna Semple, "Harriet Quimby, America's First Woman Aviator," *Overland Monthly* (1911).
263. *"I was not a bit nervous"*: Hiatt Gregory, "Woman's Record."
264. *"But, greatly to my relief"*: Quimby, "American Girl's Daring Exploit."
265. *Her eastern course to France:* Leslie Kerr, *Harriet Quimby: Flying Fair Lady* (Atglen, PA: Schiffer Publishing, 2016), 57.

Chapter 20: Women are more fearless than men

266. *On a wide stretch of sandy beach:* Harriet Quimby, "American Girl's Daring Exploit," *Leslie's Illustrated Weekly* (May 16, 1912).
267. *A photograph of the moment:* Giacinta Bradley Koontz, *The Harriet Quimby Scrapbook* (Prescott, AZ: Running Iron Publications, 2003), 123.

267. *"helpful and thoughtful"*: Quimby, "An American Girl's Daring Exploit."
268. *Immortalized by the Gaumont: Flying* (35 mm film from the National Film and Sound Archive, Australia).
269. *On the evening of April 14:* Richard R. Paton, "The Final Board of Inquiry: A Cold Case Investigation into the Loss of the Steamship Titanic," The Steamship Historical Society of America, http://www.sshsa.org/media/media/splash/TheFinalBoardofInquiry.pdf.
272. *Harriet burrowed deep:* "First to Fly the English Channel," publication unknown, 1912.
272. *"The Editor of Leslie's"*: Quimby, "American Girl's Daring Exploit."
272. *political passions, too:* "Suffrage Army Out on Parade," *New York Times*, May 5, 1912.
273. *"the only thing worse"*: Weston George, "Beauty and the Bleriot: The Story of Harriet Quimby, Pioneer Aviatrix," *Aviation Quarterly* (1980).
273. *"Miss Quimby assured me"*: Elizabeth Anna Semple, "Harriet Quimby, America's First Woman Aviator," *Overland Monthly* (1911).
273. *"Even at a time"*: George, "Beauty and the Bleriot."
274. *Gustav Hamel himself disappeared:* "Body Surely Hamel's; Corpse Found and Abandoned by Fisherman That of Airman," *New York Times*, July 9, 1914.
276. *"Woman's advent into the aviation field"*: Elizabeth Hiatt Gregory, "Woman's Record in Aviation," *Good Housekeeping* (September 1912).
276. *"Any woman with sufficient self-confidence"*: Harriet Quimby, "American Bird Woman: Aviation as a Feminine Sport," *Good Housekeeping* (1912).
277. *Matilde Moisant, tracked down in California:* Doris L. Rich, *The Magnificent Moisants: Champions of Early Flight* (Washington, DC: Smithsonian Institution Press, 1998), 188.
277. *In an odd twist:* Claudia M. Oakes, *United States Women in Aviation through World War I* (Washington, DC: Smithsonian Institution Press, 1978), 2.
277. *Once back in the United States:* Ed. Y. Hall, *Harriet Quimby: America's First Lady of the Air* (Spartanburg, SC: Honoribus Press, 1993), 117.
278. *Leo Stevens was busy:* Leslie Kerr, *Harriet Quimby: Flying Fair Lady* (Atglen, PA: Schiffer Publishing, 2016) 64.
278. *Unfortunately, the drink's pure cane:* "Vin Fiz Reborn," posted October 1, 2007, Airport Journals, http://airportjournals.com/vin-fiz-reborn/.
278. *"America is the birthplace of aviation"*: Harriet Quimby, "New Things in the Aviation World," *Leslie's Illustrated Weekly* (June 6, 1912).
278. *Her outlook hadn't always:* Bradley Koontz, *Harriet Quimby Scrapbook*, 144.
278. *It was the brass figure of a Hindu deity:* Hall, *Harriet Quimby*, 151.
279. *"It is a curious thing"*: Harriet Quimby, "We Girls Who Fly and What We're Afraid Of," *World* (1912).
280. *the clay head of an ancient Aztec deity:* Bradley Koontz, *Harriet Quimby Scrapbook*, 151.

Chapter 21:
We accept what will be, will be

281. *When it opened in 1906:* Charles De Kay, "The New York Custom House," *Century* (1906).
281. *After considerable negotiations:* Harriet Quimby, "New Things in the Aviation World," *Leslie's Illustrated Weekly* (June 6, 1912).
282. *The Blériot Type XI-2 "Artillerie"*: Henry M. Holden, *Her Mentor Was an Albatross: The Autobiography of Pioneer Pilot Harriet Quimby* (Mt. Freedom, NJ: Black Hawk Publishing, 1993), 110.

284. *She took Shakir S. Jerwan:* Eileen F. Lebow, *Before Amelia: Women Pilots in the Early Days of Aviation* (Washington, DC: Brassey's, Inc., 2002), 162. See also Editor, "The Fatal Aeroplane Accident at Boston," *Scientific American* (1912).

284. *During Harriet's second flight:* Holden, *Her Mentor Was an Albatross*, 112.

284. *"If you wish to be a pilot":* Arthur H. Gleason (likely Harriet Quimby), "How to Learn to Fly: What the Sky Chauffeurs Say, A Remarkable Interview with the Noted Birdmen," *Leslie's Illustrated Weekly* (December 29, 1910).

285. *Four months earlier:* Percy E. Noel, "Preparing for Boston Meet on Novel Basis," *Aero: America's Aviation Weekly* (1912).

286. *After raising $8,000 in seed money:* "Annual Aviation Meet," *Harvard Crimson*, 1912.

286. *The advertised price of admission:* Noel, "Preparing for Boston Meet."

286. *Leo Stevens was well aware:* Giacinta Bradley Koontz, *The Harriet Quimby Scrapbook* (Prescott, AZ: Running Iron Publications, 2003), 160.

286. *He drove a hard bargain:* Leslie Kerr, *Harriet Quimby: Flying Fair Lady* (Atglen, PA: Schiffer Publishing, 2016), 65.

286. *As an additional publicity:* Hugh Powell, "Harriet Quimby: America's First Woman Pilot," *AAHS Journal* (1982).

286. *"I will [quit]":* Lebow, *Before Amelia*, 163.

287. *Hardelot, the French resort:* "Little Miss Dresden China Doll Broken at Last," *Omaha Sunday Bee Magazine*, 1912.

287. *Squantum Aviation Meet:* Doris L. Rich, *The Magnificent Moisants: Champions of Early Flight* (Washington, DC: Smithsonian Institution Press, 1998), 189.

287. *"An aeroplane close at hand":* Spectator, "First Impressions of the Aero Meet," *Outlook* (1911).

288. *"A water landing is alright":* "Miss Quimby Dies in Airship Fall," *New York Times*, July 2, 1912.

288. *"I'll be back":* Gertrude Stevenson, "Herald Woman Reporter Was to Be Next Passenger," *Boston Herald*, July 3, 1912.

291. *It was either Harriet or Leo:* Samuel S. Whitt. "Miss Harriet Quimby," *National Aeronautics* (1973).

291. *"Willard's getting his flight":* Stevenson, "Herald Woman Reporter."

292. *"It was one of the most beautiful":* Terry Gwynn-Jones, *Aviation's Magnificent Gamblers* (Sydney: Landsdowne Press, 1981), 20.

292. *"cries of horror":* Stevenson, "Herald Woman Reporter."

292. *"The next instant":* A. Leo Stevens, "On the Death of Miss Quimby," *Aeronautics* (1912).

293. *Harriet wrestled with the now-unstable Blériot:* Terry Gwynn-Jones, "For a Brief Moment the World Seemed Wild about Harriet," *Smithsonian* (January 1984).

293. *The monoplane followed:* Whitt, "Miss Harriet Quimby." .

293. *"My God, they're killed":* A. J. Philpott, "Tragedy Near Finish of Boston Light Flight—Cause of the Accident Mystery—Meet to Continue," *Boston Globe*, July 2, 1912.

293. *"They placed her":* Myron G. Savage, "An Unforgettable Experience," *Yankee* (1979).

295. *Photographs show:* Giacinta Bradley Koontz, *The Harriet Quimby Scrapbook* (Prescott, AZ: Running Iron Publications, 2003).

295. *As a crowd of spectators:* Kerr, *Harriet Quimby*, 70.

295. *The watch that graced her wrist:* Stevenson, "Herald Woman Reporter."

295. *"A dozen people":* Holden, *Her Mentor Was an Albatross*, 119.

295. *"If aviators choose to stay":* Kerr, *Harriet Quimby*, 70.

Epilogue:
Something tells me that I shall do something some day

296. *On the evening of July 4, 1912:* Giacinta Bradley Koontz, *The Harriet Quimby Scrapbook* (Prescott, AZ: Running Iron Publications, 2003), 184.
296. *"And I wanted the Smithsonian":* Jean Adams and Margaret Kimball, *Heroines of the Sky* (Garden City, NY: Doubleday, Doran & Company, 1942), 24.
296. *The Reverend James B. Wasson:* "Eulogizes Harriet Quimby," *New York Times*, July 5, 1912.
297. *Pilot Lincoln Beachey:* Bradley Koontz, *Harriet Quimby Scrapbook.*
297. *Mr. Hardy, Harriet's mechanic, fiercely rejected:* Frank J. Delear, "What Killed Harriet Quimby?" *Yankee* (1979).
297. *A cruel rumor spread:* Weston George, "Beauty and the Bleriot: The Story of Harriet Quimby, Pioneer Aviatrix," *Aviation Quarterly* (1980).
298. *"When we reached the wreck":* Earle L. Ovington, "The Cause of the Quimby Accident," *Scientific American* (1912).
298. *"The tragic deaths":* A. Leo Stevens, "On the Death of Miss Quimby," *Aeronautics* (1912).
300. *A month before her accident:* Henry M. Holden, *Her Mentor Was an Albatross: The Autobiography of Pioneer Pilot Harriet Quimby* (Mt. Freedom, NJ: Black Hawk Publishing, 1993), 123.
300. *Almost immediately:* Samuel S. Whitt. "Miss Harriet Quimby," *National Aeronautics* (1973).
300. *"Women are temperamentally unfit":* Holden, *Her Mentor Was an Albatross*, 126.
302. *"Without any of the modern":* Ed. Y. Hall, *Harriet Quimby: America's First Lady of the Air* (Spartanburg, SC: Honoribus Press, 1993), 12.
302. *"A brilliant light":* Ibid., 141.
302. *"Nobody likes to be":* Harriet Quimby, "Lost!" *Leslie's Illustrated Weekly* (November 28, 1912).
303. *"Stricken before her mission was fulfilled":* Lilita Lever Younge, "Harriet Quimby's Monument," *Leslie's Illustrated Weekly* (January 2, 1913).
303. *And Matilde Moisant:* "Miss Mathilde Moisant to Go to France," *Air Service Journal* (1917).
303. *"It is with a peculiar":* Clara Bell Brown, "America's First Woman Aviator" (The nineteenth Amendment Victory: A Newspaper History, 1762–1922, Frank Leslie's Weekly, July 5, 1919).
305. *"If bad luck should befall me":* "Lost in the Sky," *Aero and Hydro* (1912).

INDEX

Page numbers in **bold** indicate photographs or their captions.

IMAGE CREDITS

2, 12, 15, 134, 164, 198, 200, 215, 220, 258, 283, 306:
Smithsonian National Air and Space Museum

10:
Pictorial Press Ltd / Alamy Stock Photo

20:
Robert Webb, Courtesy of Giacinta Bradley Koontz. Photo taken at Conat's Riverside Gallery, Manistee, Michigan, around 1883. The inscription reads, "Harriet Quimby—One—if not the first licensed Aviatrix of the world—Lost in Boston Harbor. Your mother's school mate. To Eloise."

77:
Brown Brothers, Sterling, PA

147, 244, 275:
Library of Congress

156, 191, 238:
Houpert family

255, 270:
National Film and Sound Archives of Australia

294, 301:
Boston Public Library, Leslie Jones Collection